Popular

Arthurian

Traditions

Popular
Arthurian
Traditions

Edited by

Sally K. Slocum

Bowling Green State University Popular Press
Bowling Green, Ohio 43403

Dedication

To Emmie P. Kennedy and in memory of W. Craig Kennedy.

Acknowledgment

I am grateful to the Popular Culture Association for welcoming Arthurian Legend to its Subject Areas of Study and thus furthering scholarly interest in the Matter of Britain. Alan Lupack especially encouraged me to pursue this quest. To him and the other tireless contributors to this volume, my sincere thanks.

I am grateful to Eric Birdsall, Head of The University of Akron Department of English, for his generosity in support of typing and Xeroxing costs. Sonia Dial has provided help and advice far beyond her typing skills. I owe her special thanks. Thanks also to Tiffini Morton.

To my colleagues in the English Department, I am thankful for helpful support: Dawn Trouard, Diana Reep, Elton Glaser. I am indebted to Mike W. Barr, my former student, who taught me that "funny books" are to be taken seriously.

Pat and Ray Browne of the Popular Culture Association have been gracious and helpful in this effort.

Finally, to Tom and Andy Slocum, I am most appreciative for their impatience in urging me onward and for their patience while I worked on this project.

Contents

Introduction

The students of Arthurian Legend must be tireless, for there is apparently to be no end to its treatment. It is easy to find reference to Arthurian matter in the popular culture—one TV ad supporting the Marines' quest to find a few good men features a sword that could only be Excalibur, most communities enjoy a Round Table Restaurant or Pub, the final "Twin Peaks" episode centers on events that occur within a West Coast "Glastonbury grove." If scholars have been unable to positively identify the original, the "real" King Arthur, it seems unlikely that anyone will be around to identify the final King Arthur; fortunately that King Arthur will also be "real." He is truly the Once and Future King, and the wealth of material surrounding his legend continues to be popular.

The Popular Culture Association has provided a vehicle for the study of popular Arthuriana since 1987, when Arthurian Legend was added to the Subject Areas of Study at the National Convention. Interest in the subject has been strong and the contributions varied, demonstrating broad treatments of the legend and its interpretations. This volume explores some uses of Arthurian Legend in popular culture and through the analytical approaches of popular culture.

Ladies first. Treatment of women is thought to be a courtly concern of Arthurian materials. The first essays concern women whose treatment is not so courtly as it may seem. Maureen Fries redefines the categories of women in medieval Arthurian legends according to their roles, especially their actions. Definitions of heroines, female heroes and counter-heroes provide a new and useful revaluation of the women and their functions. The females of Malory and Chrétien de Troyes seen through new eyes illuminate and inform medieval and modern texts alike. Relying on the traditional, medieval bifurcation of the character of Morgan le Fey into contradictory roles, Charlotte Spivack assesses Morgan's character as it appears in modern prose fiction of the Arthurian legend and finds a remarkable consistency in old and new concepts of Morgan as healer and destroyer. Ancient Celtic goddess lore merges in the character of Morgan and, especially in Bradley's *Mists of Avalon*, Morgan's powers bring her full circle. Elizabeth Sklar reconstructs Morgan le Fey's actions and character as they are sketched in Malory and transformed by modern fantasy texts—role-playing games, films and most specifically comic books—into the thoroughly wicked modern Morgan. Sklar seeks an understanding of why Morgan has become the sinister figure we now expect. Her essay "is an anatomy of popular culture's Morgan le Fey."

Turning to more recent fiction we see popular plotlines skillfully considered. Jesse Nash, inspired by the questions of young people, examines Batman old and new as representations of the Arthurian mythos. Recently, the new Batman with a postmodern approach transforms the old caped crusader into a hero more

1

attuned to postmodern awareness, a "Dark Knight" whose goal is not to prop up the established authority, but to champion the newly recognized needs of the earth and its people. The questions Nash raises here are addressed by other contributors to this volume. Dispelling a positivist reading of Twain's *Connecticut Yankee in King Arthur's Court,* Donald Hoffman shows that *the boss* is an Oedipal rival to Merlin. Hank's imperialist ambitions run out of control as his increased acquisition of technological authority reduces him to an inhuman, petty, deceitful and spiritually blind wizard.

The focus on prose fiction continues as Rebecca Beal shows how the works of C.J. Cherryh use Arthurian legend to further the freedom of human nature and expand human self-definition in the Science Fiction of *Port Eternity, The Book of Morgain* and *Sunfall.* In her essay Beal demonstrates that Malorean characters, themes and objects are subsumed into the SFF realm to illuminate both the medieval and futuristic worlds. Tom Hoberg credits Parke Godwin's character of Guenevere in *Firelord* and *Beloved Exile* as an advancement of the strength and intelligence of the queen, especially as Godwin departs from Tennyson's portrayal and develops that of William Morris. Godwin goes beyond the legend to fit both queen and history into a comprehensible frame. Suzanne MacRae discusses Thomas Berger's satiric impulse in portraying characters living between good and evil without absolute control over either one in their human natures. The success of *Arthur Rex* lies in part in his deft handling of the tragic ironies of the legend and its characters. Drawing on two novels that vary greatly in their reliance on the legend, Sally K. Slocum shows that whether three Arthurian plots—as in Davies' *Lyre of Orpheus*—or a mere two references—as in Burns' *Cold Sassy Tree*—the legend lends strong material to its subject.

Music has long been a popular vehicle for Arthurian legend. Michael Rewa takes us down memory lane with his essay that chronicles the high popularity of the Matter of Britain in English and American popular music of recent years. Arthurian elements suggest the hopes and disillusions—and more—of a popular culture through its music.

Religious experience being prominent in Arthurian works, it is nevertheless surprising to see religion drawn from the Arthurian experience. Kathleen Ely shows that The Church Universal and Triumphant has drawn from Arthurian materials, for better or worse.

The camera has provided another conduit for Arthurian legend. Constance Relihan's discussion of the difficulties faced by Julia Margaret Cameron in her effort to provide photographic illustrations for Tennyson's *Idylls of the King* clarifies the difficulties intrinsic to photography. Tennyson's treatment of women in his poem and Cameron's uses of her photographic models become of interest in themselves. The camera becomes another participant in disseminating Arthurian legend. Richard C. Bartone's analysis of two Arthurian films, Bresson's *Lancelot du Lac* and Boorman's *Excalibur,* explores how distinctive and highly contrasting cinematic styles reveal modern interpretations of the legend's meanings. Bresson's minimalism underscores his "bleak vision" while Boorman, using visionary myth and dream, presents themes of imaginative redemption. Both film and tradition are clarified in Bartone's essay.

Boorman's vision of the might-and-right-making power of the sword Excalibur, however, trivializes the real strength of medieval practice according to Liam Purdon and Bob Blanch. Though supposedly based on Malory, *Excalibur* ignores strong feudal custom and historical legal ramifications relying instead on the miraculous and box office appeal for Arthur's success.

Dramatic elements of Arthurian legend are successfully expressed in theatrical works as well as in poetry. Alan Lupack reviews the Tristan and Isolde plays written between 1900-1930, a period that found drama a popular vehicle of Arthurian lore. Lupack's analysis distinguishes the successful plays from the others and helps determine what features make the difference. Some of these dramas foreshadow post WWII themes and approaches that have become familiar and expected in more recent developments of Arthuriana. Charles Beach's focus on the narrative voices of Charles Williams' Arthurian poetry reveals that Taliessin is the most effective knight-poet of the fellowship, while the other seven knights achieve varying measures of success as poets according to their personal weaknesses or strengths. Taliessin's place as true court poet becomes clear as Beach distinguishes the roles of the knights.

To bring the collection to an end while pointing to the future, Mildred Leake Day, through Joseph Campbell's life and work, extends popular Arthurian traditions into the mythic realm. Although Campbell has been criticized as a "popularizer," Day emphasizes that "Campbell teaches us to read the Arthurian legend as the central myth of Western Culture..."

Arthurian legend has proven itself to be a finely cut gem: multi-faceted, it shines in use, can be remounted to suit new tastes without losing its worth or beauty and embellishes the new setting. The popularity of the legend defies efforts to limit its uses, to limit its traditions, to limit its life or meaning.

I would like to thank all of the contributors to this volume, whose views, expressed here, demonstrate the long popularity of Arthurian traditions. Their diligence and effort have made the Arthurian star, already very high in our time, shine brightly.

Female Heroes, Heroines and Counter-Heroes: Images of Women in Arthurian Tradition

Maureen Fries

To discuss images of women in Arthurian tradition raises problems of role-definition. In all early European vernacular literature, as Georges Dumézil and his disciples have shown, male heroic roles fall into well-defined types, drawn from actual male functions in Indo-European society.[1] Such characteristically mimetic functions encompass sovereignty, including the lawgiver and seer; battle, embodied in the warrior; and agriculture, with whose third-function figure Dumézil believes the first two warred and over whom they achieved a victory. While female figures are sometimes found in the third function, their usual position is vague and contrapuntal—often tripartite, as if they had no permanent home, and identified with evil and the color green, as in the Celtic Otherworld and the Druidic as opposed to the Christian religion.[2] I want here to investigate some women in Arthurian literature, to determine whether such negative images are universal or whether there are other female images—both heroic and positive—to be discovered.

Certainly there were very few heroic role models for females in medieval life: they were only infrequently rulers and forbidden to bear arms or enter the priesthood. Additionally, women bore the burden of numerous negative stereotypes. While some of these predated Christianity (witness Hesiod, Demosthenes and others of the ancients), the Church added to its Judaic heritage in elaborating upon the supposed universal faults of the daughters of Eve. To all women, philosophers, theologians, moral writers and even romancers ascribed the sins of Adam's partner: they were said to be weak, vain, lustful and needful of the guidance and headship of men, who were supposed to curb their pride and insubordination in order to make them pure, humble and submissive.[3] In real life, however, women sometimes proved themselves the social equals of men. Eleanor of Aquitaine, married serially to the Kings of France and England, ruled more land than either of her husbands. Joan of Arc led armies, shocking the Middle Ages not so much by her mysticism as by cutting off her hair and wearing men's clothes. Margaret Paston defended one of her husband's estates, alone with only nineteen servants for support, against a thousand men for over a day.

While most such women are rarely acknowledged in the public records, they do offer historical images of female heroism. "Female hero" may seem at first a paradoxical term, since we are accustomed by long literary tradition to think of the word "hero" as masculine and the word "heroine" as feminine. Yet a structural analysis of any plot reveals that these are, in essence, functional

5

terms: that is, they operate in character slots determined by the significance of actions to the narrative as a whole. A heroine is thus recognizable by her performance of a traditionally identified, female sex-role. But any woman who, by choice, by circumstance, or even by accident, escapes definition exclusively in terms of such a traditional role is capable of heroism, as opposed to heroinism. Even in literature, men are not the only world-changers, nor women only their helpers: Antigone is there, and Alice in Wonderland, and Jane Eyre. All three of these—and others—assume the usual male role of exploring the unknown beyond their assigned place in society; and all three reject to various degrees the usual female role of preserving order (principally by forgoing adventure to stay at home). The adventurous paths Antigone, Alice and Jane choose require the males who surround them to fill subordinate, non-protagonist roles in their stories.

Such female protagonists fit various critics' definitions of the hero. In Northrup Frye's term, they are superior in degree to other men (*Anatomy* 33: the terminology is Frye's). Even more aptly, they fill Joseph Campbell's formulation of the hero as "the man or woman who has been able to battle past his personal and local historical limitations to the...primary springs of human life and thought" (*Hero* 20). In their most complete quests, such female heroes, like their male counterparts, are able to undertake journeys to knowledge in which encounters with that which is Other lead ultimately to the decisive encounter with the Self. If completely successful, female (like male) heroes return to their original societies with the prized gift of renewal.

Heroines neither venture forth nor return. They are not knowers but—in Campbell's phrase—"what can be known" (116). The heroine "lures," "guides," and "bids [the hero] burst his fetters"; if he can "take her as she is...with the kindness and assurance she requires," he "is potentially the king, the incarnate god, of her created world" (116). The heroine is Snow White or Sleeping Beauty; she is Andrew Marvell's Coy Mistress; she is (after the fact) William Faulkner's Emily. If the rose is so often her icon, it is because her greatest virtue is her beauty. And her most desired end is marriage, the target for which that beauty is poised.

Marriage is either absent from, or (at most) incidental to, the literary career of the counter-hero. Over a decade ago I defined this type for Arthurian males ("Malory's Tristram"). I want now to redefine it for Arthurian females. Characteristically, the counter-hero possesses the hero's superior power of action without possessing his or her adherence to the dominant culture or capability of renewing its values. While the hero proper transcends and yet respects the norms of the patriarchy, the counter-hero violates them in some way. For the male Arthurian counter-hero, such violation usually entails wrongful force; for the female, usually powers of magic. The counter-hero is the Witch in *Hansel and Gretel*; she is Keat's Belle Dame Sans Merci; she is Becky Sharp, in the novel Thackeray proclaimed was without a hero. Always she is preternaturally alluring or preternaturally repelling, or sometimes both, as in Chaucer's *Wife of Bath's Tale*. But her putative beauty does not as a rule complete the hero's valor, as does the heroine's. Rather, it often threatens to destroy him, because of her refusal of the usual female role.

And more: she does not fight like a man. Male roles corresponding to the Indo-European heroic functions are easy to identify in Arthurian literature: Arthur enacts the king; Merlin, the seer; and Gawain, Lancelot and others, the warrior. But female roles are more fluid and far more ambivalent. Arthurian women are essentially ancillary to the male actors of that literary tradition, and must therefore be considered in relation to the male heroic roles they complement or defy: as heroine, female hero or counter-hero. As the heroine represents the most culturally familiar of these female presences, at her (to paraphrase Chaucer in the *General Prologue*) I will begin.

I

The first and most perdurable heroine of Arthurian literature is Guinevere. While she appears by name in fragmentary Welsh writings of uncertain date, such as the triads, her first important role is in the Arthurian section of Geoffrey of Monmouth's twelfth-century *History of the Kings of Britain*. Geoffrey used the fluid medieval genre of *historia*, with its allowance for more invention than would later be decorous, to tell the story of Arthur's marriage. Guinevere, descended from a noble Roman family, is the most beautiful woman "in the entire island" (221). This heroine's beauty and aristocracy are initially seen as an impetus to virtue. At Arthur's recrowning at Caerleon, Guinevere keeps separate but equal status to her husband's, as they banquet in sex-specific groups, the King with his knights and the Queen with her ladies (presumably to emphasize chastity). The Arthurian women attending Guinevere "scorned to give their love to any man who had not proved himself three times in battle. In this way the womenfolk became chaste and more virtuous and for their love the knights were ever more daring" (229). In the mock war of the first Arthurian tournaments, the ladies further arouse their knights to that valor necessary to the achievement and maintenance of their honor.

But honor begins a decline as Arthur decides to wage an offensive war on Rome and appoints his queen and his nephew, Modred, as co-regents. This precaution, in which the queenship has its Celtic significance of sovereignty and the male co-rule its Pauline significance of protection against womanly weakness, comes to naught. "The news was brought to [Arthur] that his nephew, Modred, in whose care he had left Britain, had placed the crown upon his own head...[and] was living adulterously and out of wedlock with Queen Guinevere, who had broken the vows of her earlier marriage" (257).

This social, nuptial and feudal fraud—at the same time incest, bigamy and treason—repeats at a deeper structural level Uther's earlier adultery with Arthur's mother, Ygerna, and is a reminder of Original Sin with its consequences for all fallen human nature. It negates the virtue of Guinevere, Arthur's prime personal and social emblem of control of self and others. Modred, as king's sister's son a shadow side of Arthur he has overlooked at his peril (Garbaty), is the first of several subsequent antagonists to the King who seize the Queen. Guinevere is here, and is to remain, the instrument around whom the action turns, the other seducers and/or abductors bearing different names but a like function to Modred. That Geoffrey's Guinevere ends her life as a nun vowed to chastity at Caerleon, the scene of her co-coronation with Arthur, indicates her conformation to the heroine's role as reflector of the male hero's values.

The performance of penitence for oneself and/or as surrogate for a male was a function of the female in romance as it was in real life.[4]

Such penitence seems to disappear from Guinevere's next appearance as heroine in the twelfth-century *Lancelot* of Chrétien de Troyes. The original role of lover/abductor assigned to Modred is here divided, more or less permanently (an exception being the fourteenth-century *Alliterative Morte Arthure*). To Lancelot falls the function of amorous rescuer, and to a new character, Meleaganz, that of usurper of husbandly prerogatives. In the *Lancelot*, Guinevere would at first appear to be the dominant character, especially in terms of the doctrine of courtly love which informs the romance. His horse killed beneath him, Lancelot mounts near the beginning of the tale a shameful cart because of his eagerness to see the queen; faints upon finding Guinevere's comb, complete with a few strands of her golden hair; pretends to lose his first battle with Meleaganz when the Queen commands him to; and—at a later tournament—begins to win at a similar command. Additionally, he patiently suffers her rejection (because of his hesitation in mounting the cart), attempts suicide at a false report of her death, and breaks through iron bars at her invitation to lovemaking. *Frauendienst*, with its doctrine of womanly superiority, seems to inform the story.

But only on its surface, as further analysis discloses. Romance, as a depiction of the warrior class's idealization of itself, actually centers upon male heroes and not female love-objects. As was consistent with medieval religious, political and moral theories, men are the agents of the action and women—when they are heroines—the instruments. On the level of deep structure, Lancelot glorifies himself in his campaign to save the Queen. Guinevere exists, like other heroines of Arthurian and other romance, to get into trouble the hero must get her out of. The incentive to heroic action, she is at the same time its reward. Functionally, Guinevere is unable to act on her own. She is carried off and imprisoned; fought for and defended; freed and returned home, and fought for again: all at the will of and/or agreement between the males in the tale.

Romance females are patriarchally predicated by passive verbs; to romance males belong the active ones. In the course of Chrétien's romance, Lancelot successfully suffers and survives a death-dealing bed and a lethal sword bridge; defeats various minor knights and succors various minor ladies; lifts a symbolic tombstone to free Arthur's imprisoned subjects, whom he later releases again; attracts admiring younger knights; breaks iron bars to join the Queen; escapes from an inescapable tower. And these are but a sample of his deeds, which climax in his joyous welcome by Arthur and his court after he finally dispatches the abductor Meleaganz. Chrétien's narrative is obviously not *about* Guinevere, no matter how much she is its heroine: it is *about* Lancelot.

To ramify the portrait of Arthurian heroinehood, Guinevere may profitably be compared to two others of Chrétien's characters, Laudine and Enide. Of all Arthurian women, Laudine is the most bound into patriarchal custom. Her fate is tied to the magic fountain which is the heart of her patrimony. Once Yvain kills her husband, Esclados, she is obliged to find another defender for the fountain, to protect her land, since she—as a woman—is forbidden to bear arms. Through the schemes of her damsel, Lunete (of whom more under the rubric of female hero), she is brought to rationalize her hate for Yvain into a love which allows her acceptance of him as a new husband/fountain-defender.

Like the initial Guinevere, Laudine serves as a pivot for Yvain's growth in knightly prowess. Warned by Gawain of the dangers of uxoriousness, he receives permission from his spouse to renew his skill at arms, for the space of one year. Overstaying his leave, Yvain is publicly rebuked by Laudine's free-roaming damsel (note: not by his wife herself, since she is bound to the patriarchal fountain). The rebuke drives him mad—in Arthurian romance, a cipher for the recognition of sexual transgression (Doob). Cured and aided by a wonderful lion, he performs various deeds of knightly valor, particularly in service to ladies and including Lunete, who again reconciles him to Laudine.

If Laudine represents the ultimate Arthurian heroine, in her extreme passivity and submission to patriarchal custom, then Enide—the only female character in Chrétien whose name is usually linked to her hero's as the title of a romance— is an anomaly: the only heroine who, for part of her story, is also a female hero. The dialectic of this essay requires me to consider the earlier part of Enide's career separately from the latter, to which I turn in my next section.

As heroine, Enide seems at first even more archetypal than Laudine. Not a great lady like the latter and Guinevere, she is so genteelly, Cinderella-ish poor that Erec first sees her in a garment full of holes. Nor is her name ever given until she marries Erec—not unusual for medieval romance, in which so many women are known merely as someone's wife or lover,[5] and certainly an indicator of her status as instrument of Erec's glorious career. Yet, once married, she displays the same spurious power as Chrétien's other heroines, as Erec— in an opposite and complementary movement to Yvain's—falls into an uxoriousness so prolonged that his father's whole court talks of it. Only when he hears Enide blaming herself for his falling away from knightly activity does Erec take the decisive action which is to turn the character I will designate as Enide I—a heroine—at least temporarily into Enide II—a hero.

But before turning to Enide II's heroic career, let me catalog the characteristics of the Arthurian heroine. Whether the archetypal Guinevere, or Laudine, or Enide I, she is an instrument and not an agent: the still point around which the real action (of the male universe) turns. Her virtues are those universally recommended to medieval women in real life: chastity, obedience, silence (one does well to remember that Enide's troubles as a heroine begin when she speaks too openly). Her chief virtue, however, is always her beauty, the prime impelling force behind her hero's activity. In the case of Chrétien's Guinevere, it is more important than any real virtue and even supersedes the usually important one of chastity. For Chrétien never condemns the adultery of Lancelot and Guinevere. In a romance world where the hero's virtue depended so much upon amorous encouragement from the heroine, a monogamous relationship accompanied by infrequent sexual consummation sufficed as well as marriage (Lanham passim). With the female hero, however, absolute chastity seems necessary, and her relationship with the male hero is quite another matter. To this matter I now turn.

II

Female heroes in Arthurian romance fall into two sub-types: the wife-hero, and the virgin. The former role is self-evident, the latter perhaps needs clarification. By "virgin" both I and Arthurian romance understand a woman living with no permanent attachment to a man, and to some extent with a man's freedom of action (as in the original meaning of the word). Arthurian virgin-heroes remain single, at least for the duration of their capacity for heroic action. But, like Arthurian heroines and wife-heroes, they nevertheless share the prime function of devoted service to patriarchal culture.

Arthurian wife-heroes, on the other hand, never play a consistently heroic role in romance. The wife's social definition as *femme couverte*—the legal term for the married woman's identity as a chattel of her husband—allows her only intermittent access to those activities ordinarily (and "properly") associated with males. The most interesting of all such wife-heroes is the character I have designated Enide II.

I left off my discussion of Enide I at the point when she woke her husband with what she thought was a private lament. Her exaggeration of her own responsibility for what is—after all—Erec's choice of uxoriousness focuses attention upon the distinction her beauty brings to her heroinehood. But her self-accusation is also a blaming of that husband who is so attached to that beauty; and Erec's self-pride in his knightly honor is wounded by it. To Erec her remarks indicate that Enide as well as the world has underestimated him, and that therefore she does not love him enough. His subsequent trial of Enide not only matures her and his characters and restores their mutual love but also—and more to my present purpose—turns Enide for a time into a wife-hero.

Enide II's actions during this part of the romance are certainly not the "purgatory of obedience" Jean Frappier has denominated them (72) but rather a loyal and loving *dis*obedience, as well as an assertion of real female prowess. Commanded to wear her best dress (in contrast to her earlier rags) and ride forth with her husband, alone, and—most important—to say no word under any circumstances without his permission, Enide proves her affection and good judgment by defying the medieval wife's expected submission to the male command. In repeated though forbidden speech, she warns Erec of danger and treachery, allowing him to conquer numerous robber knights, two lecherous counts who covet her love, and a dwarf knight who becomes her and Erec's useful friend. Enide further performs incidental, nonheroinic actions such as watching their horses while her husband sleeps and subsisting like a male in the forest, without the lady's usually requisite servants. Impressed by such heroism, Erec assures her he now knows her love is perfect. But his kiss turns her again, as in the archetypal fairy tale, into a heroine. Forsaking heroic action, Enide assumes once again the female roles of nurse and admired beauty—a beauty she had lost while playing the hero. Adventures continue, but henceforth only for Erec.

Like Enide, Guinevere in later versions of her story evinces incidental heroism. Wherever Lancelot and not Modred is her lover, she resists her nephew's attempted incest. In the thirteenth-century *Mort Artu*, the fourteenth-century *Stanzaic Morte Arthur* and Malory's fifteenth-century *Morte Darthur*, Guinevere outwits Modred with the excuse that she must go to London to ready her trousseau; then she seizes the White Tower and holds it successfully against her would-be spouse. Grail-influenced works with their repeated motif of repentance from worldly values also allow for an incidentally heroic Guinevere. In both the *Stanzaic Morte* and Malory, Guinevere's taking of the veil emerges even more specifically than in Geoffrey of Monmouth as a rejection of the worldly heroine's role: Guinevere refuses Lancelot's love in an attempt at salvation for them both. Her spurning of his offer of marriage and even of a final kiss casts her into a heroic mold, but it is a male-inspired one: that of the repentant worldly woman, on the model of Mary Magdalene, Mary of Egypt and other formerly sexual females. As with Enide, this version of Guinevere is at best only partially heroic.

In Arthurian romance, only women who are not married are capable of consistent heroism. These virgins escape male domination and, for a time at least, actualize their title by acting the man. An ancient archetype influencing this model is that of the huntress goddess Artemis/Diana, whose very occupation implies freedom from women's usual social bonds—especially from the house symbolic of woman's role as keeper of the patriarchal flame. Thus such Arthurian women are frequently connected with both the forest and the moon.

The moon gives her very name to Chrétien's Lunete, the first of the virgin-heroes in Arthurian romance. Like the goddess who stands behind her, she possesses magic powers: her initial gift of a magic ring to Yvain makes him invisible to his pursuers and enables his subsequent success. Additionally, Lunete displays the wit which will come to distinguish Arthurian female heroes—she not only talks her mistress, the heroine Laudine, into marrying Yvain but, at the end of the romance and with similar guile, successfully reconciles husband and wife. Part of Lunete's persuasion of Laudine to marriage is an alleged letter from a certain *Damsel Sauvage*—obviously a counterfeit and covert reference to Lunete's own unbound and comparatively powerful, undomesticated presence. Active where Laudine is passive, she manipulates not only her mistress but Yvain himself. Her freedom emerges also in her physical mobility; at will she is able to leave the fountain to which the patriarchally predicated Laudine is bound. At one point Chrétien even calls her *maistre*, a rare designation—with its connotation of both skill and learning—for a woman during the Middle Ages. In spite of this preternatural cleverness, Lunete is loyal both to Laudine and Yvain. Only when she is condemned to the stake for treason can Yvain aid her as much as she does him, since she is precluded from waging trial by combat (a perquisite of the warrior class).

That combat can nevertheless be mounted in distinctively feminine ways is proved not only by Lunete but by another female character, Malory's Lyonet (the similarity in names is probably no accident). Attached like Lunete to a great lady, in this case her sister, Lyonesse, Lyonet comes to Arthur's court (the mobile virgin as compared to the static lady) to ask him to send her sister relief from a siege by an unwanted suitor. Given Gareth, Arthur's disguised nephew, as a champion, Lyonet derides him for having spent a year (his deliberate choice) as Arthur's kitchen boy. Her sustained scorn spurs Gareth to numerous victories and eventually to marriage with Lyonesse. Like Lunete, Lyonet uses both verbal guile and magic—the latter to ensure the young couple's chastity—as weapons. But, at the end of Gareth's tale, she is wed to his brother Gaheris. Malory's comment here, that she *"was* called *damsel sauvage"* (1:363, italics mine) is both an echo of Lunete's appellation and a reminder that she will be tamed by marriage—as Lunete, at least within Chrétien's tale, was not. Even virgin-heroes have their limits, Lunete in her inability to defend herself against the treason charge, Lyonet in her ultimate fate as a *femme couverte*.

But if they are not as free as males, and also few in number, virgin-heroes have for a time—unlike heroines—the power to change their environments. In their fruitful use of tongue and wit, they resemble the sometime wife-heroes; in their (however limited) magical powers and their mobility, the female counter-heroes. But these latter—the freest, most potent and most feared of Arthurian women—deserve a discussion all their own.

III

Like the heroine, the female hero, whether virgin or wife, exists to encourage male prowess: her agency is "selfless" in that it exists for patriarchal—male rather than female—purposes. Contrariwise, the female counter-hero holds values which are not necessarily those of the male culture in which she must exist. Her actions are as likely to hurt the hero as to help him. Rather than only occasionally exhibiting powers greater than most women, like the female hero, the counter-hero consistently fills roles ordinarily attributable only to men.

Such female power, like the female virgin-hero's, has its roots in a mythological archetype. If the virgin-hero is an avatar of Artemis, the female counter-hero derives from a much more powerful figure, the Magna Dea, the Great Mother whose religious worship the early Christian hierarchy found so dangerous that it tolerated, and eventually encouraged, the cult of the Blessed Virgin Mary as a counterbalance. The Arthurian female counter-hero is a fluid figure, always at least double and usually multiple in her manifestations. She appears—as Campbell notes of her mythological forebears—under "a multitude of guises," serving both as "mother of life" and "at the same time mother of death" (302-03).

Her sexually-initiated status is her hallmark: I know of no Arthurian counter-hero who is maiden. Even in marriage, she exhibits an indifference to patriarchal values and a sexual freedom unknown and unknowable to the female hero or the monogamous heroine. Her double nature as nurturer and destroyer illustrates even more aptly than the figures of heroine or female hero the ambiguity and ambivalence of medieval male authors generally, and Arthurian writers particularly, toward women. Thus she can be at the same time the most alluring of presences (her aspect as supernatural beauty) and the most revolting (her aspect as hag).

Both alluring beauty and loathsome haghood appear in the most influential Arthurian female counter-hero, Morgan le Fay. More beneficent splittings-off from her original role emerge in the several Ladies of the Lake who later develop from her archetype: literally watered-down from Morgan (whose name indicates her origins in the greater body of water, the sea), they exhibit that tenet of medieval misogyny which held that no woman should be as strong as a man, or *could* be without some supernatural power. In Morgan's movement as a character in Arthurian tradition emerges such misogyny at work, as she develops from an entirely wholesome into a mainly maleficent presence.

Her literal wholesomeness marks her first literary appearance in Geoffrey of Monmouth's *Vita Merlini* where—not yet Arthur's sister—she performs the office of carrying the dying King to Avalon for healing. As objective correlative to this nurturing function stands the nourishing ambience of her *insula pomorum*. A typical Celtic Otherworld, it is free from death, full of earthly delights, and inhabited by women who—in contrast to the patriarchal actuality of the real world—are its absolute rulers. This second Eden thrives under the reign of Morgan herself—beautiful, a shape-shifter who can change her appearance at will, and learned not only in the healing medicine she hopes to use on Arthur but in such recondite studies as astrology.

This portrait of Morgan as a lovely, learned and potent woman changes early in Arthurian tradition. Incidentally a healer in Chrétien, she acquires (in *Erec*) a lover, Guiomar, upon which liaison the worldly poet makes no comment. In the thirteenth-century Prose *Lancelot*, however, Guiomar becomes Guinevere's cousin and his affair with Morgan a source of shame to them both—and to Arthur, since Morgan is now his sister. Renounced by Guiomar at Guinevere's instigation, an embittered Morgan bears her lover's son after exile from the court. In an obvious quest for power over those who have hurt her, she seeks out Merlin, who also loves her, to teach her many enchantments. In a later work, the *Livre d'Artus*, she uses this newly-learned skill to found her *val sanz retour*, to keep Guiomar in her power and—with the valley's capacity for preventing, through a magic curtain of air, the escape of any knight who enters it—to foil Guinevere and Arthur by entrapping Round Table adventurers. This character elaboration, incidentally coinciding with the growth of women-hatred in the latter Middle Ages (Heer, ch. 13), turns Morgan from a nurturing ruler of a sea-girt paradise into a destructive sorceress who entraps men sexually rather than healing them.

Not only Morgan's healing powers are transformed: even her beauty is put in question. In the Prose *Lancelot*, while her loveliness is praised, she is also seen as ugly, hot (the bodily quality medievals associated with sexuality) and lecherous. To this portrait the Vulgate *Merlin* adds that she was very brown of face. Morgan thus diverges from the pink-and-white complexion and golden hair of the heroine (Harris). Since physical beauty is a coefficient of moral goodness in medieval literature, her darkness emerges as spiritual as well as corporeal. In the *Suite de Merlin*, she is said to have acquired permanent ugliness after yielding to lechery and the devil. In versions influenced by this idea of her ugliness, only through enchantment could she appear beautiful. Such a formulation is clearly an echo of the widespread medieval theological perception of the beautiful woman as the Devil in drag.

Many of these negative themes of hypersexuality, misused power and ugliness masquerading as beauty are summed up in Morgan's appearance in the fourteenth-century English poem, *Sir Gawain and the Green Knight*. Here, the Fay is a repulsive old crone who manipulates the lovely young Lady Bertilak and her husband in an attempted seduction of Gawain, who represents the entire Arthurian ethos. At the end of the poem, Bertilak reveals Morgan's role to Gawain, who (not without blemish) has survived the double beheading and triple hunting/ boudoir tests, as an attempted blow against Guinevere. Female counter-heroes are often as much counter to heroines as to male heroes.

Even when married, Morgan refuses male values. While she has variously named husbands in various Arthurian works, her most persistent spouse is Urien, and Yvain becomes their son. But marriage cannot tame her voracious sexual appetite. Taking a lover, Accolon, she gives him Arthur's sword and its even more powerful sheath (it prevents bleeding to death) after having promised her brother to keep it safe. Arthur's regaining of the sword and slaying of Accolon motivate Morgan to even further dirty work against the Round Table. With various other sorceress-queens who serve as narrative doubles to her personality (in Malory three others), she abducts Lancelot in an attempt to seduce him. She also abducts and vamps Alexander le Orphelin, a Cornish hero who vows to cut off his testicles rather than sleep with her in Malory's version of his adventures. Adultery is compounded by her plot to kill Urien, prevented only by the intervention of Yvain.

In spite of this murderous and adulterous career, Morgan retains her nurturing function as Arthur's conductress to Avalon after his wounding. But this "good" Morgan is overshadowed by the ubiquitous "bad" woman. She is the most extreme villain of Arthurian romance—even worse than the infamous Sir Breunz sans Pitié. Her gradual change (one can hardly call it growth) from a connector of life with healing, as mistress of Avalon, into a connector of death with illicit sex indicates the inability of male Arthurian authors to cope with the image of a woman of power in positive terms.

Reduction of that power seems to have influenced the later development of the various Ladies of the Lake—also counter-heroes but less strong and much more beneficent than Morgan. The original of these is the great ruler of a sea-kingdom—like Morgan's, a watery version of the Celtic Underworld—who kidnaps the baby Lancelot and rears him among her ten thousand maidens. Taught courtesy, valor, music, and simple, non-knightly combat, Lancelot is sent—at fifteen—to conquer the enemy of the Lady's cowardly son (the purpose of his abduction and fosterage). In terms of the male ethic which governs romance, the Lady's purpose is selfish—not the furtherance of the knight's own career, but a settling of her private grudge, as with Morgan's ultimate manifestations. Unlike Morgan, however, the Lady is eventually refined to the norms of her male culture. In the Prose *Lancelot*, for instance, her purpose alters and her sending Lancelot to Arthur's court to be knighted is its climax. She—or a further avatar (Holbrook)—also gives Arthur Excalibur and, at the end of his career, receives it again from him, besides earlier restoring it to him as he fights Accolon. Obviously the Lady has been retailored to represent the (mostly) nurturing side of the split mother-image, as Morgan has become the (mostly) devouring side.

A combination of these split images appears in the figure of Nimue (also called Niniane and Viviane), who first serves as a devourer and then as a restorer of Arthurian males. Like her sister-avatar, she is called the Lady of the Lake. In a borrowing from Morgan's career, she has the besotted Merlin teach her his magic, but without yielding to him sexually. Shutting Merlin away in a cave, she deprives the male Arthurians of their counselor and reveals her own cunning ambition. But Nimue then becomes the devoted and influential friend of Arthurian society: she saves the King and his knights from Morgan's death-dealing magic mantle; reverses the infatuation of Pelleas and Etard; and, taking Pelleas as her lover, makes him a knight of the Round Table and protects him all his life. Yet even settling down with one man does not hinder her power: she reveals Guinevere's innocence of a murder charge and emerges as one of the three (or nine, depending on the work) queens who bear the King away to Avalon. This last function allies her, of course, with her original—Morgan le Fay.

Whether maleficent like Morgan or (mostly) beneficent like Nimue and the other Ladies of the Lake, all Arthurian female counter-heroes reveal a split tendency. Never completely committed to the knightly ethos which dominates their world, they often act in their own interest instead of the males' (thus differing from the female heroes). Their actions are bold and often sexual. More than the female heroes, they are capable of transforming their environment(s) and doing so for their own benefit. Examined in terms of the prime function of romance as a mirror of the male warrior ideal, these Arthurian women are truly counter-cultural.

IV

And now to sum up. Arthurian heroines are conservative, passive, instrumental non-actors, useful for provoking, renewing and rewarding the actions of their knight-agents. Arthurian female heroes may, indirectly and for a specified time, consciously play female parts to effect transformation of their male-dominant world, but they always act only for knightly benefit. Arthurian female counter-heroes openly refuse to be seen in womanly supportive roles in what is essentially a male drama and attempt to change their woman-hostile world by direct and not indirect action. All of these women, even the comparatively powerful counter-heroes, are limited by their inability to assume such traditional male roles as the warrior one of physical combat. Once, for instance, when Lancelot is wounded with an arrow by a comparatively unimportant *damsel sauvage*, both the Vulgate and Malory make clear that it is only by accident. In place of such usual male roles as warrior and seer, female heroes and counter-heroes must use guile, both verbal and magical. Yet even this does not earn them honor: what is wisdom in the seer is reduced to mere sorcery in his female counterpart. As for heroines, they have only their beauty, a chancy weapon at best.

All three female types hold up a mirror to male social values, not female ones. What goes counter to the predominant and longstanding male-glorifying bias of the tradition, such as the power of the female counter-hero, is seen as subversive. Both society and literature in the Middle Ages so neglected or distorted women's values that female heroes begin as scarce and dwindle practically into non-existence. As Chaucer had his Wife of Bath note, the portrait depends on who paints it, the lion or the man. In medieval Arthurian literature, to make this figure further ironic, the image of the woman is not ever the product of the lioness, but always of the lion.[6]

Notes

[1]Dumézil's ultraproductive corpus spans over half a century, and dozens—probably hundreds—of books and articles. For a convenient summary of his (changing) ideas, see Littleton.

[2]See, for example, Dumézil, "Le Trio des Macha." An earlier and differently focused study of female tripartition is Lucy Paton's.

[3]For further discussion, see Fries, "Feminae Populi."

[4]Perhaps the most vivid enactment of this theme, common in romance as well as in female saint's life, is in the Middle English *Athelston* (ca. 1355-80), where the wife of the Earl of Stane must submit—although pregnant—to ordeal by fire to prove her husband's innocence of treason.

[5]An egregious example is the Middle English *Sir Isumbras*, in which an abducted wife survives a forced royal (and bigamous) marriage she insists remain chaste, and makes her original husband a sovereign upon his successor's death—all with no name except "the wife of Sir Isumbras."

[6]This paper was presented in a somewhat different form as The Kasling Memorial Lecture for 1985 at the State University of New York College at Fredonia.

Works Cited

Athelston. Ed. A. McI. Trounce. EETS 224. London: Oxford, 1951.

Campbell, Joseph. *The Hero with a Thousand Faces*. 2nd ed. Princeton: Princeton UP, 1968.

Chrétien, de Troyes. *Les Romans de Chrétien de Troyes: Erec et Enide, Le Chevalier de la charrete [Lancelot], Le Chevalier au lion [Yvain]*. Ed. Mario Roques. Paris: Champion, 1952, 1958, 1960.

Doob, Penelope B.R. *Nebuchadnezzar's Children: Conventions of Madness in Middle English Literature*. New Haven: Yale, 1975.

Dumézil, Georges. "Le trio des Macha." *RHR* 146: 5-17.

Frappier, Jean. *Chrétien de Troyes: The Man and His Work*. Trans. Raymond J. Cormier. Athens: U of Ohio P, 1982.

Fries, Maureen. "*Feminae Populi*: Popular Images of Women in Medieval Literature." *Journal of Popular Culture* 14 (1980): 79-86.

———. "Malory's Tristram as Counter-Hero to the *Morte Darthur*." *NM* 76 (1975): 605-13.

Frye, Northrup. *Anatomy of Criticism: Four Essays*. Princeton: Princeton UP, 1971.

Garbaty, T.A. "The Uncle-Nephew Relationship: Origin and Development." *Folklore* 88 (1977): 221-235.

Geoffrey of Monmouth. *History of the Kings of Britain*. Trans. Lewis Thorpe. London: Penguin, 1966.

———. *Vita Merlini*. Ed. and trans. J.J. Parry. Urbana: U of Illinois P, 1925.

Harris, Adelaide Evans. *The Heroine of the Middle English Romances*. Cleveland: Western Reserve UP, 1969.

Heer, Friedrich. *The Medieval World: Europe 1100-1350*. Trans. Janet Sondheimer. New York: Mentor, 1962.

Holbrook, S.E. "Nymue, the Chief Lady of the Lake, in Malory's *Le Morte Darthur*." *Speculum* 53 (1978): 761-77.

Lancelot de Lac. Ed. Elspeth Kennedy. 2 vols. Oxford: Clarendon, 1980.

Lanham, Margaret. "Chastity: A Study of Sexual Morality in the English Medieval Romance." Diss. Vanderbilt, 1948.

Littleton, C. Scott. *The New Comparative Mythology: An Anthropological Assessment of the Theories of Georges Dumézil*. Rev. ed. Berkeley: U of Cal. P, 1973.

Livre d'Artus, Le. The Vulgate Version of the Arthurian Romances. Ed. H. Oskar Sommer. 8 vols. Washington: Carnegie Institution, 1908-16. Vol. 7.

Malory, Sir Thomas. *The Works*. Ed. Eugéne Vinaver. 3rd ed., rev. P.J.C. Field. Oxford: Clarendon, 1990.

[Estoire de] Merlin. The Vulgate Version of the Arthurian Romances. Ed. H. Oskar Sommer. 8 vols. Washington: Carnegie Institution, 1908-16. Vol. 2.

[Suite de] Merlin. Ed. Gaston Paris and J. Ulrich. 2 vols. Paris: Didot, 1886.

[La] Mort [le roi] Artu. The Vulgate Version of the Arthurian Romances. Ed. H. Oskar Sommer. 8 vols. Washington: Carnegie Institution, 1908-16. Vol. 8.

[Stanzaic] Morte Arthur. Ed. P.F. Hissiger. The Hague: Mouton, 1975.

[Alliterative] Morte Arthure. Ed. Mary Hamel. New York: Garland, 1984.

Paton, Lucy. *Studies in the Fairy Mythology of Arthurian Romance*. 2nd ed. New York: Franklin, 1960.

Sir Gawain and the Green Knight. Ed. J.R.R. Tolkien and E.V. Gordon. 2nd ed., rev. Norman Davis. Oxford: Clarendon, 1967.

Sir Isumbras. The Thornton Romances. Ed. J.O. Halliwell [-Philips]. London: Camden Society, 1844.

Morgan Le Fay:
Goddess or Witch?

Charlotte Spivack

The origins of Morgan le Fay are obscured in the mists of Avalon, that mysterious veil between the Celtic Otherworld and our mundane one, which Marion Zimmer Bradley so movingly penetrated in her novel of that name. Arthurian scholars, such as Lucy Paton and Roger Sherman Loomis, speculate that she derived from a goddess figure—the mother goddess Modron or the war goddess Morrigan.[1] In four medieval texts she is actually referred to as a goddess. But these in turn are but facets of "the" goddess, the feminine deity who in her totality represents the life cycle and the psychic dimensions of all women as maiden, mother, wise woman, and warrior.[2]

Mythic figures, however, descend from their mountain tops to take on roles in human society, and in popular literature gods and goddesses become men and women—a kind of euhemerism in reverse. When we first encounter Morgan le Fay in the pages of that most imaginative historian, Geoffrey of Monmouth, she is one of the nine sisters of the holy Isle of Avalon where the mortally wounded Arthur goes to be healed and whence he will one day return. Subsequently in the various French verse romances based on the Matter of Britain she is portrayed as a benevolent figure, and the greatest of the French romanciers, Chrétien de Troyes, stresses her remarkable healing powers. As Loomis observes, "There is no attribute of Morgan's better authenticated than her power of healing" (*Grail*, 161). From her first appearance in literature, then, Morgan seems identified with the Wise Woman aspect of the goddess. Indeed in some versions of the Grail legend, she is even cited as the Grail bearer.

Beginning with the French prose romances, however, her character changes dramatically. She degenerates both in her purposes and in her powers, becoming a malicious master of the black arts, using her magic both to harm others and, somewhat pathetically, to conceal her own advancing age. In the Vulgate *Lancelot* she splits into two selves, sending a younger version of herself to seduce Lancelot when the older person proves incapable of doing so. Similarly, in the well-known English romance, *Sir Gawain and the Green Knight*, many readers find her again in a double role, at once the aged, ugly aunt and the beautiful young wife. "Most unlike to look on these ladies were,/For if the one was winsome, then withered was the other" (57).

The reasons for Morgan's degeneration are complex, but one clear fact emerges from the emphasis on her healing power. As a feature of the goddess, associated with the Wise Old Woman, this is a benign gift, even when associated

18

with death. The Celtic goddess as crone used her arts mercifully to ease the aged and suffering on to the next stage of life, which was death only when seen from this side but actually a higher level of existence in the Otherworld beyond.

In a Christian milieu, however, the arts of healing with herbs and other natural remedies became in the Middle Ages and early Renaissance associated with older women who were accused of witchcraft. Furthermore their skills as midwives and healers conflicted with the rise of medicine as well as with the teachings of the Catholic church. As a result in Europe between the thirteenth and seventeenth centuries nine million women were burned as witches.[3]

Recent years, however, have brought a revival of the benevolent witch. A frequently seen bumper sticker reads, "Witches heal." Charlie Murphy's song "The Burning Time" from the album *Catch the Fire* describes the meeting of a coven, focusing on one woman, "One of the many we call witches, the/ Healers and teachers of the wisdom of the earth/ The people grew through the knowledge she gave them/ Herbs to heal their bodies,/ Spells to make their spirits whole" (335). The increasingly popular neo-pagan movement has helped much to revamp our notions of witches and witchcraft.[4]

Not surprisingly, therefore, in many works of contemporary fantasy fiction, benign witches are depicted as healers. The old fear is still there, however, for the same herbs that cure can also kill. As the noted Renaissance physician and alchemist, Paracelsus, long ago warned, everything is potentially poison. In Vonda McIntyre's *Dream Snake*, for example, the healer is rejected by society, partly because of the traditional antipathy toward snakes. Furthermore the old disjunction between "witch" and "wizard", words which should have identical meanings but in popular usage do not, contrasts the witch's homely, domestic knowledge and skills unfavorably with the wizard's more intellectual learning. In Ursula Le Guin's *Earthsea* trilogy and its sequel *Tehanu*, the witches are portrayed as adept at food, herbs and handiwork, but the wizards cast the significant spells. On the other hand, whereas the work of the witches is largely benevolent, there is vast danger in the potential for destructive sorcery on the part of the talented but self-seeking wizards.

Goddess or witch? Morgan le Fay as depicted in recent popular fiction reveals the ambivalence of her heritage. In a few works she is a total villain. In Ruth Nichol's *Marrow of the World* she is a cruel witch who transforms herself into a beautiful young maiden in order to capture young men whom she lures to her castle. In this double role she closely resembles her divided portrayal in the Vulgate *Lancelot*, where she is split between the maiden and the crone aspects of the goddess. Morgan is also a malignant witch in Penelope Lively's *The Whispering Knights*, where she represents "the bad side of things" (17). Her appearance is a virtual iconography of darkness. She drives a black Rolls-Royce, "her skin was bone-white, and slightly gleaming, and the (black) hair hung straight to her shoulders and shone like water...her eyes were terrible. They were black, and cold as frost, and quite empty of anything but a furious intent to destroy" (73). Although summoned forth by a casual spell, Morgan has tremendous powers that make her eventual defeat a formidable challenge.

In several novels Morgan's portrayal is much more complex in its ambivalence. In Poul Anderson's *Three Hearts and Three Lions* her role combines that of a servant of Chaos with that of the mistress of the hero, Ogier the Dane, who defends the Law against Chaos. She is thus inwardly divided between her love for the hero and her destructive impulses. Unfortunately her character is not sufficiently well-developed to fulfill its potential complexity.

In Sanders Anne Laubenthal's *Excalibur* Morgan is portrayed with a much deeper ambivalence as a result of the goddess dimension in her role. The novel is set in Mobile, Alabama, where the Holy Grail and Arthur's magic sword have resurfaced, and Morgan is a contemporary woman infused with the personality of the legendary fay. As she explains her former life, however, she is also a reincarnation of Arianrhod, the sorceress and daughter of the goddess Don. The modern Morgan, who recalls her long-ago life, attributes her carrying of Arthur to Avalon to be healed to the instructions of the goddess Cerridwen, to whom she was and is still dedicated.[5]

Morgan's antagonist is Morgause, who is depicted as a terrible figure, identified with Lilith and Hecate and Anu. At some points in the narrative she enters into the body of the protagonist, Lynette. At first Morgan and Morgause as sisters are allied with the dark, but Morgan's devotion to the goddess turns her to the light. In a climactic scene, Morgause announces herself as "Anu, Bobh, and Macha, the triple sovereign of Darkness" (223), challenging her sister Morgan, who responds heroically, determined to destroy the "Mistress of Darkness." In a final dramatic confrontation their battle assumes epic-mythic proportions. Morgan stands firm while Morgause becomes a parody of rage. Biting her lips, foaming at the mouth, "her eyes scorched like blue coals in her haggard face" (223), she demands to be worshipped. "Light is only a mask of darkness!" (224) she screams, but Morgan, inspired by a sudden vision of the cauldron and of the goddess Cerridwen, the All-Wise, finds the strength to seize the sword and dismiss Morgause, who simply fades into the dark.

The living woman, who has incorporated Morgan into her own body, however, is burned to death in the flames which ensue. The body is reduced to dust and fine ash, much more than the normal effects of fire, as the fireman notes with astonishment. But Morgan's sacrifice has saved Excalibur for the Pendragon. In this novel Morgan moves from the role of witch, or mistress of the dark arts, to that of a devotee of the goddess, who leads her to the light.

Another ambivalent portrayal appears in Phyllis Karr's *Idylls of the Queen*, which deals with Malory's story of the poisoning of Sir Patrice by an apple at a banquet given by the Queen. Suspicion falls on Guenevere, but her innocence is proved by Sir Kay, the first-person narrator, with the help of his aunt, Morgan le Fay. Herself a reputed specialist in poisons, Morgan is a logical resource, and in this case her motives are sincere. By studying the vision in her magical basin she is able to determine the real culprit.

This Morgan is austere, somewhat resembling a nun, and attends compline when Sir Kay comes to call. She has an ecumenical view of religion, asserting that there is but one Divine, although known by many names. "I join myself to God under all His names, explore all His aspects, study all scriptures, choose myself symbols wherever I find them" (184). In her earthenware basin of water she can summon images of past and present. Unlike Merlin, she cannot prophecy the future. In her basin Kay and Mordred watch the enactment of the past event of the murder.

Throughout the episode Morgan is friendly yet distant, aloof yet witty, arrogant yet sympathetic. Her action is well-intentioned toward helping the queen, yet her pride in her necromancy and her teasing manner suggest someone not to be trusted. Clearly this is no villain, nor is it even an enemy of Camelot. On the other hand, this is not the incarnation of the goddess out to destroy the new patriarchal religion. In fact her reference to godhood, although supposedly all-inclusive, is clearly a masculine image. Karr's Morgan is the sly but genial sorceress whom anyone would like to have for an aunt.

Yet a different—and wholly sympathetic—portrayal of Morgan le Fay appears in Parke Godwin's *Firelord*. Here Morgana, as she is called, is one of the Prydn, the "little people," whom Arthur comes to love. The Prydns, or Britons, were regarded as Faerie Folk because of their diminutive size and supposedly magical powers. Morgana is described as "a tiny girl less than five feet tall, soft and vulnerable in a mass of black hair, leaves, and vines" (75). Arthur comes to love her, but she, along with several of the Prydn, are victims of Guenevere's murder plot. Unfortunately the characterization of Morgana is not developed, for the dominant female role is that of Guenevere.

Numerous other versions of Morgan le Fay have appeared in the burgeoning world of the Arthurian novel, some villainous, some sympathetic and some ambivalent, but an overall pattern emerges. Morgan seems to have been originally a goddess who evolved into one facet of the archetypal fourfold feminine—maiden, mother, wise woman and warrior. One side of the goddess, as of the human psyche, was dark and negative. Hence Morgan as the wise woman devolved in her negative manifestation into a treacherous figure who used her knowledge of herbal healing destructively—and to preserve her own youthful appearance— hence as a witch. In contemporary fiction, however, the witch is not necessarily an evil being. With the current popularity of neo-paganism, witches have been at least partially redeemed from the centuries old prejudice against them.

As we have seen, in some novels, such as Laubenthal's *Excalibur*, the character of Morgan is redeemed through her devotion to the goddess. What remains is for her to become once more a goddess. This is achieved in Marion Zimmer Bradley's *The Mists of Avalon*, the most complex and satisfying revisioning of this tantalizingly paradoxical fay. Morgaine, the first-person narrator of the novel, begins by asserting in recollection her totality: "In my time I have been called many things: sister, lover, priestess, wise-man, queen" (ix). Shortly into the retrospective narrative, when Morgaine is but a child, Viviane identifies her as the maiden facet of the goddess. Speaking to Igraine, Morgaine's mother, she explains, "She is not yet a maiden, and I not yet a wise woman...but we are the Three, Igraine. Together we make up the Goddess, and she is present among us" (23), adding ominously that their other sister, Morgause, may be the fourth dark hidden face. In the course of the novel, Morgaine moves through all four phases of the feminine, embracing in turn all of those roles, maiden, mother, wise-woman, and warrior, each of which is revealed in a negative as well as a positive manifestation.

First we see her as maiden. Blessed with the gift of Sight, she displays remarkable visionary powers. While yet a child, she is able to summon visions of people and events at a great remove in time or space. Viviane is so impressed with her skills that she takes the girl with her to Avalon for a period of seven years training in the House of Maidens. Morgaine later recalls these years which culminated in the mark of the crescent moon set between her brows. "Seven times Beltane eve came and went; seven times the winters shrivelled us all with cold. The Sight came easily" (136). Then, at age eighteen, she dedicates her life—and her chastity—to the goddess.

After she reaches maturity, she is chosen to mate with the King Stag, one whom she does not know ahead of time, in the sacred marriage. It is not until after the ritual that she discovers the identity of her lover: he is her brother Arthur. Both are horrified, but although she feels tricked into committing incest, she resists the temptation to abort the pregnancy and becomes the mother of Mordred.[6] Although this child is immediately taken away from her by Morgause, she also experiences motherhood in her subsequent marriage to Uriens, whose son comes to love her as his own mother.

Although Morgaine for a time renounces her role as priestess of Avalon, she eventually returns to her beloved goddess and becomes the wise old woman. For a time she thinks of the world outside of the sacred isle as distant and unreal. "I do not know how many years I dwelt in Avalon before the end. I remember only that I floated in a vast and nameless place, beyond joy and sorrow, knowing only serenity and the little tasks of everyday" (758).

When her tranquil life as priestess in Avalon is disrupted by events in Camelot, she becomes the Morrigan, the Celtic goddess of war and death. It becomes her mission to destroy Arthur, who has banned the matriarchal religion in favor of patriarchal Christianity. In possession of the magic sword Excalibur, he also steals the remaining Holy Regalia, the cup, the dish and the spear. Because of Morgaine in her warrior role, not only Arthur but also Mordred, Uriens' two older sons and many others die. Even her close friend, Raven, who helps her to recover the Holy Grail, dies at her behest, albeit indirectly.

Morgaine ultimately realizes the identity of goddess and total self. "I have called on the goddess and found her within myself" (803). The four women on the barge which receives the wounded Arthur are all facets of her. "Morgaine the Maiden, who had summoned Arthur to the running of the deer and the challenge of the King Stag, and Morgaine the Mother who had been torn asunder when Gwydion was born, and the Queen of North Wales, summoning the eclipse to send Accolon raging against Arthur, and the Dark Queen of Fairy" (867).

With Bradley, the role of Morgan le Fay thus comes full circle. Originally a mythic goddess, encompassing all sides of the feminine nature, then fragmented into the wise old woman aspect, who quickly deteriorates into a witch, with her healing powers employed destructively, then reemerging as a benevolent witch redeemed through her belief in the goddess, she at last once more becomes the goddess, i.e., the total woman.

Notes

[1]Loomis argues that the descent of the fays in medieval romance and modern folklore from the goddesses of the pre-Christian era explains Morgan le Fay's multiple personality. "She has acquired not only the attributes and activities of Macha, the Morrigan, and Matrona, but also the mythic heritage of other Celtic deities. She is a female pantheon in miniature" (*Wales* 127).

[2]According to the typology of psychologist Carl G. Jung, the female psyche is structured as a quaternity, with polarized dimensions representing the maiden and the mother, the wise woman and warrior. Similarly, the male psyche is represented as son and father, wise man and warrior.

[3]Although scholars do not agree on the exact number of witch burnings—inevitably a speculative figure—most recent studies of the subject agree that it was probably in the range of four to nine million.

[4]An example of a recent non-Arthurian novel which features a sympathetic witch is Elizabeth Arthur's *Binding Spell* (New York: Doubleday, 1988).

[5]In Merlin Stone's study of early matriarchy, Cerridwen is identified as "the Goddess of Intelligence and Knowledge in the pre-Christian legends of Ireland" (4).

[6]Morgaine's infant son is originally named Gwydion but later assumes the Latinized name of Mordred.

Works Cited

Anderson, Poul. *Three Hearts and Three Lions*. Garden City, New York: Doubleday, 1953.

Bradley, Marion Zimmer. *The Mists of Avalon*. New York: Knopf, 1982.

Chrétien de Troyes. *Arthurian Romances*. Trans. D.D.R. Owen. London: J.M. Dent, 1987.

Geoffrey of Monmouth. *The History of the King of Britain*. Trans. Lewis Thorpe. Harmondsworth: Penguin, 1966.

Godwin, Parke. *Firelord*. Garden City, NY: Doubleday, 1980.

Karr, Phyllis Ann. *The Idylls of the Queen*. New York: Ace Books, 1982.

Laubenthal, Sanders Anne. *Excalibur*. New York: Ballantine, 1973.

Le Guin, Ursula K. *Tehanu*. New York: Atheneum, 1990.

Lively, Penelope. *The Whispering Knights*. London: Wm. Heinemann, 1971.

Loomis, Roger Sherman. *The Grail from Celtic Myth to Christian Symbol*. New York: Columbia U, 1965.

_____ *Wales and the Arthurian Tradition*. Cardiff: U of Wales, 136.

McIntyre, Vonda. *Dream Snake*. New York: Dell, 1986.

Micha, Alexandre, ed. *Lancelot, roman en prose du XIIIe Siecle*, 7 vols. Geneva: Droz, 1978-80.

Murphy, Charlie. "The Burning Time." *Extrapolation* 31 (1990): 334-335.

Nichols, Ruth. *Marrow of the World*. New York: Atheneum, 1972.

Paton, Lucy Allen. *Studies in the Fairy Mythology of Arthurian Romance*. Boston: Ginn, 1903.

Sir Gawain and the Green Knight. Trans. Brian Stone. Harmondsworth: Penguin, 1959.

Stone, Merlin. *When God Was a Woman*. New York and London: Harcourt Brace Jovanovich, 1976.

Thoroughly Modern Morgan:
Morgan le Fey in Twentieth-Century
Popular Arthuriana

Elizabeth S. Sklar

For better or worse, Morgan le Fey appears to have cast a glamour on creators and consumers of twentieth-century Arthuriana. Currently a cornerstone of the new Arthurian mythos, she has made her presence felt in neo-Arthurian literature throughout this century, from E.A. Robinson's *Tristram*, to White's *Once and Future King*, to Berger's *Arthur Rex*, and is easily recognizable in such pseudonymous incarnations as Walker Percy's Margo (*Lancelot*) and Memo Paris in Malamud's *The Natural*. Morgan is also featured in at least ten fantasy-fiction novels,[1] achieving star status in Bradley's *Mists of Avalon*, and more recently in *White Nun's Telling*, by Fay Sampson. In one form or another, Morgan has become an obligatory feature of Arthurian films, even such off-center productions as Disney's *The Sword and the Stone*, where she surfaces as the protean Mad Madame Mim, and *Knight Riders*, where she becomes a he. In both astral manifestation and physical incarnation Morgan has invaded the comic book universe, and she inhabits the world of fantasy role-playing and board games as well. In short, Morgan occupies a secure position in the contemporary Arthurian pantheon, as familiar a figure to modern enthusiasts as Merlin, Lancelot, or King Arthur himself.

But Morgan le Fey is different from Merlin, Lancelot, Arthur or any other major figure in Arthurian tradition in one important respect: for all practical purposes she is deficient in literary lineage, a virtual unknown to pre-modern Anglophone Arthurian literature. In Middle English Arthurian romance, for example, aside from her *dea ex machina* role in *Sir Gawain and the Green Knight*, explicable only by reference to the French Vulgate Arthurian cycle, and a passing allusion to her as "Arthour's soster" in *Of Arthour and of Merlin* (4444), Morgan is notable primarily for her absence. Only in Malory's *Morte Darthur* can Morgan be accounted a viable fictional figure; and even in Malory, where she serves an important thematic function, turning up like the proverbial bad penny for a good two-thirds of the narrative, Morgan is accorded only a single tale of her own.[2] Curiously, despite Malory's crucial influence on the nineteenth-century Arthurian revival, Victorian and post-Victorian revivalists had little or no truck with Morgan le Fey, opting instead to embody their gynophobic anxieties in the seductress figure of Nimue/Vivien.[3] While Morgan is occasionally represented in the Victorian and post-Victorian visual arts, especially by the great illustrators of Malory's *Morte* (Beardsley, Rackham, Pyle), and is presumably present as one of the mourning queens in various pictorial representations of the death of Arthur (e.g. James Archer's "Le Mort D'Arthur"), only rarely does she serve as protagonist, as in Frederick Sandys' "Morgan le Fey" (1864). Her literary representations are also relatively rare during this period and tend to be confined to obscure, non-canonical texts, such as a narrative poem entitled "Accolon of Gaul" by one Madison J. Cawein (1889), or *King Arthur* (1897), a trilogy of lyrical dramas whose author was afflicted with the unlikely moniker F.B. Money Coutts.[4] Indeed, the tangentiality of Morgan to the "serious" medieval and pre-modern Anglophone Arthurian tradition is indicated by the entries for Morgan in two recent Arthurian reference books. The only allusion to her in the first edition of *The Arthurian Handbook*, for example, turns up under the entry for Geoffrey of Monmouth's *Vita Merlini*; and *The Arthurian Encyclopedia* merely observes that "She was paid little attention in English literature...until rediscovered by modern fantasy writers" (395).[5]

It is this rediscovery, or rather one facet of this rediscovery, that I want to explore here. We have made Morgan our own in a rather interesting way: in the process of transforming her from a virtual nonentity into a fictionally viable persona we have actually created two Morgans, both reflexes, I think, of the same cultural phenomenon: the Morgan of fantasy fiction, where feminist ideology accords her varying degrees of sympathy; and the Morgan of texts designated for mass audiences—films, comic books, and role-playing games— a Morgan who, as the very embodiment of evil dedicated to the subversion of all forms of governance, expresses the fears that inevitably accompany the sort of radical cultural change represented by the social realities and ideological imperatives of escalating female empowerment during this century. This latter Morgan is my subject here. What follows, after a brief but necessary digression on her Malorean progenetrix, is an anatomy of popular culture's Morgan le Fey.

Malory's Morgan

Unlike the Morgan of modern fantasy narratives, which more often than not capitalize on her associations with a romanticized and largely unrecorded Celtic tradition, the Morgan of the genres under consideration here is based primarily on the account of her character and actions in Malory's *Morte Darthur*. Indeed, Malory is the acknowledged source for all the more serious-minded contemporary productions, especially the fantasy role-playing and board games, the most self-consciously "authentic" of popular culture's Arthuriana. For example, *King Arthur and the Knights of the Round Table* includes, in addition to a four-page disquisition on the early historical and literary sources of Arthurian legend and on conditions in subroman Britain (21-24), a seven-paragraph summary of the *Morte Darthur* (3), and incorporates quotations from the *Morte* in its rule book (eg. 5, 7). Although Morgan le Fey is not a player-character in this game, "Morgana's Scabbard" is featured as a major game artifact; the description of this object (28) alludes to Malory's account of Morgan's antics in "Arthur and Accolon," where Morgan steals, and subsequently disposes of, Arthur's life-protecting sword sheath. Equally indebted to Malory are the authors of *Knights of Camelot*, who acknowledge having drawn "extensively from the works of Sir Thomas Malory" (contents page); and in this game, Morgan is a player-character, albeit a tangential one, in that she is forced to share a game-chit with Merlin. The setting and most of the characters of *Pendragon*, as well, are avowedly based on the *Morte Darthur*; moreover, the ample marginalia of the *Pendragon Player's Book* frequently quote verbatim from Malory's work, and one marginal note offers a substantial collection of "Malorean Male Names" (11). Additionally, the bibliography on page 11 of the *Pendragon Game Master's Book* lists three different editions of Malory's work, accompanied by brief comments on the relative readability of these texts. The source reading list provided by the *Prince Valiant* game is headed by Malory, and even *Dungeons & Dragons*, a fundamentally non-Arthurian game, enumerates in the *Advanced Dungeons & Dragons Deities & Demigods Cyclopedia* over one hundred knights of Arthurian tradition, specifying in a prefatory note that in his *Morte*, Malory "collected all the legends and tales of Arthur and his Knights of the Round Table, and first presented the stories in the forms we are familiar with today" (17-18). Less reverential than the foregoing, perhaps, is the author of the *Grey Knight* scenario for *Pendragon*, who grudgingly confesses to having "dutifully slogged through Malory" (2).

Although such explicit acknowledgements are less frequent in comic-book and cinematic treatments of the Arthurian legends (perhaps because the intertext is more diffuse in these genres), Mike Barr's introduction to the single-volume edition of *Camelot 3000* includes several paragraphs on Malory, and the *Marvel Handbook* provides both an accurate genealogy for Morgan and a summary of "Arthur and Accolon" in its entry under Morgan le Fey (13). Amongst the cinematic treatments of the legend, John Boorman's almost sycophantic attribution of his material to Malory is well known; and although *Camelot*, like the stage play from which it derives, is based on White's *Once and Future King*, Malory himself, as it were, makes a brief guest appearance in the final scene in the guise of young "Tom of Warwick." Even the self-indulgent producers of *Knights of the Round Table* solemnly indicate that their script is "Based on Sir Thomas Malory's 'Le Morte D'Arthur'," and, despite its over-fanciful reworking of the legend, the film occasionally offers up surprisingly accurate details from the *Morte*: a version of the poisoned apple episode from Book VII, for example, or the adder whose fateful appearance precipitates the final battle between Arthur and Mordred.

Given, then, the heavy reliance of these texts on Malory's *Morte Darthur*, and given that I want to argue for the ideological "authenticity" of the contemporary Morgan, it may be useful here to provide a brief description of Malory's Morgan le Fey. In general terms, Malory's Morgan represents all that is structurally subversive within Arthurian society as a whole. The quintessential anarchist, Morgan obsessively devotes her not inconsiderable energies to opposing and attempting to sabotage all aspects of the structure, both social and political. Enabled through her possession of supernatural powers to violate "natural" gender-boundaries and constraints, she is known to the Logrian inhabitants as the "wycche most that is now lyving" (327), doggedly dedicated to malfeasance, a woman who "ded never good by yll" (382). Malice is her metier—she collaborates in the boiling of Elaine of Corbin, for example, merely "bycause she was called the fayryst lady of that countrey" (582). Driven to "false treson" (383) by her equally "fals lustes" (107), Morgan engages in an unremitting attempt to depose

King Arthur and sabotage his realm, for "ever as she myght, she made warre on kyng Arthure" (446); and like any saboteuse worth her salt, Morgan operates by indirection and subterfuge, manipulating others into unwittingly doing her dirty work for her. She also forms alliances with empowered male antitypes, "daungerous knyghtes" such as Brewnys Saunz Pyte and King Mark, in her attempt to harrass the structure and "dystroy all thos knyghtes that Kynge Arthure lovyth" (446). Her speciality is the ambush, and at various times throughout the narrative she succeeds in capturing and imprisoning a number of chief knights of the realm, including Sir Trystram and Sir Lancelot.

Malory's Morgan is a veritable congeries of primal drives, whose literary antecedents include a host of unsavory prototypes, among whom Cain holds pride of place. For the source of Morgan's antipathy to her half-brother Arthur and all that he represents evidently consists in a particularly virulent form of sibling rivalry. King Arthur, we are told, is "the man in the worlde that she hatyth moste, because he is moste of worship and of prouesse of ony of hir blood" (106). Her most concerted effort to reenact Cain's crime is recounted in the tale of "Arthur and Accolon," in which Morgan concocts a truly byzantine plot, the objective of which, after disposing of Arthur, is to place her lover, Accolon, on Arthur's throne so that she might become queen of Logres. To implement this scenario, Morgan supplies her unsuspecting lover with Excalibur and its life-protecting scabbard, both of which Arthur, displaying a trust more endearing than admirable, has given into her safekeeping. That achieving her objectives entails not only an appalling combination of regicide and fratricide but husband-slaying as well—part of Morgan's plan is to "sle hir husbonde kynge Uryence lyghtly" (106)—deters her not a whit. Nor is she deterred by the death of Accolon, which short-circuits her immediate political agenda; to the contrary, failure only fuels her determination to savage the Arthurian dream.[6]

In relation to the Morgan of popular culture Arthuriana, one feature of Malory's Morgan is worth separate mention here, and that is her sexual appetite, which underscores the fundamental gynophobia that marks both the Malorean and the modern Arthurian tradition. In Malory's book, female sexuality—active or passive—is by its very nature structurally threatening; by invoking desire and engendering masculine sexual competition, thereby deflecting loyalty from its proper channels and dislocating culturally-endorsed priorities, it subverts the male-male bonding and the allegiance to ethical imperatives upon which the survival of the realm depends. In her combination of randomly destructive and purposefully subversive behaviors with aggressive sexuality, Malory's Morgan becomes the perfect repository for this gynophobic anxiety. Thus, although Accolon functions more or less as a pawn in Morgan's push towards checkmate, it is Morgan's lust that led her to so deploy him in the first place, for she loved him "oute of mesure as paramour" (106). Subsequently, with Accolon out of the picture, Morgan turns to Lancelot as lust-object, whom she chronically kidnaps and imprisons in the hopes of diverting his amorous attentions from Guinevere to herself, for "quene Morgan loved sir Launcelot best, and ever she desired hym" (413). But sexual desire for Morgan does not necessarily entail love; at one point in Malory's narrative she imprisons young Alysaundir l'Orphelin "for none other entente but for to do hir plesure whan hit lykyth hir" (480). All told, Morgan's is an essentially sociopathic personality, respecting no boundaries and acknowledging no rules save those dictated by her own ambitions, envy and lust.

Modern Morgan

Like her Malorean prototype, the Morgan of contemporary popular texts is a thoroughly bad egg, a composite of all the patriarchal nightmare-women of literary tradition: Eve, Circe, Medea and Lady Macbeth compressed into a single, infinitely menacing package. In terms of the external features of that package, there seems to be little current consensus. The Dark Lady paradigm, which we would predict from literary tradition, tends to predominate in the source-conscious Arthurian fantasy role-playing and board games. In the character insert accompanying *Pendragon*, for example, Morgan is said to have "dark skin, black hair, black eyes, piercing glance" (5), a descriptor replicated in the *Grey Knight* scenario for the same game (insert C, np), while the *Prince Valiant* script limns her as "A very tall, willowy brunette" (84). Although the gospel according to Marvel Comics fancifully endows her with magenta tresses (and a daunting 6'2" frame), comic book portrayals of Morgan also generally adhere to the Dark Lady paradigm: in both *Iron Man* and *Camelot 3000*, Morgan is depicted as a raven-haired, feline beauty, albeit given to highly immodest fashion choices. The one anomaly here is the Morgan of *Swamp Thing*, whose creators have opted for a style that can only be identified as Flash Gordon futuristic, in which Morgan's coloring is obscured by a bizarre and fundamentally indescribable headpiece. Cinematic representations of Morgan tend to be more varied, determined in part by the exigencies of casting. Films that choose to offer up a Celtic—hence dark-haired—Guenevere, such as *Knights of the Round Table* and *Excalibur*, counterpose a fair-haired Morgan le Fey. Conversely, blonde Guineveres (as in *Sword of Lancelot*) dictate dark Morgans. Morgan's self-presentation in films varies even more widely than her coloring, ranging from Candace Bergen's superannuated hippie *cum* Wicked-Witch-of-the-West get-up in *Merlin and the Sword* to Helen Mirren's S&M iron bikini in *Excalibur*, to the severe, nun-like garb sported by Maureen O'Brien in the BBC's *Legend of King Arthur*.

Given Morgan's supernatural powers, perhaps such shape-shifting is to be expected. But despite the variety of the pop-Morgan's physical manifestations, there is remarkable intergeneric consistency in terms of her character and behaviors, for all of which Malory serves as the principal model. The Morgan le Fey of film, comics and gaming is id incarnate, anarchic and obsessive, deploying a devastating combination of sexuality and sorcery in a single-minded campaign of structural subversion. Like Malory's Morgan, ours is an implacable enemy to Arthur: *Pendragon* notes Morgan's "passionately developed contempt for Arthur," and one of her dominant character traits in the *Prince Valiant* game is "Hatred for Arthur." Similarly, the *Marvel Handbook* notes that "Morgan hated King Arthur and frequently attacked him and his knights" (13). Unmodified over the course of five centuries, Morgan's agenda retains as its major objective the subversion of Arthur's realm and all that it represents. The scenario for *The Grey Knight*, for example, calls for Morgan to "launch major plots against Arthur," and both film and comic-book treatments of Arthurian legend consistently portray Morgan in her role as saboteuse and Arthurian adversary; indeed, the Arthur of *Camelot 3000* confesses that "Of all my enemies, [Morgan] is the only one I fear" (6.7). Morgan is all the more threatening in that, like her prototype, she rarely operates in the open; forced by the limitations of her gender into covert opposition to the establishment, she works exclusively by indirection, manipulating others (usually male, occasionally extraterrestrial) to execute her dastardly deeds: in films, she is generally portrayed as a sneaky voyeuse, whose favorite pastimes consist of spying on Lancelot and Guinevere and whispering in the ear of whomever she has selected as her current instrument of destruction. Our Morgan also enters into alliances with empowered males, although Mordred (of whom more shortly) and in one instance Dr. Doom (*Iron Man*) have replaced such "daungerous knyghtes" as Brewnys Saunz Pyte and King Mark as her co-conspiritors.

Where we can discern a motive for her subversive activities, it is consonant with that of Malory's Morgan, that is, political aspiration. The Morgan of *Advanced Dungeons & Dragons*, for instance, "constantly uses her power of illusion to attempt to become queen of the British Isles" (20) (an obvious allusion to "Arthur and Accolon"); the *Marvel Handbook* avers that "[Morgan] wished to rule Britain herself" (13), and in *Knights of the Round Table* Morgan incites Mordred to ever-greater feats of treachery in order to come into her rights as self-proclaimed only heir to Uther. One difference between our Morgan and Malory's is that the Cain paradigm which served as partial motivation for the medieval Morgan has been supplanted by a more contemporary (i.e. post-Freudian) explanation of her hostility: *Excalibur*, *Camelot 3000* and the *Marvel Handbook* ascribe her animosity towards Arthur to Morgan's desire to even the score with the Pendragon clan for Uther's rape of her mother, Ygerne.

The genesis of her malice, however, is of minor significance in our narrativization of Morgan as compared to the destructive potential and consequences of its enactment. What is foregrounded in both Malory and in Morgan's contemporary incarnations is the threat she represents to the ethical and moral foundations of society as a whole. At her most anarchic, the modern Morgan becomes the very embodiment of motiveless malignancy, the archetypal *animus* run rampant. Her designated character-type in *Pendragon*, for instance, is that of "Wicked Witch" (echoing Malory's "wycche moste that is now lyvyng"), and, like her progenetrix who "ded never goode but yll," she bears a richly-earned reputation for reflexive malfeasance: the gamemaster of *Pendragon*, for example, is enjoined to "always blame evil events on [Morgan], even if she is not responsible. Any suspected ill-doing is her fault..." (39). Morgan specializes in gratuitous violence as well as structural sabotage, especially in her comic-book persona, where she can be found casually vaporizing one of the aliens in her thrall for approaching her "without permission" (*Camelot 3000*, 3.4), or transforming men into beasts at whim: the sinister simian "pet" who accompanies Morgan in *Camelot 3000* "was once a man—before he displeased me" (7.12); and one must suspect that her hawk-familiar in *Iron Man* suffered a similar fate—the bird's name, it would seem, is Accolon.

It is no accident that the victims of the modern Morgan's malice are exclusively male, for her overdetermined sexuality exceeds even that of her prototype and serves as the chief vehicle for her manipulation of others. Predictably, lust features high on the list of character traits enumerated for the pop-Morgan in role-playing games: *Pendragon*, for instance, assigns her a lust quotient of 18 (as compared, say, to an honesty quotient of 3), and the *Prince Valiant* game narrative describes her as "the sinister, lustful enchantress of legend," although curiously her lust-object here is the "handsome Sir Gawain" (84), rather than Sir Lancelot. The *Marvel Handbook* puts it most succinctly: "Morgan had many lovers" (13). While her sexual aggression is muted in most cinematic and comic-book treatments of Morgan, in that she tends to inspire rather than enact desire, her sexuality is given ample play in all three genres; she is with only one exception uniformly depicted as seductive in both appearance and behavior, particularly in comic-books, where her physical sexuality is grotesquely displayed: big-breasted, wasp-waisted, long-legged, she is an adolescent wet-dream gone awry. The degree to which Morgan le Fey is reflexively associated with sexuality nowadays is indicated by the program preview for a recent revival of the BBC's *Legend of King Arthur*, anomalous in its interpretation of Morgan as an asexual, brooding ascetic. Yet the program preview, with wanton inaccuracy, promises that the first episode will offer the spectacle of "Arthur...seduced by the evil Morgan" (Ann Arbor News *TV Guide* 1/1/90).

The New History of Morgan le Fey

In all the features enumerated above, the pop-Morgan replicates the character traits and behaviors of her Malorean progenetrix with admirable fidelity; she is far more "authentic" in this respect than the more sympathetic Morgan of fantasy fiction. But although Morgan landed on our doorstep with a predetermined character, she arrived with no narrative to speak of: she is a woman with a past (in both senses of the word) but a woman without a history. What little narrative did accompany her in her time travels—the story of "Arthur and Accolon," whose primary concerns are regnal succession and aristocratic inheritance rights—has not proven very useful for modern treatments of Morgan, and turns up only in bits and pieces: the hawk-familiar named Accolon, for example, or "Morgana's Scabbard" as an artifact in the *King Arthur* game, or the shard of Excalibur which the Morgan in *Iron Man* uses to resurrect the decayed bodies of those killed by that sword in a past life.[7] Thus we have been forced to narrativize Morgan le Fey, to create for her a fictive history that accommodates her inherited character and function while enabling the promotion of Morgan from bit-player to major actor in the modern Arthurian saga.

Although its details vary from source to source, the new history of Morgan le Fey is comprised of three fundamental features, all of which represent non-canonical and even anti-canonical contributions to the fictive history of Arthur. The first, consistently enacted in both film and comic-book renditions of Morgan, is her entirely non-traditional association with Mordred as her collaborator in the sabotage of Camelot. Whereas in Malory's account Mordred is one of the few major antagonists with whom Morgan has no association, in the sources under consideration here the presence of the one necessarily entails the other; they are inseparable as henchpeople joined in antipathy to Camelot. A corollary constant is that Morgan is invariably both the brains and the backbone of the operation, a phenomenon that not only signals, through its inversion of accepted dominance patterns, the extent of Morgan's violation of patriarchal order, but also conveniently shifts the burden of guilt for Camelot's collapse from the masculine to the feminine, from Mordred to Morgan. The creation of this new Morgan/Mordred axis facilitates yet another displacement as well, one which likewise serves to launder a masculine figure's reputation while further sullying Morgan le Fey's. Inspired, no doubt, by residual queasiness regarding Mordred's canonical parentage—his incestuous conception as the result of a random coupling between King Arthur and Arthur's half-sister Morgawse (Malory 32)—many of the neo-Arthurians have felt constrained to re-invent Mordred's genealogy and, perforce, Morgan's as well.[8] In the process, the precise nature of the blood-relationship between Mordred and Morgan has become a matter of some uncertainty. While *Camelot 3000* and *Merlin and the Sword* quite properly identify Mordred as Morgan's nephew (although the latter remains mum concerning the troublesome issue of Mordred's parentage, as does *Swamp Thing* which represents Mordred as Arthur's cousin), some treatments move to strengthen the blood-ties between them. Thus *Knights of the Round Table* converts Mordred and Morgan into half-siblings: in the opening scene of the film, Morgan proudly identifies herself as the only legitimate heir to Uther Pendragon, while Mordred is evidently a bend-sinister production of the same king, and in *Excalibur*, as in some of the fantasy fiction accounts, Mordred becomes Morgan's son, in this case the product of Morgan's cold-blooded seduction of Arthur as part of her carefully-crafted plan to destroy the kingdom. Whatever the posited familial relationship between Mordred and Morgan, however, we are usually given to infer sexual interaction of one sort or another between them. As a result, the uncomfortable issue of sexual taboo is displaced, with Mordred serving as kind of a genetic conduit, from Arthur to Morgan le Fey.

The second non-traditional constant in our narrativization of Morgan le Fey is her adversarial relationship with Merlin, who, according to traditional chronology, had long since been entombed by Nyneve/Nimue/Nimiane when Morgan began her career as a guerilla warrior against Arthur and his knights (Malory 92-93). In the current popular Arthurian mythos, however, undoubtedly because of the premium placed on sorcery and magic by the genres under consideration here, Merlin has been granted non-canonical longevity; his own history has been revised to allow him to function for the majority of Arthur's long reign, where he serves as protector of and advisor to the king, ofttimes more crucial to the survival of the realm than Arthur himself. Nowhere is this more evident than in his role as principal obstacle to our modern Morgan, whose nefarious agenda he persistently foils through his superior magic. Thus, in *Excalibur*, it is Merlin's withholding of the spell to awaken the Dragon of Power that delays the implementation of Morgan's elegant plot against Arthur and his kingdom. Merlin also impedes Morgan's conspiracy with Mordred to entrap Lancelot and Guenivere in *Knights of the Round Table*; and in *Merlin and the Sword*, Merlin is so effective in short-circuiting Morgan's plans that she is constrained to pressure Nyneve to "neutralize Merlin with a magic spell" in order to give free rein to her own evil enchantments. The adversarial relationship between Morgan and Merlin is even more explicit in comic-book treatments of the legend. The extensive biography of Morgan le Fey in the *Marvel Handbook* notes that "Morgan's many attempts to bring ruin upon Camelot were continually thwarted by Arthur [and] Merlin"; ultimately, we are informed,

"Morgan was imprisoned by Merlin in her Earthly palace," whence she was able to escape only by projecting her astral self into a different dimension (14).[9] Similarly, King Arthur in *Iron Man* boasts that historically, despite his half-sister's worst efforts against him, "with the aid of my mystic sword, Excalibur, and my own wizard, Merlin, Morgana was always thwarted." The Morgan of *Camelot 3000* puts the case most succinctly; all of her attempts on Arthur's life have been futile, she avers, because "the thrice-damned Merlin provided a defense against my magicks" (5.10).

Given this adversarial relationship between the two enchanters, it is hardly surprising to find that in some contemporary renditions of the new Arthurian mythos, Morgan has become instrumental in the demise of the new Merlin. In *Merlin and the Sword*, for example, Morgan puts Nyneve's hapless father to the rack in order to force the girl to seduce and entrap Merlin. In *Camelot 3000* (11.15), Morgan goes so far as to recreate Nyneve—visually represented as a rather horrible parody of the *vagina dentata*—in order that Nyneve may re-enact her seduction and entombment of Merlin. In several instances, Morgan herself has supplanted Nyneve in the role of Merlin's nemesis: in *Knights of the Round Table* she ensures his demise by ordering Mordred to treat Merlin to a poisoned apple, and in *Excalibur* she waits only until she has wrested the precious spell from Merlin to permanently entrap him in the bowels of the Dragon's Cave.

The third essential feature of Morgan's new history is her active and largely successful role in the destruction of Camelot. In Malory, despite her determination and palpable ill-will, Morgan le Fey plays no role whatsoever in the final demise of Arthur's kingdom: her machinations are usually foiled, and most of her malicious activities ultimately come to nought. Indeed, she disappears from Malory's narrative prior to the "Book of the Sankgreal," long before the suppressed tensions of Logres erupt into civil war and political chaos. In her modern manifestations, however, Morgan le Fey, like Merlin, is granted non-canonical longevity and is usually portrayed as the orchestrator of Camelot's collapse. In both *Knights of the Round Table* and *Merlin and the Sword*, it is Morgan who first observes the suppressed sexual tensions between Lancelot and Guenivere, which she ultimately uses as a wedge to weaken the foundations of the realm; in *Knights of the Round Table* Morgan herself contrives the entrapment of the lovers and is present at the denouement. The more ambitious and highly motivated Morgana of *Excalibur* deals the kingdom a double whammy, getting Lancelot banished through her manipulation of Sir Gawain, and seducing Arthur to engender Mordred, whom she grooms as Arthur's nemesis. Although *Swamp Thing* tends to waffle a bit on this matter, having Morgan foresee rather than engineer the collapse of Camelot, it does grant Morgan (and us) the gratifying sight of Camelot literally falling—from Swamp Thing's back—as it happens.

With her meager fictive history and her lack of literary lineage, Morgan le Fey has served as a kind of *tabula rasa* upon which we have been able to inscribe our peculiarly modern cultural aspirations and anxieties. One might wonder why we have selected Morgan for such intensive play in our times; tradition provides for any number of masculine figures with minimally-developed fictive histories, many of whom would have served equally well as structural antagonists. The phenomenon may be partially explained by the current fascination with magic and sorcery—a response, perhaps, to our technology-intensive age—that has also granted Merlin a non-canonically important role in our collective version of Arthurian legend. But one senses that the cultural encoding runs deeper than this, and I suspect that the key to that encoding lies in Morgan's gender. I would suggest that our rendering of Morgan le Fey, in both her positive and her negative incarnations, may be read as a response to the increased empowerment of women in the course of this century, that the feminist ideology that informs the rehabilitative treatments of Morgan in fantasy fiction, generally produced by and for women, has reciprocally engendered the gynophobic response of those mass-cultural texts whose primary target audience is adolescent and post-adolescent males. One unifying feature of the new history of Morgan le Fey that differentiates her from the Morgan of historical tradition is her greatly increased empowerment. Although the structure still dictates that she operate covertly, we have given her a far more powerful ally in Mordred, whose fictive history is inextricably bound to the destruction of Camelot, than Malory allowed his Morgan, whose henchmen in subversion—Sir Malagryne, Brewnys Saunz Pyte, and even King Mark—proved to be containable by the structure. Thus, through Mordred, a male whose malice matches her own, Morgan has been able to transcend the structurally-imposed limitations of her gender, and achieve, as her medieval prototype could not, full realization of her anarchic agenda.[10]

The other constant in the new history of Morgan le Fey, her overdetermined sexuality, encodes the traditionally gynophobic attitude towards uncontained female sexuality, which, if liberated, is perceived as having the power—graphically represented in the Circean transformations wrought by the comic-book Morgan— to literally turn men into beasts.[11] Her adversarial relationship with Merlin is equally suggestive. In a sense, while he is able, Merlin plays superego to Morgan's id, containing as best he can her anarchic impulses: it is no accident that Merlin, with his aged countenance and flowing white beard, is the visual embodiment of the patriarchal ideal. The fact that this containment is only temporary, however, that Merlin is ultimately defeated by Morgan's primal energy, by her essential femaleness, suggests a truly apocalyptic gynophobic vision, predicating as the inevitable outcome of female empowerment and uncontained female sexuality the successful sabotage of all the structures controlled by the masculine establishment, familial, social, ethical and political. The end-product of female empowerment, according to this gloomy gospel, is the irredeemable collapse of human civilization, a return to the primal world of bestiality, anarchy, and chaos.

Thus we come to the fundamental irony of popular culture's Morgan le Fey: despite the ostensibly subversive nature of at least two of the three genres under consideration here, and despite their deviations from the surface features of traditional Arthurian lore, their menacing Morgan inscribes an intensely conservative ideology, subtextually consonant with the pervasive gynophobia that has marked most Anglophone Arthurian literature from Malory to the present. Beneath the playful surfaces of the games, films and comic books that constitute much of our Arthurian entertainment lurk anxieties and biases that bring us full circle to medieval sexual politics.

Notes

[1]See Thompson for titles and summaries.

[2]"Arthur and Accolon," Book I, 98-112.

[3]The notable exception here, of course, is Twain's carelessly sadistic Mrs. le Fey (*Connecticut Yankee*, chapter 16).

[4]On Cawein and Coutts, see Taylor and Brewer 169, 210. The paintings by Sandys and Archer are reproduced in Barber, *The Arthurian Legends*. The plates among which they appear, unnumbered and unpaginated, immediately precede page 167. One point of interest concerning the literary interpretations of Morgan is that Coutts appears to have been the first Arthurian redactor to convert Morgan into Mordred's mother, evidently a bowdlerizing gesture to remove "the taint of parenthood" from King Arthur (Taylor and Brewer 210).

[5]By far the most substantial and thoroughly-researched reference entry on Morgan le Fey is found in Phyllis Ann Karr's *The King Arthur Companion* (76), a sourcebook for fantasy role-playing gamers.

[6]It is, for example, immediately following this episode that Morgan steals and disposes of Excalibur's protective scabbard.

[7]A few other bits and pieces of traditional Arthuriana concerning Morgan appear from time to time. One of the fortune cards in *King Arthur and the Knights of the Round Table*, for example, stipulates that the player "may invite Morgan le Fey to one of [his/ her] estates. If Sir Lancelot strays to within 1 area of it he will be captured." The *Grey Knight* scenario alludes to Morgan's penchant for setting ambushes for Arthur's knights. Notwithstanding these occasional nods to tradition, however, we find nothing approaching a connected narrative based on earlier materials.

[8]Morgawse and Morgan le Fey are sisters, offspring of the union between Ygerne and Duke Gorlois of Cornwell; Ygerne also bore Arthur, although his sire was, of course, Uther Pendragon. Mordred is thus nephew to Morgan, nephew-and-son to King Arthur.

[9]Morgan's comic-book debut occurred in the August 5, 1978 issue of *Spider Woman*, where the protagonist becomes unwitting host to Morgan's astral manifestation.

[10]The notion that fully-realized female empowerment can be achieved only through alliance with status males is made explicit in *Iron Man* by Arthur himself, who expresses his concern that that "should Morgana ally herself with this King Doom, she could possibly find the power to succeed where so often before she failed."

[11]In one instance, Morgan's sexuality is literally contagious, as well, for in *Camelot 3000* she is the carrier of a unique variety of sexually-transmitted disease: any man daring to embrace her immediately finds his body covered with a gross, and instantly lethal, fungoid growth.

Works Cited

Books

The Arthurian Encyclopedia. Ed. Norris J. Lacy. New York: Garland, 1986.

The Arthurian Handbook. Ed. Norris J. Lacy and Geoffrey Ashe. New York: Garland, 1988.

Barber, Richard. *The Arthurian Legends: An Illustrated Anthology*. Totowa, NJ: Littlefield Adams & Co., 1979.

Karr, Phyllis Ann. *The King Arthur Companion*. Reston, VA: Reston Publishing Co, Inc., 1983.

Malory, Sir Thomas. *Works*. Ed. Eugene Vinaver. London: Oxford UP, 1964.

Taylor, Beverly and Elisabeth Brewer. *The Return of King Arthur*. Cambridge: Boydell and Brewer Ltd., 1983.

Games

Advanced Dungeons & Dragons Deities & Demigods Cyclopedia. James M. Ward with Robert J. Kuntz. Ed. Lawrence Shick. Lake Geneva, WI: TSR Games, 1980.

"The Grey Knight" (*Pendragon* scenario). Larry DiTillio. Albany, CA: Chaosium, 1986.

King Arthur and the Knights of the Round Table. Matthew Hill et al. London: Wotan Games, 1986.

Knights of Camelot Fantasy Boardgame. Lake Geneva, WI: TSR Hobbies, Inc., 1980.

Pendragon. Greg Stafford et al. Albany, CA: Chaosium, 1985.

Prince Valiant: The Story-Telling Game. Greg Stafford et al. Albany, CA: Chaosium, 1989.

Films

Excalibur. Dir. John Boorman. With Nicol Williamson and Nigel Terry. Orion/Warner, 1981.

Knights of the Round Table. Dir. Richard Thorpe. With Robert Taylor and Ava Gardner. Loew's/MGM, 1953.

The Legend of King Arthur (TV series). Dir. Rodney Bennett. With Robert Eddison and Andrew Burt. BBC/Time Life, 1974.

Merlin and the Sword (originally titled *Arthur the King*). Dir. Clive Donner. With Malcolm McDowell and Candice Bergen. Martin Poll and Jadran/Comworld, 1985.

Sword of Lancelot (originally titled *Lancelot and Guinevere*). Dir. Cornel Wilde. With Cornel Wilde and Brian Aherne. Universal, 1963.

Comics

Camelot 3000. Mike W. Barr and Brian Bolland. New York, NY: DC Comics Inc./Warner Books, 1988.

Handbook of the Marvel Universe #9. New York, NY: Marvel Comics Group, 1985.

Iron Man #150. New York, NY: Marvel Comics Group, Sept. 1981.

Swamp Thing #87. New York, NY: DC Comics, June 1989.

Gotham's Dark Knight:
The Postmodern Transformation
of the Arthurian Mythos

Jesse W. Nash

All too often, our insights into the nature of popular culture are the result of accidental encounters with the very people professional academics talk to the least—children and young people. Students of culture, and not just anthropologists, tend to operate as if culture is something adults transmit to children. According to that logic, to understand culture we need to talk to adults or study their artifacts. Popular culture, however, is an entirely different matter. Unlike the "culture" of classical anthropological and humanistic studies, contemporary popular culture is increasingly for, about and by young people (King).

A case in point is the fate of the Arthurian legends in contemporary American popular culture. Arthurian themes and symbolism continue to be widely disseminated throughout popular culture, the culture of our young people. Although few specifically *King Arthur and the Knights of the Round Table* movies are being made, interest in Arthuriana can be detected in the themes, motifs, and symbols of many science fiction and fantasy films, from *Star Wars* to *Willow*. The heroic fantasy novels that crowd the shelves in our bookstores are essentially variations on the Arthurian legends. Comic books as well feed on Arthurian themes, symbols and artifacts. Series with such titles as *Camelot 3000, The Knights of Pendragon, Excalibur, The Legends of the Dark Knight*, etc. are highly praised and well-read, my own local comics dealer tells me.

The Batman comic books, and perhaps popular culture in general, exploit traditional Arthuriana to such a degree they actually replace more "classical" Arthuriana artifacts. A local book dealer tells me that very few copies of such works as *King Arthur and the Knights of the Round Table* are sold anymore, and when they are bought, they are normally bought by adults buying them for unsuspecting and perhaps unappreciative children and young people. Young people, my book dealer tells me, rarely buy any of the many available traditional versions of the Arthurian legends.

Ironically, popular American culture is suffused by Arthurian-sounding titles and images. But the classical artifacts of Arthuriana, such as Malory's text, for example, are neglected, especially by younger people. A high school teacher explains that this neglect is due to the "cultural illiteracy" of her students. "Besides," she adds, "that King Arthur stuff is really boring."

36

Her students, of course, disagree. One student told me: "Man, they're not, like, you know, realistic." I was intrigued. Not realistic? "No, like, the story's for the birds. King Arthur, his dad, Merlin, the whole crew are real crooks." Another student was a little more articulate: "I can't really respect Lancelot either. How could someone be willing to die for King Arthur?" Still another student rescued me from total confusion by telling me: "Check out Frank Miller's Batman, not the old caped crusader crap, but the new Dark Knight. Miller's got the story right."[1]

I did "check out" Miller's Batman and compared him to the older Batman. There was a difference. With the help of my youthful informants, I was able to confirm that the difference does have something to do with "getting the story right." And that difference helps explain that generational gap in the appreciation of Arthuriana artifacts, textual and otherwise, classical and popular. We will find that the Arthuriana of popular culture has undergone a considerable transformation.

Classical Arthuriana materials and the old Batman comic books belong to what might be called an Arthurian "mythos."[2] My youthful informants reject this classical mythos as "unrealistic." The "new" Batman, Frank Miller's recent version, is more than a simple variation on the Arthurian theme(s) but is rather a "postmodern" transformation of that mythos (Collins, 33-34; Nash). Why call this Batman postmodern? Miller's *Dark Knight* and other popular culture artifacts are postmodern precisely because they have rejected and/or transformed the older Arthurian mythos. This fact makes Miller's Batman and other popular culture artifacts of a similar nature somewhat revolutionary, if not unAmerican.

The Arthurian mythos is part and parcel of American culture. The Arthurian mythos *is* the ideology of the American political system.[3] The elements of that ideology are so woven into the narrative of American culture that we can still speak of President John F. Kennedy's tenure as that of a "Camelot."[4] Ronald Reagan, too, although very different, appealed to the Kennedy myth to justify his own revolution and would have occasion to refer to America as the "city" on the hill, a Camelot. It is no surprise, then, that Reagan could be described in Arthurian language. He was an outsider, a knight in shiny armor, like Kennedy and King Arthur, riding in to rescue the system (Wills, 299). At his first state of the union address to Congress after the revelations concerning the "Iran-Contra Affair" were made public, Reagan would be referred to by one news commentator as "a wounded leader." In keeping with the logic of the Arthurian mythos, both Kennedy's assassination and Reagan's problems are understood not so much as personal problems but as threats to the system. As Peter Jennings made clear in his analysis of Reagan's difficulties, what is at stake in such situations is the presidency and the system, not the man but the president, as in the older story, not Arthur so much as kingship itself. And that is the central element of the Arthurian mythos: the health of the system, its maintenance, its periodic degeneration and consequent regeneration. In one sense, because the system is so paramount, the sins of the two presidential-kings, like those of Arthur and his predecessors, only add to the mythic luster of their reigns.

Summarizing, the Arthurian mythos indicates that there was a golden age of politics and culture than can be relived, especially when inaugurated by a politician deemed to be an "outsider" to the political system, but who has "blood ties" to that system as a bastard child of sorts and who because of his uncertain status rejuvenates the system. This outsider doesn't function to tear down the system but to reform it, to make it stronger. A fundamental element of this mythos then is the periodic decline and resurrection of the system, but no matter what, the system must be preserved. As in both the Kennedy and Reagan cases, some will argue that the "evils" they committed, they committed for the "good" of the system and for its survival. Finally, that system must exist because there are forces, the forces of evil and chaos, an "evil empire," antithetical to civilization, which would triumph if the Arthurian political system were not in place. Above all, the Arthurian mythos fears the triumph of these "evil forces" knocking at the gates of Camelot, and a crucial element in the self-definition of the Arthurian president is his opposition to these evil forces. The Arthurian king and/or president doesn't simply oppose evil, he, by virtue of who he is, regenerates the earth.

My young informants, on the other hand, do not only think that Washington, D.C. is no Camelot and Ronald Reagan is no King Arthur, they doubt if there ever was a Camelot or if such a place is even desirable. They have rejected at least partially the Arthurian mythos. In a way, Batman's Gotham City *is* Camelot, and that is a frightening thought. Camelot unmasked is Gotham City. And Gotham City is America disabused of the American dream. Camelot, one young woman told me, is a "trick" of the system. The new Batman is postmodern precisely because there is no Camelot-like Gotham to return to or work toward. Miller's Dark Knight, first introduced in 1986 as a revision of the Batman materials, is not a return to an older, more pristine Batman of the late thirties and early forties. The older Batman necessitates a postmodern rewriting because the older Batman himself has become politically problematic.

The old Batman is an ideal part of the Arthurian mythos. He is orphaned by a criminal, but he is wealthy, thus aristocratic, the victim of the unrestrained greed of the poor. He becomes a "dark knight" to pursue criminals at night, the ideal time for crime, and dresses as a "bat" to induce fear in the "superstitious" minds of the criminal class. Crime itself represents the activities of a "hidden world."[5] He is a caped crusader, which likewise evokes the image of the knight. He is chivalric and single. He has his own squire, Robin the Boy Wonder. He eventually belongs to a round table of sorts, the Justice League of America. And he works for both police commissioner Gordon and the president of the United States.

His wealth and his status as a spokesman for the system become politically untenable. As a superhero, he is only an industrialist protecting the wealth and property of other wealthy Gothamites. At the end of one of the first cases, Batman tells Robin that a certain company of criminals thought they could acquire wealth the "easy way," that is, by crime (Kane 304). Bob Kane, the creator of the series, portrays a criminal class that threatens Gotham and its upright and usually wealthy citizens. As a spokesman for the wealthy and the political system, the old Batman is preachy, self-righteous and largely unconcerned with the life and rights of the criminal class. All of this makes perfect sense within the framework of the Arthurian mythos, which neatly divides the world up into binary characteristics such as good and evil, right and wrong, law and crime, wealth and poverty, etc.

The difficulty with these binary characteristics and the political system reliant on them is their naivete. They presume that crime is only something one willingly chooses. They presume that the political, judicial and legal system are just and impartial. More ominously, they are ahistorical and immune to criticism. The binary characteristics, being binary characteristics, are also doubles of each other. The Arthurian King is both savior and tempter, just and tyrannical.[6] Batman himself is an ambiguous, almost shady figure, working for the law but outside the legal system and occasionally sought by the police. Being Arthurian, the old Batman and the rulers of his Gotham can rule precisely because they already rule. When we can ask why they rule and if they should rule, we are ready for a change in perspective. Miller's Batman is decidedly postmodern because he no longer buys the myth of power Gotham's leaders utter. All postmodern analysis will presume the fictional or mystical basis for legal authority in the first place (Derrida 944-945).

The ambiguity plaguing the Arthurian conceptual apparatus can be seen in the figure of Batman himself, who was once described as: "Count (Dracula) cleansed of his evil and endowed with a social conscience" (Leatherdale 224). Such a description is more apt for the old Batman, the Arthurian Batman, and the description also touches on the problematic nature of the Arthurian mythos. To begin with, it is odd for a system fearful of "evil forces" and "evil empires" to have heroes who are themselves of ambiguous or dubious origin and all too easily labeled criminal. Note that this labeling is equally possible of Arthur, Parzival, Lancelot and Batman. The Arthurian mythos needs this cloak of indecipherability, this air that law is the mystery of authority and not fiction (Nash 9). When he first made his appearance in the May, 1939 issue of *Detective Comics* as "the Bat-Man," Batman is introduced as "a mysterious and adventurous figure fighting for righteousness and apprehending the wrong doer, in his lone battle against the evil forces of society..." (Kane 8). For the old Batman and his creators, evil is antithetical to society—the two descriptions are mutually exclusive. Historically, Kane is naive as to the nature of American society. When that society becomes problematic, the old Batman will become embarrassing, and the Arthurian mythos will be seen as an uncritical and perhaps unhealthy authoritarianism.

This early description of Batman as a loner, however, is really misleading. Batman rarely works alone. Almost immediately in his comic book career, he is adopted by the police and police commissioner Gordon. From a postmodern perspective his cozy relationship with the "Man" is troubling, and telling indeed is the fact that the legal and police system of Gotham City needs his help. Why he becomes the caped crusader is itself intriguing and terribly Arthurian. He tells Robin: "My parents too were killed by a criminal. That's why I've devoted my life to exterminate [sic] them" (Kane 131). He becomes the Batman to seek vengeance against criminals, which could also serve as a description of the political and legal system of Gotham. Although revenge is illegal, the law seeks revenge. Batman's revenge then justifies the system in a strange way. The old Batman protects the system from having to face its own inadequacies, especially the inadequacy of the legal system and police force. It is almost a religious affirmation of sorts: even if the police or courts fail, there is a higher justice which will even all the scores. But the score in the old Batman is always evened out in favor of the wealthy.

As an outsider, Batman functions to keep the puzzle that is Gotham City from falling completely apart. When he first meets Robin in the April 1940 issue of *Detective Comics*, Batman tells Robin that the future Boy Wonder can't tell the police who killed his parents because "this whole town is run by Boss Zucco. If you told what you knew you'd be dead in an hour" (Kane 131). If this is true, what kind of city is Gotham? And if this is true, why fight to preserve a corrupt and uncaring system? Batman doesn't ask these questions, but my younger readers think he should have.

Gotham isn't quite the Camelot it's cracked up to be, but Batman doesn't seem to notice. He doesn't seem to be aware of the contradictions. The introduction of Robin the "Boy Wonder" only adds to the problematic nature of those contradictions. At the end of their first caper together, Batman mildly scolds Robin for being too eager and not waiting for him before engaging a group of criminals. Robin replies smiling: "Aw! I didn't want to miss any of the fun! Say, I can hardly wait till we go on our next case. I bet it'll be a corker" (Kane 140). Batman and Robin, like the knights of the old round table, have become part of the problem. The heroic mythos, whether it is Arthurian or Homeric, masks the contradictions of society and by masking them allows them to persist. Batman not only becomes part of the problem that is Gotham City; his activities are misdirected. The real problem in Gotham City is not the penny-ante criminals he chases about the nightscape of the city or the masked and costumed super-villains he battles with alarming frequency, again like the knights of old, not dueling to save the city so much as to prove who is stronger, Batman or the Joker. No, the structures of Gotham City itself are the problem. If that is the case, to battle crime and evil, Batman must do the unthinkable for an Arthurian hero. He must rebel against the system. To do that, he must become, not a criminal, but postmodern, since the criminal is already a functioning part of the system.

Which is the starting point of Frank Miller's *The Dark Knight Returns*. Batman has disappeared from the scene for ten years, having retired to become Bruce Wayne, not because his job was finished but because his job had become too complex. The Gotham of this series of Batman adventures is very different from the Gotham of the past. The contrast, for the uninitiated reader, is remarkable. This Gotham, the Gotham of the new Batman, is truly dangerous. At the beginning of *Batman Year One*, which is a rewriting of Batman's origins after the appearance of *The Dark Knight Returns*, Commissioner Gordon describes his entry into the city: "Gotham City. Maybe it's all I deserve, now. Maybe it's just my time in Hell...in an airplane, from above, all you'd see are the streets and buildings. Fool you into thinking it's civilized" (Miller, *Year One* 2). Bruce Wayne, who is also flying into the city, is thinking: "I should have taken the train. I should be closer. I should see the enemy" (Miller 2).

The enemy in the *Dark Knight* texts is also Gotham City. Its very structures and history engender crime. The nature of the criminal hasn't changed. The nature of Batman's perceptions has changed. In *Batman: Year One*, Batman returns to the "enemy camp," a slum area. That's what the old Batman would have naively thought: crime is where poverty is, thus the criminal is the poor man wanting the wealth of the wealthy. This postmodern Batman quickly discovers that crime is a structural feature of the city as a whole and not simply the willful actions of the have-nots, who isolate themselves from the wealthy and proper citizens of Gotham.

Crime is something the rich and powerful also practice. And this new Batman declares war. He crashes a party of the wealthy who routinely finance and run the city's politicians. After having destroyed much of the ballroom, Batman announces: "Ladies and gentlemen, you have eaten well. You've eaten Gotham's wealth. Its spirit. Your feast is nearly over. From this moment on—none of you are safe" (Miller 38). The leader, a wealthy gangster-type, named, appropriately enough, Roman, calls Batman "a damned Robin Hood" (Miller 40). But unlike the Robin Hood of legend, the new Dark Knight has no loyalty to the system, and he doesn't just wage his war against the wealthy and politically affluent. He wages his war against any and all who threaten human survival.

Having noted this war, we must hasten to point out that Batman as a child of postmodernity is hard pressed to justify his stance. As is pointed out in the *Dark Knight* texts, Batman's existence, from the perspective of the Arthurian mythos, is a thorn in the side of the legal and political structures. Batman's activities are quite illegal. According to the logic of the Arthurian mythos, Batman has no right to wage war against either the full-fledged criminals or the quasi-criminals of the upper class and the nouveau-riche gangsters of Gotham City. He holds no office of law enforcement and has received no appropriate delegation. According to the logic of the system, Batman too is a criminal. In short, to crusade against crime, the caped avenger must break the law, must defy the law and eventually even fight federal troops.

Batman's stance is not easily taken. Nor is Police Commissioner Gordon's. In the *Dark Knight* texts, the commissioner is naturally opposed to Batman's involvement in the criminal scene, but Gordon shares Batman's/Bruce Wayne's uneasiness with the system. Both men become more complex in these texts. To adequately express that complexity, the *Dark Knight* texts must become more complex in terms of their narrative strategy. Unlike the texts of the Arthurian mythos, the *Dark Knight* texts are retrospective, uncertain. They reveal a change in the understanding of the person, an understanding which is postmodern in that it is reminiscent of Foucault, Derrida, Lacan, Kristeva, etc. (Taylor). In the older Batman stories, Batman is a nifty schizophrenic, moving easily from rugged superhero to effeminate jetsetter. Identity is monolithic, a given, naive, we might say.

Frank Miller's Dark Knight is not comfortable with his schizoid state. But it is not something he can really control. There is a "bat" within that limits his control; the bat is no longer a model; it is now a totem. This Batman is more realistic. Fighting crime of whatever stripe in Gotham isn't a picnic. One cannot be nice or flippant in such a pursuit. One does become a bat, a hunter, a dark knight, a knight whose own interiority is labyrinthine and less than godly. As Delueze and Guattari formulate the matter, the human civilization of Gotham City is a sham; what is required is that one become an animal, a human-becoming-animal, a human-becoming-intense. Miller's Dark Knight is such a "becoming," a creature no longer under rational control, because rationality as a convention only protects the powerful and refuses to address the issues at hand—a city of human beings threatened by the various criminal elements, including the city itself, innocent human beings who aren't really all that innocent. At times, as in the "graphic novel" *Arkham Asylum*, Batman fears that he is as bad as the Joker (Morrison and McKean).

To express this transformation of the Batman character and the reality of Gotham City, the *Dark Knight* texts are polyphonous. There is no one narrator. These texts are truly heterogeneous in that no one person, including Batman, owns the texts and speaks unequivocally (Kristeva 10; Collins 60-64). Sometimes Batman or Bruce Wayne speaks. Sometimes Gordon narrates. Quite often, newscasts inform us of what has happened. Even the criminals are given a narrative voice. And no one voice is authoritative, not even Batman's. The absence of one narrative voice reflects the rejection of the Arthurian mythos. There is no one narrative voice because there is no one structure of authority in the city. In *The Dark Knight Returns*, the various criminals have as much claim to authority as the mayor or the police. As the leader of the gang known as the "mutants" says: "Don't call us a gang. Don't call us criminals. We are the law. We are the future. Gotham City belongs to the mutants. Soon the world will be ours" (Miller 36). Who can dispute their claim? In a postmodern universe, we realize that authority belongs to those who control the city. In an Arthurian universe, those who control the city control it by the will of God. No one is that naive in Frank Miller's Gotham City, not even the mayor who knows he rules by virtue of criminal support and their complicity with the duly elected political officials.

Moreover, the lack of one narrative voice forces us to demythologize or deconstruct our notion of "the people" or "innocent citizens." Media interviews with men and women in the street highlight the absence of innocence and the problematic nature of democratic or popular approval of Batman's vigilante actions. One man interviewed enthusiastically supports Batman: "Batman? Yeah, I think he's a-okay. He's kicking just the right butts—butts the cops ain't kicking, that's for sure. Hope he goes after the homos next" (Miller 37).

Who runs Gotham City? No one, and everyone. It depends on what part of town one happens to find oneself in. Batman's vigilante efforts are directed toward the wealthy criminal class and the mutants, a gang threatening to take over. Oddly enough, the police negotiate with the mutants and the gangsters. They don't really try to eliminate them. Even in the midst of the mutants' crime wave, the police and legal authorities are more concerned with Batman's interfering than they are with protecting lives. The gangsters and the mutants, aptly named given their punk hair styles, scarification rituals and filed-down teeth, justify the existence of the police force. Batman by virtue of his vigilante actions calls into question the need for the police force. Batman forces us to realize that the Law is designed to protect Itself, not citizens (Nash 9). In this sense, Batman is decidedly anti-Arthurian and postmodern.

The mutants understand the system. Their leader, the archetypal "black knight," even issues a vaguely Arthurian-sounding challenge: "We will kill the old man Gordon. His woman will weep for him. We will chop him. We will grind him. We will bathe in his blood. I myself will kill the fool Batman. I will rip the meat from his bones and suck them dry. I will eat his heart and drag his body through the street" (Miller 36). The mutants are products of the system, and then they receive what they need to aid in their takeover of the city. A general, himself depressed and angry with the system, sells munitions to them (Miller 14-15). Reminiscent of political scandals in the Reagan administration, these scenes set the stage for Batman's battle with the mutant leader, his eventual branding as a federal problem, and the appearance of Ronald Reagan and his ambassador to Batman, Superman.

At the end of an early case (February, 1941), a military figure tells Batman and Robin: "You've done your country a great service! I'll see that the president hears of this and gives you both a suitable award" (Kane 276)! To which Batman responds: "That's not necessary. Being Americans is enough of an award!" That patriotism is a necessary part of the Arthurian mythos. The old Batman naturally thought that the enemies of the United States were evil and the President of the United States was the standard-bearer of truth and justice. With the appearance of Reagan in the pages of *The Dark Knight Returns*, those old ideas fade. Ronald Reagan's Iran-Contra affair is parodied by the story of the general selling arms to the mutants. The comic's Reagan even gets the United States involved in a nuclear war, and Gotham City is engulfed by a nuclear winter. It is not that Reagan is any different from the other presidents Batman served under; he's not. It's Batman who is different. He is a superhero without a president, which is perhaps the ultimate transformation of the Arthurian mythos, the rejection of the need for a leader, a king, a president. But Batman *can't* have a president, knowing what he knows, believing what he believes, history being what it is.

While Batman is battling city hall and the mutants in the city's streets, Superman is working for President Reagan in a little dispute with the Russians. Batman's troubles escalate, and he must fight Gotham's finest just to survive. In an Arthurian universe, Batman would have to surrender to the authorities. In a postmodern universe, Batman *cannot* surrender. In an Arthurian universe, Batman would be vindicated. In a postmodern universe, Batman too is guilty. When he defeats the mutant leader, Batman unknowingly creates a monster: "the sons of the Batman." Superman unknowingly helps Reagan start a nuclear winter. Unknowingly. Still, both superheroes are complicitous.

When Batman defeats the mutant leader, many of the mutants disband and become the sons of the Batman, a new breed of vigilantes. Again, it's the mutants who are truly Arthurian. Batman, because he has won, should rule and be followed. The king is dead. Long live the king. The sons of the Batman make a chilling media announcement: "The mutants are dead. The mutants are history. This is the mark of the future [pointing to a blue bat painted on their faces]. Gotham City belongs to the Batman. Do not expect any further statements. The sons of the Batman do not talk. We act. Let Gotham's criminals beware. They are about to enter hell" (Miller 46).

The sons of the Batman proceed to clean up Gotham City, much to the displeasure of the authorities *and* Batman. The sons of the Batman punish and punish harshly, making it difficult for readers to determine what they prefer, justice or crime. But these youthful vigilantes come in handy during the nuclear winter. The streets of Gotham are quiet and safe while cities elsewhere experience the expected panic and chaos. In a scene my young informants literally drool over, Batman and the former mutants ride on horses down Gotham's streets restoring and assuring order. They are no knights. The Dark Knight has no lord. The order they bring is of a different kind; we don't really have categories to describe an order without a legitimate political structure to obey, so Arthurian is our political language.

Because they aren't Arthurian, the order Batman and the sons of the Batman bring is, legally, disorder. Reagan sends in federal troops and Superman to bring Batman to "justice." Batman fights though as Bruce Wayne. Early in the battle, Superman pulls Batman's mask off. He is no longer a superhero. Only Superman is a superhero, and superheroes work for emperors like Reagan. Batman works for no one, especially no political authority. He accuses Superman: "You sold us out, Clark...I've become a political liability and you...you're a joke" (Miller 41-42). Predictably, Batman/Bruce Wayne loses the battle; he is after all only human; Reagan, America's King Arthur, wins. The TV news announces fittingly enough: "The spectacular career of the Batman came to a tragic conclusion as the crimefighter suffered a heart attack while battling government troops" (Miller 45).

Battling government troops? No one reading Batman twenty years ago or in 1939 could have imagined Batman a federal renegade, but the changed nature of the political situation of the late eighties necessitated a reimaging of Batman. In particular, the Arthurian mythos that provided the framework for the old stories and the justification for Batman's existence is rejected and transformed. The Arthurian mythos of authority and law is decidedly rejected, but the Arthurian desire for order is not rejected so much as transformed. Batman does not leave Gotham City to chaos. At the end of *The Dark Knight Returns*, there is a postmodern transformation of the Arthurian apocalyptic ending. Batman stages his own death, and upon reviving sets about the task of training the former mutants and whoever else is willing to listen how to survive in a post-nuclear world, lessons not in authority and obedience—look where that got the Reagan generation—but in recreating society and a crippled earth.

With Miller's *Dark Knight* texts, popular culture provides American society with a brilliant and powerful critique of our Arthurian mythos and a transformation of that mythos. The story concludes with the hero gone, but the human Bruce Wayne working to restore the earth. Unlike the Arthur of legend or the movie *Excalibur*, Reagan, the king of Batman's America, is still alive but the earth is dying, dying because of the king. To Batman though, the king is dead, and the earth must live. There can be no more kings after the nuclear winter. The king is dead. Long live the earth. The postmodern transformation of the Arthurian mythos is not a retreat into nihilism but an affirmation of the worthwhileness of being human and committing to care for the earth.[7]

Notes

[1]Miller's *Dark Knight* texts are conveniently collected in Frank Miller, *The Complete Frank Miller*, which places *Batman: Year One* first and then *The Dark Knight Returns*, reversing their original chronological order. My reference to Miller's texts will be to this edition.

²By mythos I do not refer to Jungian archetypes but to the often unarticulated and unavowed mythological presuppositions of a culture. As Levi-Strauss makes quite clear this "mythos" is often quite contradictory and ambivalent.

³It goes without saying that a deconstructive reading of the Arthurian texts is possible which would point out the difficulties I am referring to at the mythical and cultural levels.

⁴Garry Wills (200-204) uses the phrase "Hollywood on the Potomac" to refer to the mythical, Arthurian air of both Kennedy's and Reagan's Washington, D.C. The point is that none of these Camelots, King Arthur's in the legends, Kennedy's or Reagan's, were healthy places.

⁵In the older Batman materials, the criminal world is a double of sorts of the world of law and order, Gotham; they aren't a part of Gotham. It is sometimes thought that the earliest Batman episodes were more realistic than those seen in the campy 60s, but that isn't really the case. One will be disabused of that notion by a casual glance through the first volume of Bob Kane's *Batman Archives*.

⁶See Campbell's (53, 345) somewhat naive discussion of the symbolism; it would be intriguing to take Walter Burkert's more critical and politically mature reading of myth and apply that to the Arthurian mythos.

⁷See Derrida (933) who notes that a deconstructionist or postmodernist agenda has as its goal the transformation of the world and its protection. Similarly, Miller's Batman's agenda is no longer simply one of vengeance.

Works Cited

Burkert, Walter. *Structure and History in Greek Mythology and Ritual*. Berkeley: U of California P, 1979.

Campbell, Joseph. *The Hero with a Thousand Faces*. Princeton: Princeton UP, 1949.

Collins, Jim. *Uncommon Cultures: Popular Culture and Post-Modernism*. New York: Routledge, 1989.

Deleuze, Giles and Felix Guattari. *A Thousand Plateaus*. Minneapolis: U of Minnesota P, 1987.

Derrida, Jacques. "Force de Loi: Le 'Fondement Mystique De L'Autorite'/ Force of Law: The 'Mystical Foundation of Authority'." *Cardoza Law Review* 11 (1990): 919-1045.

Kane, Bob. *Batman Archives*, vol. I. New York: DC Comics, 1990.

King, Arden. "Modern Civilization and the Evolution of Personality: We Have Collapsed Infancy into Senility." *The Burden of Being Civilized: An Anthropological Perspective on the Discontents of Civilization*. Ed. Miles Richardson and Malcolm C. Webb. Athens, GA: U of Georgia P.

Kristeva, Julia. *Powers of Horror: An Essay on Abjection*. New York: Columbia U P, 1982.

Leatherdale, Clive. *Dracula: The Novel and the Legend*. Wellingborough, Northamptonshire: The Aquarian P, 1985.

Levi-Strauss, Claude. *Le Cru et Le Cuit*. Paris: Plon, 1964.

Miller, Frank. *The Complete Frank Miller*. Stamford, CT: Longmeadow P, 1989.

Morrison, Grant and Dave McKean. *Arkham Asylum*. New York: DC Comics, 1989.

Nash, Jesse W. "Postmodern Gothic: Batman." *The New Orleans Art Review* Aug. 1989: 8-9.

Taylor, Mark C. *Altarity*. Chicago: U of Chicago P, 1987.

Wills, Garry. *Reagan's America: Innocents at Home*. Garden City: Doubleday, 1987.

Mark's Merlin:
Magic vs. Technology in
A Connecticut Yankee in King Arthur's Court

Donald L. Hoffman

When *A Connecticut Yankee* confronts us with such oppositions as magic vs. technology, science vs. superstition, regress vs. progress, autocracy vs. democracy, Europe vs. America, Merlin vs. Hank, we know where our sympathies ought to lie. Everett Carter, for example, is quite clear that "the meaning of *A Connecticut Yankee* is, as the author repeatedly said it was, that the American nineteenth-century, devoted to political and religious liberalism and to technology, was better than the traditional past...saying to the reader: you've been poor following European models; you've become rich following American models, rich is better" (Carter 440). What Carter and his fellow positivists overlook, however, is that those who follow the lead of the Connecticut Yankee do not end up rich; they end up dead. Ultimately, the promises of Hank's technology are as dubious as those of Merlin's magic. Merlin may be what Hank detests but is also what he becomes. The novel then is not about a conflict of ideologies, but an Oedipal contest for world domination, and Hank is less the *übermensch* than the Sorcerer's Apprentice.

When we first meet Merlin, he matches our perceptions of the great enchanter: "a very old and white-bearded man, clothed in a flowing black gown...standing...upon unsteady legs, and feebly swaying his ancient head...surveying the company with his watery and wandering eye" (16) and beginning to tell his inevitable story one more time. But this sixth-century Merlin is not much different from the nineteenth-century Hank we meet in Warwick Castle as an old man intimately familiar with ancient armor, a relentless talker, who "as he talked along...seemed to drift away imperceptibly out of this world and time" and came to seem "unspeakably old and faded and dry and musty and ancient" (1).

Hank never acknowledges his likeness to Merlin, but his scorn for the enchanter cannot disguise the fact that Hank's original struggle with Merlin is not just for his own life, but also for Merlin's job. He explains to Clarence, "I'm a magician myself," and he goes on to invent a mythic history that both parodies Merlin's style and legitimizes his profession. "I knew him in Egypt three hundred years ago; I knew him in India five hundred years ago—he is always blethering around in my way, everywhere I go; he makes me tired" (23).

Critics seem to assume that Hank had no other choice than Merlin as the object of his attack. But the notoriously malicious Sir Kay was responsible for his imprisonment, while Merlin, rather than incarnating the malice of a savage age, relates in his first speech, the one no one wanted to listen to, his account of the recovery of Excalibur that makes the point that the scabbard is more valuable than the sword, peace more profitable than war. In contrast to Merlin's implicitly pacifist narrative, Hank has arrived in Camelot as the result of a crowbar combat with the Hartford Hercules.

In the episode of Merlin's tower, Hank rivals Merlin more directly than seems to have been recognized, for the encounter reconstructs Geoffrey of Monmouth's tale of Merlin and Vortigern. In Geoffrey, Vortigern's Druids explain that to prevent the nightly collapse of his tower, he must sprinkle it with the blood of a fatherless boy. When such a child is discovered, he reveals to Vortigern the actual cause of the tower's collapse is the nocturnal combat of a red and a white dragon in the pool beneath the tower. Merlin is saved and the inaccurate Druids are put to death.

Hank's attack on Merlin's tower restructures this archetypal tale. Hank, arriving in Camelot a millennium before the birth of his father, is as innocent of genealogy as the fatherless Merlin. And both are challenged by the magical establishment. Thus, Hank challenges Merlin as Merlin had earlier challenged the Druids. While both episodes involve a contest between magicians, Merlin is forced into his contest, but Hank initiates his; and, while Merlin restores a tower, Hank destroys one. This phallic deflation hints that Hank's struggle with Merlin is an Oedipal one, and implies Twain's allegory of the nineteenth century struggling to obliterate its memory of and indebtedness to its sixth-century father and the superstition and brutality associated with it.

Merlin's tower enshrines his patriarchal authority and the blind obedience that supports it. Hank's shattering of that tower is meant to be liberating, but the destruction of the phallic father, as Oedipus proved, does not guarantee the innocence of the son, or provide reason to believe he will not himself become a tyrant. This contest is also the first confrontation of magic and technology. Merlin prepares his little spells, drawing "an imaginary circle on the stones of the roof, and [burning] a pinch of powder in it which sent up a small cloud of aromatic smoke,...Then he began to mutter and made passes in the air with his hands. He worked himself up slowly and gradually into a sort of frenzy, and got to thrashing around with his arms like the sails of a windmill" (35). Hank's magic is more straightforward: "...a few bushels of first-rate blasting powder,...a lightning rod and some wires" (34). After a few passes in the air, "there was an awful crash and that old tower leaped into the sky in chunks, along with a vast volcanic fountain of fire that turned night into noonday, and showed a thousand acres of human beings groveling on the ground..." (35-36). Hank here establishes TNT as the antidote to superstition.

As a result, Hank has the power to dominate Camelot but lacks the moral authority to lead it. His power, as he himself acknowledges, results from an accident of chronology and a crowbar that creates a dark age prodigy out of a modern mediocrity. "What would I amount to in the twentieth century?" he asks. "I should be a foreman of a factory, that is about all" (37). What Hank, the child of "progress," is never able to grasp is that his views are as limited, as culture-bound, as Merlin's. His democratic principles are grounded in a longing for a totalitarian state, albeit with a necessary proviso:

Unlimited power *is* the ideal thing when it is in safe hands. The despotism of heaven is the one absolutely perfect government. An earthly despotism would be the absolutely perfect earthly government, if the conditions were the same, namely, the despot the perfectest individual of the human race, and his lease on life perpetual. (47)

As Hank comes to forget his position in the Colt factory and to totally identify with his role as THE BOSS, he forgets his own fallibility and concentrates on the greater failure of the poor, beknighted denizens of the sixth century, whose primary defect is their inability to think like Hank. Although he may not believe his lease on life is perpetual, he does have good reason to believe it spans a millennium, and while he many not believe he is "the perfectest individual of the human race," he is all but convinced he is the "perfectest individual" of the next several centuries. When to his technological improvements (a patent office, newspaper, schools, Protestantism, telegraph, telephone, Persimmon's Soap and sandwich boards), he adds a secret military academy, he has moved well past his rivalry with Merlin. With the best will in the world, and with none of the intellectual baggage that weighed down "Mistah Kurtz," Hank begins to undertake Kurtz' project, not in the jungles of Africa but in the heart of "brightness," becoming a tyrant in the name of democracy, a divinity in the struggle against idolatry.

Hank's conflict between democracy and despotism undergoes a significant transformation when he meets Morgan le Fay, who exercises autocratic cruelty with such graceful elegance that Hank feels "persuaded that this woman must have been misrepresented, lied about." This impression lasted until "a handsome young page, clothed like the rainbow" made an error in etiquette, and "she slipped a dirk into him in as matter-of-course a way as another person would have harpooned a rat!...Meanwhile madame went rippling sweetly along with her talk." As she does so, Hank notices "that she was a good housekeeper, for while she kept a corner of her eye on the servants to see that they made no balks in handling the body and getting it out; when they came with fresh clean towels, she sent back for the other kind; and when they had finished wiping the floor and were going, she indicated a crimson fleck the size of a tear which their duller eyes had overlooked...Marvelous woman" (80-81).

Those who, like Everett Carter, wish to seek no further than "the nineteenth-century assumptions that *A Connecticut Yankee* was a satire on English chivalry" (419), are forced to see in episodes such as this what Pressman refers to as the Yankee's "split personality" (59). Chadwick Hansen, however, has persuasively argued that such episodes "are inconsistencies of surface, beneath which there lies a really frightening coherence of vision" (62). Through his meeting with Morgan le Fay, Hank's professed democratic vision is altered into an admiration for naked power, *if* combined with a certain delicacy; it is a moment when Robespierre, allowed to eat cake with Marie Antoinette, is transformed into Edmund Burke.

While Clark Griffith's attempt to trace Hank's progress "from Faustian selfishness toward Promethean altruism" is, if anything, an inversion of the actual demonic movement of the novel, he is fundamentally correct in his perception that "the main drift of the narrative [is] more lucid and coherent than has hitherto been supposed" (29, n. 1). But even those critics who have seen a dark consistency to Hank's progress seem not to have noticed the crucial conversion effected in the encounter with Morgan. If he has been baffled by the combination of barbarism and chivalry in Arthur, he is enthralled by the combination of evil and elegance in the dainty demon, Morgan. Hank, appalled by the degrading condition of the medieval peasant, challenged by the mediocre showmanship of Merlin, is totally won over by Mme. le Fay, who kills with the grace of a *femme fatale* and tyrannizes the domestics like a thrifty *hausfrau*.

When Hank too becomes the object of her whimsical wrath, he is saved only by his reputation as a magician and her call to prayers. While Hank marvels at the bloodthirsty penitent, a praying Morgan may be no less a wonder than the democrat who loathes most of humankind, the liberator who annihilates a kingdom.

In a complementary pair of episodes, Hank intercedes on behalf of an old woman who accuses Morgan of having murdered her grandchild but feels a certain sympathy with Morgan's loathing of a medieval band. Having "considered the matter thoughtfully," Hank finally decides "that she was right, and gave her permission to hang the whole band. This little relaxation of sternness had a good effect upon the queen...A little concession, now and then, where it can do no harm, is the wiser policy" (85). While medievalists, satiated with revivals of *Robin et Marion* may sympathize with Morgan's resolution of the problem, Hank's concession marks a change in the style and the target of his scornful wit, his first collaboration with the cruelties of the Middle Ages.

When she takes Hank to see one of her favorite toys, the rack, he is shocked to see stretched upon it "a native young giant of thirty or thereabouts...with his wrists and ankles tied to ropes which led over windlasses at either end. There was no color in him; his features were contorted and set, and sweat drops stood upon his forehead" (87). The elegant Morgan and the sweating giant serve as icons of Hank's tendencies toward both autocracy and democracy. In both episodes, there is a submerged eroticism and more than a hint of sado-masochistic uncertainty, as Hank wavers between identifying with the torturer or the tortured. Hank's sojourn in Morgan's castle pointedly underlines the conflicts in his own character and points up the extreme fragility of his commitment to democracy once THE BOSS discovers the delights of power.

Both the fragility and insensitivity of his "commitment" are revealed in his noble and cruel experiment when he releases from Sir Bruce's prison a husband and wife who had been imprisoned for nine years "within fifty feet of each other" (94) without knowing it. Hank is incapable of understanding why, after nine years of solitary confinement, the man is numb, dumb and unresponsive. He arranges the reunion of husband and wife like the stage-manager of a bathetic melodrama, displaying a taste for cheap art consistent with his earlier nostalgia for chromos (32), blending his own taste for showmanship with Morgan's contempt for other people. Nevertheless, Hank must finally acknowledge that "it was a disappointment. They sat together on the ground and looked dimly wondering into each other's faces awhile, with a sort of weak animal curiosity; then forgot each other's presence, and dropped their eyes, and you saw that they were away again and wandering in some far land of dreams and shadows that we know nothing about" (94-95). The poignancy of the description almost but not quite removes some of the sting of Hank's first reaction, disappointment that his carefully arranged entertainment did not quite come off.

A short time later, when Hank reflects on revolution, he incorporates what he has learned from Morgan—that bloodshed should be no impediment to success. "No people in the world," he argues, "ever did achieve their freedom by goody-goody talk and moral suasion; it being immutable law that all revolutions that will succeed, must *begin* in blood, whatever may answer afterward. If history teaches anything, it teaches that. What this folk needed, then, was a Reign of Terror and a guillotine, and I was the wrong man for them" (103). In Morgan's castle, Hank begins to become that sort of man: (1) he acquires a taste for blood, and (2) discovers that the bodies, hearts and minds of others are his to dispose of. Armed in this way, he is set on the path towards his final solution, one more efficient than a mere guillotine.

Set on this path, he is confronted once again by Merlin in the Valley of Holiness. Hank again sets the tone of professional rivalry, admitting to the abbot that "Merlin is a very good magician in a small way" (118), but while Merlin "is enchanting away like a beaver" (119-120), Hank examines the well to find the source of the blockage and is disappointed to note that "there was no occasion for the bomb" (121). But with the resources of his Yankee optimism, he consoles himself with the thought, "I am in no hurry, I can wait; that bomb will come good, yet. And it did" (121).

The bomb at bay, it is possible to see in the restoration of the Holy Well a compensation for the destruction of Merlin's tower, as creative fire replaces destructive fire, and even mystically transmutes fire into its opposite, the life-giving waters that flood the plain. Yet Hank and ultimately the people pay a heavy price for this gift. "When I started to the chapel," he relates, "the populace uncovered and fell back reverently to make a wide way for me, as if I had been some kind of superior being—*and I was*" (131). In this moment of triumph, Hank comes close to accepting himself as the one capable of imitating "the despotism of heaven."

But even as Hank maintains his sense of nineteenth-century superiority, reinventing the economy and establishing his secret military academy, he becomes susceptible to medieval mysticism, just as Twain the businessman was drawn to spiritualists and clairvoyants from his youthful visit to the "enchantress," Mme. Caprell (Webster 52), to his later interest in the Fox sisters of Chatauqua. In the vicinity of Astolat, Hank visits the site of a miracle of the Virgin, and is unable simply to dismiss it:

"...thousands of the lame and the sick came and prayed before it every year and went away whole and sound...Of course when I was told these things I did not believe them; but when I went there and saw them I had to succumb. I saw the cures effected myself, and they were real cures and not questionable. I saw cripples whom I had seen around Camelot for years on crutches, arrive and pray before that picture, and put down their crutches and walk off without a limp. There were piles of crutches there which had been left by such people as a testimony" (154).

Hank begins to feel torn between the demands of his simultaneously medieval and modern lives. But even as Hank comes to accept the miracles of healing, he begins to envy the Author of miracles, reminding us of the adventure of the Holy Well, when he noted that "the populace uncovered and fell back reverently to make a wide way for me, as if I had been some kind of superior being," adding the exultant, "—and I was" (131). But Hank's miracles are not restorative ones. His magic wand is a stick of TNT, and his next miracle, when he and the unarmed king are attacked by a group of knights, results in a fifteen-minute "drizzle of microscopic fragments of knights and hardware and horseflesh" (165-166). While Hank's robust frontier-style humor has its effect, it is the sort of humor that predicates distance and detachment. Hank cannot pose as the enlightened savior of the sixth century and be amused by a shower of "microscopic fragments" of its citizens.

His increasing detachment, the consequence of the elitism he acquired in Morgan's castle, is seen again in his encounter with the blacksmith Dowley, who had bragged about his lavish twice-yearly meat feasts. Hank lays careful plans for a dinner on a scale to quite deflate the pompous blacksmith. While we may delight in this *exemplum* of the proud man humbled, it is difficult to sympathize entirely with Hank, who takes such a great delight in such a petty triumph, who spends the wealth of an empire to embarrass a blacksmith, but who uses none of that wealth to actually improve conditions in that impoverished village. Poor Dowley is the victim of the frustrations of a factory foreman still smarting under the slights of the undeclared class system of Hartford, CT. Hank, possessing the wealth and power of a medieval noble, uses it to avenge the spite of a *petit bourgeois*.

With Hank's descent into elitism, Twain contrasts King Arthur's complementary rise to a feeling for the unity of the commonwealth, and his heroic self-sacrifice for his people during the small pox epidemic. Hank can admire but barely emulate this truly human concern. Thus, while the aristocratic Arthur actually displays the humanity that Hank only talks about, Hank becomes increasingly discouraged with the stupidity of the people he pretends to save. The more convinced he becomes of the Truth of his principles and the Necessity of his goals, the more inevitably he becomes the kind of man who will destroy the world in order to perfect it.

This tendency is underlined in his renewed rivalry with Merlin, when it becomes clear that Hank is fighting for royal favor and personal power. His tournament with Sir Sagramore is, as he says, the "final struggle between the two master enchanters of the age" (233). This is Hank in his show biz mode, crass, brassy and still appealing guise, but he loads his combat with a dangerous ideological content. "I was a champion, it was true, but not the champion of the frivolous black arts, I was the champion of hard unsentimental common sense and reason. I was entering the lists to either destroy knight-errantry or be its victim" (234). Balancing his roles as conjuror and revolutionary, Hank creates a diverting spectacle by confronting Sagramore encased in full armor like "an imposing tower of iron," with his own simple costume of "flesh-colored tights...with blue silk puffings" around the loins. This visual contrast is reinforced by the contrasting modes of magic, as Merlin casts spells and gossamer threads over Sagramore, while Hank entraps him with his rodeo lariat.

When Merlin, the master magician, resorts to basic conjuror's sleight of hand, and simply steals the lariat, Hank resorts to his more advanced enchantments. "I snatched," he tells us, "a dragoon revolver out of my holster, there was a flash and a roar, and the revolver was back in the holster before anybody could tell what had happened. Here was a riderless horse plunging by, and yonder lay Sir Sagramore, stone dead" (238).

As narrative supplants rhetoric, we see the bottom line of Hank's ideology. The ineffectual magic of Merlin's gossamer veils yields to the unsentimental magic of a dragoon revolver. Whatever his ideals, his advantage lies not in intelligence, but in explosives, in naked displays of a technology he did not invent, but smuggled backwards from the nineteenth century as he undertakes his imperialist invasion of the sixth.

When Sagramore's body is searched for wounds, nothing is found but "a hole through the breast of his chain mail" (239). With this discovery, we are whisked forward to the nineteenth century and backward to the beginning of the narrative and the anachronistic armor that caught Twain's eye in Warkwick Castle. Rather than having brought the highest achievements of the nineteenth century to Camelot, Hank had brought merely his expertise as Foreman of the Colt Factory, and the arrogance that led to his first battle, the one that Hercules fought with a crowbar in Hartford.

With the death of Sagramore, Hank rejoices. "The day was mine. Knight-errantry was a doomed institution. The march of civilization had begun. How did I feel? Ah, you never could imagine it. And Brer Merlin? His stock was flat again. Somehow, every time the magic of folderol tried conclusions with the magic of science, the magic of folderol got left" (240). Hank has indeed murdered knight-errantry, not by means of any noble advance in the culture or manners of the sixth century, but merely by the introduction of a more destructive weapon. The bullet hole in Sagramore's armor does indeed signal the end of chivalry and the feudal class system; the traditional aristocracy is naturally doomed the moment a twit in tights can bring down a knight in full armor. The revolver is more democratic, because more accessible, than medieval horses, arms and armor. But when Hank reduces ideology to weaponry and glorifies the murder of Sargramore as the "march of civilization," Twain has not given us the portrait of an idiosyncratic time-traveller, he has analyzed the basic structure of "advanced civilizations" that colonize the globe not by the truth of their teachings, but by the invincibility of their weapons. In this confrontation with the magic of science and the magic of folderol, it is almost impossible not to side with the magic of folderol, and the silly, but relatively benign, Merlin. Hank, fantasizing about becoming the President of a Republic, will really settle for nothing less than becoming its god. *Au fond*, the ingenuous Yankee is a charming, naive Kurtz, hollow at the core, and prancing about in circus tights to celebrate "the Horror."

When the fall does come, it is because of Lancelot's success in the Stock Market, another of Hank's innovations, the rumors of adultery becoming merely a weapon in an economic vendetta. Twain, aware of the dynamics of war and capitalism, knows that economics is a far more dangerous passion than the love of queens.

As Hank prepares his troops for war, he learns just how shallow his supposedly progressive education has been. "When the armies come," Clarence warns him, "the masks will fall" (255). Or as Malory's Lancelot put it, "Harde hit ys to take oute off the fleysshe that ys bredde in the boone." This knowledge comes as a surprise to Hank who, assuming the universal validity of his perceptions and prejudices, never tried to understand his subjects, and so never knew that his civilization was no more than an imposition of manners, that his "improvements" were a double lie, a misconceived project imposed on an uncomprehending populace.

Not without irony, Hank retires to fight his last defense from Merlin's cave now transformed into an electric plant and provisioned for a siege. Clarence points to the convenience of that arrangement when he remarks that "we shan't have to leave our fortress now, when we want to blow up our civilization" (256). Hank has arranged the collapse of a civilization with a thrift Morgan would have applauded. "You don't want any ground connection except the one through the negative brush. The other end of every wire must be brought back into the cave and fastened independently, and *without* any ground connection. Now, then, observe the economy of it. A cavalry charge hurls itself against the fence; you are using no power, you are spending no money, for there is only one ground connection till those horses come against the wire; the moment they touch it they form a connection with the negative brush *through the ground*, and drop dead. Don't you see—you are using no energy until it is needed; your lightning is there, and ready, like the load in a gun; but it isn't costing you a cent till you touch it off" (257). Here is the true voice of Yankee—thrifty and lethal, efficient as the New York State Legislature when it legalized electrocution in 1888 (Gardiner 454-55), while Twain was working on *Connecticut Yankee* for its publication by Charles Webster in 1889.

As the horrendous Battle of the Sand Belt is underway, Hank ignores the pleas from the boys in his Academy, who beg him to reconsider: "Oh, sir, consider! Reflect! These people are our people, they are bone of our bone, flesh of our flesh, we love them—do not ask us to destroy our nation!" (262). Hank, however, does not relent and with his companions creeps out to anticipate an electrocuted knight, motionless, "except that his plumes swished about a little in the night wind." As Hank and his companions creep closer, they "made out another knight vaguely; he was coming very stealthily, and feeling his way. He was near enough, now, for us to see him put out a hand, find an upper wire, then bend and step under it and over the lower one. Now he arrived at the first knight—and started slightly when he discovered him. He stood a moment—no doubt wondering why the other one didn't move on; then he said, in a low voice, 'Why dreamest thou here, good Sir Mar—' then he laid his hand on the corpse's shoulder—and just uttered a little soft moan and sunk down dead. Killed by a dead man, you see—killed by a dead friend, in fact. There was something awful about it" (268).

Something awful indeed! Throughout the night, Hank and his friends see the occasional "blue spark" and know that another knight has been electrocuted. Finally, they are trapped in their enclave, "enclosed with a solid wall of the dead—a bulwark, a breastwork, of corpses, you may say" (169). Hank's earlier explosion that created a drizzle of fragmented knights may have been a bit of robust frontier exaggeration, but there is nothing remotely comic in the horror of this scene in which the dead murder their friends, and our *quondam* hero huddles in fear and resignation behind a barricade of corpses, listening to the death pangs of eleven thousand men, and opening fire on the few survivors with his thirteen gatling guns. At the end of the affair, twenty-five thousand men are dead and Hank and his twenty-five companions are the masters of England.

But not for long. Having displaced Arthur as actual ruler of Britain, Hank also appropriates Arthur's death and the Oedipal conflict of Arthur and Mordred is replaced by the symbolically Oedipal conflict of Hank and Merlin. Just as the dying Arthur was watched over by the four queens, Hank is tended by his ancient rival Merlin, disguised as a peasant nurse. While Hank lies dying in the "poisonous air," poisoned by his own multiplication of putrefying corpses, Clarence finds this woman "making curious passes in the air," and pronouncing a kind of benediction and a curse on Hank and his companions. "Ye were conquerors; ye are conquered! These others are perishing—you also. Ye shall all die in this place—every one—except *him*. He sleepeth, now—and shall sleep thirteen centuries. I am Merlin!" (272). Then he too, in "a delirium of silly laughter" falls against one of the wires and is electrocuted.

In this shared death, Twain again underscores the Oedipal conflict in the rivalry of Hank and Merlin, for the scene echoes the mutual death of Arthur and Mordred on Salisbury Plain when the son dies impaled on the father's lance, as the father is run through by the son's sword. Here in this strangely Oedipal cave, a kind of paternal womb, the old and young magicians die together in a victory in which no one is triumphant despite the old magician's dying, maniacal laughter that rings for thirteen centuries until Hank awakens to meet Mark Twain in Warwick Castle, where the "son" has become the "father." Hank the Connecticut Yankeee is now the ancient mage, a figure of Merlin as alien in his own time as he had been in Camelot. Hank's allegorical journey forces us to recognize that nineteenth-century enlightenment is grounded in the darkness of the Dark Ages, when Hank first introduced technology and gunsmoke to the world. Hank confronts but never defeats the Merlin-Shadow, implying that deep within modern man the ancient mage is still enclosed.

Hank's inability to escape Merlin has from the beginning been inscribed in his being. Choosing to become *The Boss*, he seeks to acquire the authority of function freed from the fallibly human. In his desire to attain the divine objectivity he associates with the machine, Hank ignores the limits of his own subjectivity. In striving to transcend the human, Hank merely succeeds in becoming inhuman.

Finally, Hank is incapable of recognizing how much of the mother is inscribed in the *nom du père*. Born Hank Morgan, THE BOSS never acknowledges that the blood of the ancient, dangerous goddess circulates in his veins. This amnesia of origin invalidates Hank's project, since he never understood that he was not the shaper of Camelot, but that he was shaped by it. In this Oedipal confusion, Hank strives to father a new civilization, without understanding that he is the son of the old one, and that his "progress" is little more than medieval superstition armed with modern weapons. Hank, with the murderess Morgan inscribed in his paternal name, as he fruitlessly seeks to kill the magician who defines him, proves the continuing struggle for a righteous civilization to issue from the womb of the Dark Ages.

Works Cited

Briden, Earl F. "Mark Twain's *Connecticut Yankee* and the Matter of Colt." *American Notes and Queries* 24 (1985): 45-48.

Carter, Everett. "The Meaning of *A Connecticut Yankee.*" *AL* 50 (1978): 418-440.

Collins, William J. "Hank Morgan in the Garden of Forking Paths: *A Connecticut Yankee in King Arthur's Court* as Alternative History." *MFS* 32 (1986): 109-114.

Cox, James M. "*A Connecticut Yankee in King Arthur's Court*: The Machinery of Self-Preservation." *Yale Review* 50 (1960): 89-102.

Cummings, Sherwood. *Mark Twain and Science: Adventures of a Mind.* Baton Rouge, LA: Louisiana State UP, 1988.

Ensor, Allison R. "Mark Twain's Yankee and the Prophet of Baal." *ALR, 1870-1910* 14 (1981): 38-42.

Fienberg, Lorne. "Twain's Connecticut Yankee: The Entrepreneur as a Daimonic Hero." *MFS* 28 (1982): 155-167.

Gardiner, Jane. "'A More Splendid Necromancy': Mark Twain's *Connecticut Yankee* and the Electrical Revolution." *SNNTS* 19 (1987): 448-458.

Griffith, Clark. "Merlin's Grin: From 'Tom' to 'Huck' in *A Connecticut Yankee.*" *NEQ* 48 (1975): 28-46.

Hansen, Chadwick. "The Once and Future Boss: Mark Twain's Yankee." *NCF* 28 (1973): 62-73.

Hellwig, Harold Henry. "Mark Twain's Response to Democracy and Technology: A Computer-Aided Psycholinguistic Analysis of *A Connecticut Yankee in King Arthur's Court.*" *DAI* 46 (1985): 982A.

Johnson, James L. *Mark Twain and the Limits of Power: Emerson's God in Ruins.* Knoxville, TN: U of Tennessee P, 1982.

Kordecki, Lesley C. "Twain's Critique of Malory's Romance: *Forma tractandi* and *A Connecticut Yankee.*" *NCF* 41 (1986): 329-348.

Marx, Leo. *The Machine in the Garden: Technology and the Pastoral Ideal in America.* New York: OUP, 1964.

Pressman, Richard S. "A Connecticut Yankee in Merlin's Cave: The Role of Contradiction in Mark Twain's Novel." *ALR* 16 (1983): 58-72.

Shanley, Molly Lyndon and Peter G. Stillman. "Mark Twain: Technology, Social Change, and Political Power." *The Artist and Political Vision.* Ed. Benjamin R. Barber and Michael J. Gargas McGrath. New Brunswick NJ: Transaction Books, 1982. 267-289.

Smith, Henry Nash. *Mark Twain's Fable of Progress: Political and Economic Ideas in "A Connecticut Yankee."* New Brunswick NJ: Rutgers UP, 1964.

Twain, Mark. *A Connecticut Yankee in King Arthur's Court.* 1889; rpt. New York: Bantam Books, 1981.

Webster, Samuel Charles. *Mark Twain: Business Man.* Boston: Little Brown, 1946.

C.J. Cherryh's Arthurian Humanism

Rebecca S. Beal

While very much at home in modern fantasy literature, the Arthurian legend has not made much headway in science fiction, except in the case of C.J. Cherryh (Thompson 79-80). A full treatment of Cherryh's debt to the Arthurian legend has yet to be made, although Raymond Thompson, who identifies Cherryh's *Port Eternity* as the most effective treatment in the tradition of science fiction, does analyze that novel in some detail (79-82), and Marry Brizzi's survey of Cherryh's work sees certain Arthurian motifs in the first three Morgaine novels (44). This article, while not pretending to examine every instance of Cherryh's Arthurianism, will trace her debt to the legend in *Port Eternity*, certainly that work in which both the science fiction element and Arthurian material come most clearly to the foreground; the short story "The General," which concludes the collection *Sunfall*; and, finally, the "Morgaine" series of novels, especially the first of these, *Gate of Ivrel*.

Cherryh's interest in the legend emerges first in 1976, in her first novel, *Gate of Ivrel*; it continues as an influence through 1982, the year of *Port Eternity*. Her Arthurian sources range from Malory to Tennyson, but Cherryh seems most interested in the legend because it enables her to define human nature, particularly as it sheds light on how humans can achieve freedom within limits imposed by the environment, personal history, or even more circumscribed "programs" governing behavior. For Cherryh, these structures are not necessarily negative; even Arthurian legend may be imagined as a structuring element which enables those caught up in it to define themselves more clearly and go on to initiate purposeful actions.

Port Eternity's cloned humans, "made-men," Cherryh calls them, are surely the author's most radically constrained characters:

They are "made people," cloned from special genetic combinations, then conditioned with "deepteach" tapes to create a special "psych-set." These "made people" are "sold out" to "born people" when ready at sixteen or eighteen and "put down" when they pass forty years of age. The sole reason for their existence is to serve their owners, and their programming is so tight that they have very little freedom of choice. (Thompson 80)

Living within such narrow confines, the cloned humans might seem less than human. Indeed, their very names derive from a whim of their owner, Dela Kirn. The latter, entangled in a fantasy of Camelot and seeing herself as Guinevere, decorates and names her space craft "Maid of Astolat," and also names her staff of cloned humans after characters in Tennyson's version of the legend. In addition to Elaine, the narrator of the novel and Dela's maid, there are Gawain and Lynette, the ship's pilots; Modred and Percivale, the ship's engineers; Vivien, Dela's accountant. And there is Lancelot, Dela's lover when her "born-men" lovers pall.

Elaine is the first of the cloned humans to gain access to Dela Kirn's "tape" of *Idylls of the King*. Her experience shows something of the process by which these cloned, fundamentally determined, humans are transformed by the legend. Even before coming to Dela, Elaine wonders about "born" and "made" people, and believes that the two are qualitatively different: "until I was sold to Dela and until I saw Dela's secret fancies, I thought that the difference between us and born-men was that born-men lead real lives, and see what really is, and that this was the power born-men have over the likes of us" (11). After being acquired by Dela and hearing the tape of *Idylls*, she identifies the major difference between cloned and born humans as a capacity for love, action undertaken for the good of another apart from the programming which makes her who she is. Thus, she compares herself with "that other Elaine, who was absolute in love, and who was so much that I was not made to be" (55).

But, like her Tennysonian predecessor, Elaine does falls in love with Lancelot, although she sees her situation in terms of her programs:

...Elaine—the real Elaine, the one realer than I—had destroyed herself trying to turn Lancelot's love to herself, when it was fixed on Guinevere: she had to try, because in the story Elaine was fixed on him and he on his lady, and that made sense within my frame of reference. I was not supposed to fix on him, but pain always went straight to my gut and made me try to stop it; and he had the most pain of anyone aboard. (56)

Elaine's fixation on Lancelot follows immediately upon their sharing the tape of *Idylls* and the experience of the Lancelot and Elaine of the poem. Further, that experience allows her to transcend the limits of her programs: "While the tape was running, I loved, and had a soul, and believed in the born-men's God" (53).

Whatever their capacity for love, these cloned people adapt more quickly than their owner or her guest when their spacecraft, "Maid of Astolat," is stranded in sub-space.[1] Thus, when Elaine perceives chaos around her, she makes sense of it through an existential act of will learned in the laboratory:

Then, like in the time before I left that white place where I was made, I had to have something to look at, to control the images, to sort truth from illusion, and I concentrated simply on getting my hand in front of my face. Knowing what it ought to look like, I could begin to make it out...there is an advantage in being what we are, which is that wherever we are, that's what *is*....(25-26)

Cherryh seems to suggest that for all the cloned humans on board the "Maid of Astolat," the experience of sub-space is, indeed, a return to the laboratory. Now, however, an experience of uncertainty about the nature of reality, about behavior in crises unforseen by the original "deep teach" programming, challenges that programming. And experience is further complicated, programs further undercut, by the Arthurian tape which introduces uncertainty about their identities and opens possibilities for behavior previously unavailable to these characters. The tape's power for the cloned humans on board ship resides precisely in their vulnerability to programming; ironically, then, the tape of Tennyson's *Idylls* plays against the "deep-teach" programming of the laboratory and enables them to behave in opposition to that programming. Thus Elaine, conditioned to ease the pain of others, overcomes that programming enough to confront Vivien as she would not have been able to do at the beginning of the novel. She says, " 'Maybe if Viv's hydroponics don't work out, *she* can go out on the hull'...It was cruel. Deliberately. It left me shivering worse than ever, all my psych-sets in disarray" (99).

By the end of the novel, she grows beyond both the limits of Tennyson's Elaine and of her own programming into an experience that acknowledges the tentative nature of love: "Whether we dream, still falling forever, or whether the dream has shaped itself about us, we love...at least we dream we do" (191). Even if Elaine is only dreaming, her dream has taken her beyond the original legend and her own programming. According to the former, she would die for love of Lancelot; according to the latter, she should remain with and serve her mistress, Dela Kirn. But she does neither; rather, she goes with her Lancelot to a seaside tower. There she lives, loves and—in accordance with neither her tapes or the legend—prepares for combat: "And whenever the call goes out, echoing clear and brazen through the air, we take up our arms again and go" (191).

By contrast, the owners of the cloned humans, originally conditioned by their society to behave with more flexibility than their servants, at times fall short. Dela Kirn, for instance, abandons her crew to Griffin and takes to her bed while her crew struggles to cope with a new master as well as a crisis in this new space. She emerges only when Elaine shows her a lion's banner, an Arthurian symbol of courage; at that moment Dela regains the will to live. The entire ship's company adapts, adopts new identities, values and behavior, and their change may ultimately be traced to the tape of *Idylls of the King*, which Elaine first pirates from the ship's library, but which becomes the means by which the entire ship's company is transformed into the fellowship of the Round Table.

Thompson suggests that the novel describes a traditional folktale motif: "we witness the descent into complete illusion, into another world from which there is no return. Failure to return from the other world bearing the treasure of knowledge is a traditional signal of defeat in legend and folklore, a symbolic death" (82). We could, perhaps, better understand the work if we read its transformation of born and cloned humans in light of another ancient myth, that of creation. Because of a malfunctioning space craft, the characters are marooned in subspace, a location without temporal references. In this place time can only be measured in relative terms, but if days are measured by sleeping-waking cycles, the crew emerges seven days later into the rest of an edenic, prelapsarian Avalon.

The seven "days" of this creation witness Arthurian transformation in two stages. The first of these concerns Lancelot, who accidentally gains access to the tape of *Idylls* on the first night after the "Maid of Astolat" enters sub-space, and whose transformation into an analog of Tennyson's Lancelot continues through the fourth day; on that day, when the rest of the crew, also accidentally, hear the tape, they begin altering as well. Their change is completed on the sixth climactic day, the day when Modred seems to betray the ship, when, wreathed in a fog suggesting Tennyson's account, the rest fight a "last" battle before surrendering to the aliens at the hatch.

When, on the first night, Lancelot listens to the tape of *Idylls*, his reaction must be measured in light of his programming. Before, as Elaine notes, he "did sex very well and with endless invention, which was what he was made for" (19). Afterwards, however, he is unable to have intercourse with Elaine, a reaction in direct opposition to his programming for sexual prowess. As Elaine notes: "He blanked, then, which froze my heart—because blanking out from something beyond your limits is one thing; but blanking on your training, on your whole reason for being at all—" (54-55). She breaks off, apparently unable to communicate the horror of failing one's programming. Lancelot's response to the tape, then, indicates how far the tape has gone to undermine thirty-six years of programming. As Elaine ponders the outcome of his hearing the tape, she reflects for the first time upon how dangerous Lancelot really is, and her musings foreshadow the coming violence between Lancelot and Griffin, Dela's lover, who "fills the role of an aggressive Arthur" (Thompson 81). As Thompson notes, "even his name recalls Pendragon" (81).

On the second day, then, while Dela calls for the tape of *Idylls* and sleeps "the deepsleep, lost in the dream" (58), Lancelot and Griffin meet in the gym. Here Lancelot actively resists Griffin, the first time in the text that a cloned human stands up to a "born-man" (61), and his resistance shows him developing into the Lancelot of Arthurian legend. Elaine interrupts, so that the conflict is without resolution. On the next day, however, Lancelot and Griffin move into even deeper conflict, and the crew begins to be enmeshed in the legend. Thus, Lancelot fights Griffin again, but loses; Lancelot does, however, fight and defeat Percy, Gawaine, and Modred in the gym, and when Griffin takes command of the ship from Dela, she calls Lancelot to her bed. Lancelot's role as the best of Arthur's knights as well as his affair with Guinevere is thus recapitulated. Finally, on the fourth day, when Griffin decides to fight the alien force outside the ship, Lancelot recognizes Griffin's generosity and moves toward the double allegiance which marks the Lancelot of legend. As he tells Elaine, after Griffin learns about Dela's lapse with Lancelot, when Elaine and Lancelot find Dela and Griffin asleep in one another's arms: "'He's good to me—you know that? He knows, like you said. And he loves her. And all of today—he never had any spite. Nothing of the kind. And he might have. Anyone else would have. But he treats me no different for it'" (117-118).

The day ends with the rest of the crew hearing the tape of *Idylls* for the first time; on the following, fifth day, the crew begins to adapt to the conditioning of the *Idylls* tape: by the day's end Elaine can claim that "we're all lost in Dela's dream" (148), and indeed, Percy talks about finding God, Vivien discovers malice, Lancelot comes to love both Griffin and Dela, Lynette risks her life going outside the ship to "find a way to *be* that other self if it killed her" (137). And Gawain protects his "brother" Mordred as that one works on a program to contact the aliens despite Griffin's orders to the contrary. Each of the cloned people sees him or herself as a pale reflection of truer images taken from the tape: "And what did their images—but love, and want, and struggle—things far more live than they?...And oh, what was Vivien's pettiness to *that* Vivien's malice; or Percy's kindness to *that* Percivale's goodness; or Lynn's bravery to Lynette's? We tried to live, that was what; we caught sight of something brighter and more vivid than ourselves and we wanted that" (141).

The sixth and final day includes Modred's treachery—his receiving communication from the aliens and opening the forward hatch to them—and the last battle, with the loss of Griffin/Arthur. The transformation of the crew is not complete, however, until Dela Kirn affirms that transformation and enters the Arthurian dream along with her cloned humans. She does so just before the battle with the aliens outside their ship, after Percivale asks whether Dela talks to God, whether God will be able to find their souls in this place, and Elaine at last confesses that the crew has heard the tape of *Idylls*. Now Dela looks at her crew with new eyes, "as if she were seeing us for the first time, as if suddenly she knew us. The dream settled about us then, wrapped her and Griffin too" (170). When Dela looks at the crew, she seems to be recognizing the essential humanity of each; when she immediately tells Percivale, "'I've no doubt of you,'" she grants him the soul that Elaine had previously only discovered when she listened to the Arthurian legend.

At this point, before their final battle, the company of the Round Table is complete. What remains is the transition into legendary status, and this transition occurs after Griffin's disappearance, his symbolic death, in the battle, when the crew surrenders to the aliens it has been fighting, passes to the space station to which the ship has been moored, but then discovers that the aliens Mordred contacted are friendly; that Griffin is alive, saved by the aliens, and all are reconciled:

And then we shed the suits which were our last protection...And after, one by one, we settled down ourselves to sleep, absolutely undone. Griffin watched over us, his arms about our lady who slept against him. And creatures watched us strange as any heraldic beasts of our dream, but wise-eyed and armed and patient. (188-89)

The programmed people of the novel's opening have become the knights and ladies of the Round Table, but with notable differences: Modred's treachery turns out to have been reasonable action; Vivien's narrowness is expanded; Lancelot and Elaine live apart from Dela and Griffin, learning what it is to love. All things, including the Arthurian legend, are made new.

In *Sunfall*, Cherryh again makes a foray into Arthurian legend, this time without relying on a single literary source, but rather appropriating the Arthur-Guinevere-Lancelot triangle and resolving it within the Arthur-Mordred conflict of traditional Arthurian legend.

Sunfall is a collection of short stories placed in or about cities of time to come. Each tale in the collection describes the fate of one of the world's great cities at the closing of earth's history: Paris, London, Moscow, Rome, New York. The last story, "The General," concerns Peking, "The City of Heaven" to its inhabitants and "The Forbidden City" to the outside world, particularly to the barbarian hordes besieging its gates. The story moves in distinct double plots which set the ritualistic unimpassioned life of the city of Peking, at peace with its age and coming end, against the passionate, impulsive, and impatient spirit of the barbarians. Inside the city are Tao Hua and Kan Te, lovers living in a world where time at first seems endless; outside are Ylan Baba, the leader of the hordes, his beloved wife Gunesh and his warlord—her lover—Shimshek, whose lives are rapidly coming to an end.

At the beginning of the tale, few worlds could be further removed from this city, beautiful "beyond dreaming," than Ylan Baba's, with its "dust and the stink of urine" (143). And, it would seem, few worlds could be further removed from both the camp and the city than that of Arthur, Guinevere, Lancelot and Mordred. But Ylan Baba, the "The General" of the story's title, is the stuff of legends: in previous lives he has been the great conquerors of world history; he is Arthur, reborn; his wife Gunesh, is Guinevere, and his warleader, Shimshek, is Lancelot. As Ylan Baba tells Shimshek:

'I was Hannibal, hear me? And you Hasdrubal my brother; Caesar, and you Antony; I was Germanicus and Arthur and Attila; Charlemagne and William; Saladin and Genghis. I fight; I fight the world's wars...Am I not always the same? Do I ever hold long what I win?'

'Ylan Baba—' [says Shimshek]

'Do I ever truly win? Or lose? Only you and Gunesh...Roxanne and Cleopatra; Guinevere and Helen...as many shapes as mine and yours, and always you love her.'

'Boga has other names, too, you know. Agamemnon, Xerxes, Bessus...don't sell him short.'

'Modred.' [replies Shimshek]

'Him too.' (150-151)

Whether called Ylan Baba, Shimshek, Gunesh, Boga, or Arthur, Lancelot, Guinevere, Modred, these characters represent an historical pattern which operates through them and which constrains their behavior. Ylan, like Arthur, is fated to die, betrayed by Boga/Modred; Shimshek, like Lancelot, is devoted both to his lord and his love; she, in turn, must love both and lose them as well. But in these last days of the world, Gunesh/Guinevere and Shimshek/Lancelot choose to remain with Ylan Baba/Arthur and fight with him. The decision, which suggests a change in the metahistorical reality which has constrained the characters, is brought about first of all when Gunesh/Guinevere refuses to flee: " 'This time'," she says, " '—after all the world's ages—we might make the difference. We might, mightn't we? If we've been trapped before, can't we fight, this time'?" (155). The three agree to fight together, and perhaps more importantly, to return in later lives and remember: " 'Remember'," Ylan Baba says, " 'Remember! We'll fight, my old friends; we'll fight each time. We'll change the pattern on him; and you'll be by me; and you'll...someday...tip the scales. I believe that. O my friends, I do believe it' " (156). They die, killed in yet another "last battle," and they triumph over their fates by recognizing the nature of the legend which constrains them and changing it in a small way—fighting and dying together, instead of apart.

In the Prologue to *Sunfall*, Cherryh writes that the cities, "microcosms of human polity...bound their residents by habit and by love and by the invisible threads that bound the first of the species to stay together" (7). She continues, attempting to define the nature of the bond that holds people together in cities:

In all of human experience there was no word which encompassed this urge in all its aspects: it might have been love, but it was too often hate; it might have been community, but there was too little commonality; it might have been unity but there was too much of diversity. (7-8)

Ylan Baba, Shimshek, Gunesh, and even Boga, transform this definition into narrative form. They embody the various drives which have brought humanity together into cities. Ylan Baba, in particular, is associated with the growth of cities or civilizations: "I was Akkadian, Sumerian, Egyptian, Kushite, Greek, Macedonian...I brought Persia to birth; defended Greece against it at Thermopylae; built an eastern empire as Alexander; and a western one as Hannibal; checked both as Caesar, and drove north and south" (152). Each of the characters represents different human qualities which draw humanity into communities: Ylan/Arthur is associated with power; Shimshek/Lancelot with love and loyalty; Gunesh/Guinevere with sex; even Boga has a part to play. As Ylan Baba says: " 'He's the dark force. The check on me. Lest I grow too powerful' " (151). Boga limits Ylan Baba's power; according to Ylan, Gunesh and Shimshek influence Ylan in another way, despite their apparent powerlessness: " 'Shimshek, if it weren't for you—I might *be* Boga. Think of that. If not for you...and for her. Because I love you' " (153).

Although Ylan Baba, Shimshek and Gunesh at first appear arrayed against civilization, the city their hordes have come to attack, their vivifying force becomes apparent through the other plot, that of Kan Te and Tao Hua, young lovers inside Peking. These two characters synechdotally represent the entire city. Like the rest of the city's population, they prepare for war by decorating their armor with flowers; the city can imagine no other outcome than that of the last war, when "much before Tao Hua and Kan Te were born, the army had come back with its flowers unwilted, unstained, victorious" (136). War is, at first, an elaborate ritual, divorced from the realities of death and pain. But Ylan Baba's assault on Peking constrains Tao Hua and Kan Te, as well as the entire city, to emerge from dream and ritual into passion and life.

This process is itself signalled by Kan Te's account of a troubling dream: "I dreamed...that all the grass of the plains was gone; I dreamed that the Earth swarmed with men and beasts and that they were much alike; I dreamed of tents and campfires like stars across all the plains of the world; I dreamed that the moon fell, and the moon was the hope of the city" (136-37). Despite its relevance—the grass of the plains has indeed been destroyed by drought and the plains covered by the tents, campfires, and beasts of the invaders—his dream is strikingly ambiguous, particularly in its last episode, the falling of the moon. Kan Te interprets the moon's fall as a symbol of hopelessness. But though he doesn't know it, a luminary is falling outside the walls: Ylan Baba is experiencing his last battle and in that fall is, indeed, the city's hope.

After this dream, Kan Te begins to imagine his own death, with drastic consequences: "the thought of death came between" him and his beloved for the first time (137). Now, however, he also begins to wake from his dreamlike existence. When the city finally does experience war, when the hordes heap the heads of the soldiers from the Lion and Phoenix regiments outside the front gate, the city finally abandons ritual in the face of death. Thus, the lovers make love and so defy death, and do so without the traditionally sanctifying rites:

They touched, Kan Te and Tao Hua, and touches became caresses; then caresses became infinitely pleasurable, a means to defy death existed. They were not wed—it was not lawful—but there was not time left for weddings. The ashes of the dead settled on their roof and drifted in the open window to settle on their bed. (155)

On the following morning they, like the rest of the city, are transformed and purged: "No more flowers, no more ribbons; they were there to defend their home, a toughened, determined crew" (157). Ylan Baba, Arthur, "The General," has come, and his advent has again roused a city from a studied, dreamlike existence, into life. This life, as well as the promise of the hero's return, is underscored by the story's dramatic conclusion, when Tao Hua realizes that she might be carrying Kan Te's child:

she set her hand to her belly...she could have become pregnant, she realized...The warmth was strange, as if some vitality had gotten into her, some strange force of desire and will.

As if some stranger had come to dwell there, born of the death and the shaking of their world.

He had. (158)

Gunesh/Guinevere's unborn child had died with her as she fought Boga/Mordred's clan; Tao Hua's child, however, was conceived because of Arthur/Ylan Baba's violent advent; it will live because the deaths of Ylan Baba, Gunesh, and Shimshek led to the dissolution of the hordes; it will, further, be born into a radically transformed community, and the story's last line suggests that Ylan Baba, Arthur, will be the "stranger come to dwell there, born of the death and the shaking of their world" (158).

Sunfall is the only one of Cherryh's works in which Arthur plays a major role: *Port Eternity* focuses on the secondary figures in Tennyson's account, and although Arthur's role is filled by the "born-man" Griffin, we see him least clearly, for he is the only character not known intimately—whether as crewmate, mistress, or sexual partner—by the narrator, Elaine. Even in *Sunfall*, however, Arthur is less a restored version of the legendary figure than a force of history responsible for the regeneration of human society. At least this far in her career, Cherryh seems to focus her Arthurian fiction upon the power of Arthurian legend to alter characters associated with it, whether Chinese lovers or laboratory-originated space crews. But *Gate of Ivrel*, the first of her works to utilize the legend, if more allusively than *Port Eternity* or *Sunfall*, draws on the Arthurian sources in yet a different fashion. Here, the name of a major character, Morgaine, alludes to Malory's Morgan le Fay, as do details of Morgaine's equipment.[2]

Malory's text particularly emphasizes Morgan's hatred of Arthur, malice which leads her to attempt to slay Arthur by substituting an inferior sword for Excalibur, and giving the latter to her lover Accalon. After Accalon fights Arthur, the king soon knows what he's lost: "But allwayes Arthurs swerde bote nat lyke Accalons swerde...And than he demed treson, that his swerde was chonged" (Malory 85, 11. 39-44). Cherryh's Morgaine is also associated with a sword, memorably decorated and named:

> The sun shone down on him as he worked, and glittered coldly off the golden hilt of the blade he hung upon the gray's saddle. The dragon leered at him, fringed mouth agape, clenching the blade in his teeth; his spread legs made the guard; his back-winding tail guarded the fingers.
>
> He feared even to touch it. No Korish work that, whatever hand had made the plain sheath. It was alien and otherly, and when he ventured in curiosity to ease the awful thing even a little way from its sheath, he found strange letters on the blade itself like a shard of glass—even touching it threatened injury. No blade ever existed of such substance: and yet it seemed more perilous than fragile....
>
> The blade's named was *Changeling*. (*Gate of Ivrel* 22-23)

The sword's named, "Changeling," elicits associations with Malory's account, in which Arthur claims his sword has been "chonged." Its possession here by Morgaine, a character whose powerful technology causes members of the primitive cultures she visits to believe her a sorceress, underscores the Malorean underpinnings of the text. Finally, as Brizzi notes, the description of the blade, with its dragon hilt, also seems an oblique reference to Arthurian legend, specifically that of Arthur's father, Uther Pendragon (Lacy 419; Brizzi 44). In Cherryh's novels, however, both the sword's name and its description have other associations as well. "Changeling," the weapon with which Morgaine disrupts the worlds she tries to save, is her very emblem: " 'Change,' Morgaine said, 'is very possible. That is the work I do' " (*Exile's Gate* 385).

Malory's Morgan is a figure of animated malice, motivated, as even her lover Accalon admits to Arthur, by powerful emotions. Foremost among these is hatred: "for ye shall undirstonde that kynge Arthur ys the man in the worlde that she hatyth moste, because he is moste of worship and of prouesse of ony of hir bloode" (Malory 88, 11. 9-11). Lust also plays a role: "she lovyth me oute of mesure as paramour" (1. 12). Indeed, in Malory, Morgan is perceived as a demonic threat against Arthur's patriarchal society: her treachery in the Accalon episode is repeated when she sends Arthur "the rycheste mantell that ever was sene in the courte" (93, 11. 23-24), but which is intended to destroy its wearer. Her enmity against Arthur extends to his wife and companions, and she keeps a fortified castle from which to war upon Arthur: "And ever as she myght she made warre on kynge Arthur, and all daungerous knyghtes she wytholdyth with her for to dystroy all thos knyghtes that kynge Arthure lovyth" (367, 11. 23-25). Despite her sorcerous arts, used both offensively, as above, and defensively, as when she changes shape to elude pursuit, Morgan le Fay is unsuccessful, though not because Arthur outwits her, but because of the Lady of the Lake's intervention, because of knights like Sir Lamoroke, who intercepts the magic drinking horn designed to sow discord at Arthur's court, or Sir Gawayne, who saves Trystram after recognizing the maiden guiding Trystram as one of Morgan's. It would appear that the community of knights, aided of course by the Lady of the Lake, is enough to contain Morgan le Fay's evil.

Cherryh's Morgaine seems, to the inhabitants of the worlds she visits, even more dangerous and arbitrary than Morgan. Even Vanye, her sworn-man, and the character through whose perception the narrative is focused, at first sees her in light of the ancient songs which warn against her:

> When Thiye ruled in Hjemur
> came strangers riding there,
> and three were dark and one was gold,
> and one like frost was fair.
> . . .
> Fair was she, and fatal as fair,
> and cursed who gave her ear;
> now men are few and wolves are more,
> and the Winter drawing near (*Gate of Ivrel* 11)

Vanye's fear when he first meets Morgaine is that of an Arthurian knight in Malory, wary of Morgan le Fay; it is a perspective reflected in both oral and written traditions established after she leaves. The *Annals of Baien-an*, for instance, blame the deaths of an entire army on the deceit of Morgaine and her companions (*Gate of Ivrel* 4-5), and in Shiuan, a stone is inscribed in her memory: "Know that it was Morgaine kri Chya who wrought this ruin. Morgen Angharan, Men named her: the White Queen... who was the death that came to us. It was Morgaine who extinguished the last brightness in the north...and stripped the land of inhabitants" (*Fires of Azeroth* 407).

Unlike Morgan le Fay, however, Morgaine sweeps aside all resistance, contained by no force which various enemies muster against her. She is able to do so in part because of her technological superiority, but also because of the greed and corruption of her opponents, who have no community analogous to the Arthurian fellowship of Malory's account. Indeed, *Gate of Ivrel* opens with an account of Vanye's outlaw state, caused in part by his own rashness, in part by the callousness of his father and the treachery and cruelty of his brothers; Vanye's separation from his own kin calls attention to the fragmented nature of his society, and makes his devotion to Morgaine—who restores his honor and gives him a "lord" to serve—understandable.

Moreover, the reader learns to interpret Morgaine's seemingly malicious acts in light of a larger mission: she is the last member of a team sent by a human space government called Union. As the *Journal of the Union Science Bureau*, cited in the prologue to *Gate of Ivrel*, notes, Union scientists have realized that the entire inhabited universe confronts potential catastrophe, the "gates" to time and space originally set in place by an alien race called the qual. These gates destroyed qualish civilization when the gates were misused and the "whole of reality warped and shredded" (*Gate of Ivrel* 3). Some of the gates still exist; Union scientists believe that the gates may be destroyed by specially equipped humans who locate the gates on various worlds, pass through each, and seal them from "the other side."

That Morgaine is compelled to destroy the gates she passes becomes clear: in *Gate of Ivrel* and its sequel novels *Well of Shiuan*, *Fires of Azeroth*, and *Exile's Gate*, she searches for the gate dominating a world, passes through it, destroys it, and embarks upon another search. Her searches usually lead to catastrophes in gated worlds, for the gates are a source of energy, one which warps but also supplies the worlds that support the gates. Like Malory's Morgan, then, Cherryh's Morgaine often finds herself at odds with the power structure of the society she enters; the larger science fiction frame of her quest, however, provides the reader with an explanation of her behavior which moderates her otherness in terms of her function. Furthermore, the dominant point of view in the Morgaine series is that of Vanye, and his growing love for Morgaine and appreciation of the forces which compel her provide another perspective by which to judge her. In the Morgaine series, then, Cherryh mitigates the apparent capriciousness of a Morgana-like sorceress by drawing on the resources of a science fiction frame for what is basically a fantasy story, and providing a sympathetic viewpoint—Vanye's—within the fantasy.

C.J. Cherryh's career is barely fifteen years old (Grothey 139); three of her works thus far have had significant Arthurian components. In *Port Eternity* and "The General," characters defined as Arthurian are carefully defined within biological or historical contexts, then made to transcend these limits after exposure to the Arthurian tradition; in *Gate of Ivrel*, by contrast, Morgaine's Malorean context serves to measure the distance between the medieval vision of women— inscribed in *Gate* through quotations of medievally inspired literature—and the modern context which makes science fiction possible.

Notes

[1]My analysis of the cloned characters' response to crisis differs from Thompson's; he believes that their conditioning prevents them for coping well in crisis (80).

[2]This analysis differs from that of Mary T. Brizzi, who associates Morgaine with Arthur, Gawain, and Merlin, rather than with Morgan (Brizzi 44).

Works Cited

Brizzi, Mary T. "C.J. Cherryh and Tomorrow's New Sex Roles." *The Feminine Eye: Science Fiction and the Women Who Write It*. Ed. Tom Staicar. New York: Frederick Ungar, 1982. 32-47.

Cherryh, C.J. *Exile's Gate*. New York: Daw, 1988.

———— *Fires of Azeroth*. 1979. Rpt. in *The Book of Morgaine*. New York: Nelson Doubleday, 1979. 405-633.

———— *Gate of Ivrel*. 1976. Rpt. in *The Book of Morgaine*. New York: Nelson Doubleday, 1979. 1-172.

———— *Port Eternity*. New York: Daw Books, 1982.

———— *Sunfall*. New York: Daw, 1981.

———— *Well of Shiuan*. 1978. Rpt. in *The Book of Morgaine*. New York: Nelson Doubleday, 1979. 173-404.

Grothey, Mina Jane. "Cherryh, C.J." *Reader's Guide to Twentieth-Century Science Fiction*. Ed. Marilyn P. Fletcher. Chicago: American Library Association, 1989.

Lacy, Norris J. "Pendragon." *The Arthurian Encyclopedia.* Ed. Norris J. Lacy. 1986. New York: Peter Bedrick, 1987.

Malory, Thomas. *Works.* Ed. Eugene Vinaver. 2nd ed., 1971. Rpt., Oxford: Oxford University P, 1981.

Thompson, Raymond H. *The Return from Avalon: A Study of the Arthurian Legend in Modern Science Fiction.* Contributions to the Study of Science Fiction and Fantasy 14. Westport, CT: Greenwood, 1985.

In Her Own Right:
The Guenevere of Parke Godwin

Tom Hoberg

At almost the same time in the middle of the last century, William Morris and Alfred Tennyson were working on their portraits of Guenevere, Arthur's queen. Morris depicts a character the social and psychological equal of the lords she confronts; defiantly articulate, she faces down Gawain and the rest of Arthur's chivalry in array, buying time with her eloquence until Lancelot can ride to her rescue. In Tennyson's hands, contrariwise, Guinivere's defiance is clandestine, her guilt pervasive, and her extravagant abasement before her lord and husband so demeaning that it offended even some of the Laureate's admirers.

Yet it is Tennyson's Guinevere that lies behind most of her contemporary portrayals: the sullen and neglected chattel bride of Rosemary Sutcliff; the winsome but passive nonentity of Mary Stewart; and, most recently and most controversially, the Gwenhwyfar of Marion Zimmer Bradley, whose petty and ignorant bigotry robs her character of any poignancy, and whose only claim to importance is the magnitude of the disasters wrought by her myopic selfishness.

And, like Tennyson's Guinevere, these contemporary ladies are emphatically subordinate characters, competing unsuccessfully for Arthur's attention—and the reader's—with Merlin or Lancelot, or Arthur's vision of a new world order. Bereft alike of political influence and personal magnitude, each of them is consigned to cloistered seclusion when Arthur casts her off, and narrative oblivion thereafter.

There is, however, one modern Arthurian who has chosen to see Guenevere as Morris did, to incarnate the poet's vision and fulfill the promise of his dramatic vignette. In his novels, *Firelord* and *Beloved Exile*, Parke Godwin has fashioned a Guenevere of equal status and strength with Arthur, who was his friend and his lover and, if necessary, his adversary, a fit consort for this greatest of legend's kings. While not stinting his portrayal of a memorable Arthur, he has given us a Guenevere who is, in Raymond Thompson's words, "one of the most dynamic and admirable characters in Arthurian literature" (*Avalon to Camelot* 13) who stands equal with Arthur during his life and, after he dies, perseveres in her own right and shapes her own arduous but ultimately triumphant future.

From the outset, Godwin's Guenevere is not one to let others direct her life and by both nature and nurture is admirably equipped to look out for herself. "I was fourteen when my mother died," she recalls,

At an age when most Parisi women bore their first child, I began to learn government... At sixteen I knew the machinery of government; how much sovereignty Ambrosius would give us in return for holding his back door against the Picts; in whose bosom we must place trust and in whose a knife: when to bargain, when to submit; when truth could be served and when it must be adulterated. (*Beloved Exile* 80, 84)

And Guenevere knew men, enjoyed them and exploited them. Brushing aside those suitors who would have had her as a decorative and biddable incubator of heirs, she keeps close tabs on the career of the young tribune Artorius, whose person and prospects equally attract her. When he becomes front runner to succeed Ambrosius as Imperator Guenevere defies her father and casts her fortunes with Arthur. And when he is crowned and anointed, she ascends the throne with him, his wife, his consort, his *de facto* if not *de jure* equal. Their joint rule, like their marriage, is monumentally tempestuous, as they hammer together a kingdom in the face of incessant factional bickering and in the teeth of the unrelenting pressure of the Saxons. Godwin's royal couple have neither the time nor the inclination for heroic romanticism; they are much too interested in life for that, and much too interesting to each other. Besides, such spurious histrionics would be a waste of too much time for them in ruling a kingdom and on Parke Godwin's in telling a story.

In Godwin's hands, all the familiar Arthurian characters and situations are recast to be fitted around the relationship of the royal pair, even as within the story Arthur and Guenevere use others without the luxuries of either cruelty or compassion, as they create a Britain shaped to their likeness and liking. Yet they are lovers as grand as they are rulers, and it is the star-crossing of their personal lives that precipitates the political crisis from which Godwin—remaking the legend and reordering its elements—creates his own "Defence of Guenevere."

It happens like this. Early in Arthur's career, before he had even met Guenevere, Arthur had sojourned for a season with the *prydn*, the faery folk of the island, and had been taken as husband by Morgana, the young matriarch of their clan. It is a life that cannot hold Arthur forever, or even for long. When the road to power opens before him he leaves the *prydn* and Morgana, and their child to be, and chooses to climb with Guenevere to the throne. Yet he never forgets Morgana, nor denies the double debt he owes her.

It is part of Arthur's life that Guenevere has neither the will nor the wit to understand. A northern princess, she has been bred to identify the faery folk with the Pict and to regard both as a foe even more savage and loathsome than the Saxon. And as Arthur's queen and wife, she has no intention of sharing him with even the memory of a former beloved. Arthur had told her of his experience with Morgana. But in apparent deference to her barrenness following the stillborn death of *their* child, he neglected to tell her about his son by Morgana. It was a serious mistake. For one day Morgana and her people, including that son, came to Camelot to claim their heritage.

Guenevere is beside herself, the queen outraged that the king would consider giving land to these scruffy vagabonds, the wife incensed that her husband dared parade this disgusting remnant of his past before her. Most searingly and complexly, the woman in her is devastated by the appearance of the son she had been unable to give Arthur, and of which he is so achingly proud. Other

Gueneveres might have taken refuge in hysterics or revenge in adultery or even, reasoning that a greater share of the King of Britain is a greater fortune than falls to most princesses, come to a grudging acceptance of the situation. But not Godwin's queen. As intelligent, passionate and capable as her consort, she is also his equal in pride, ruthlessness and, when the occasion demands, violence. Acting under her orders, her guardsmen invade the sleeping quarters of the *prydn* and slaughter all but Modred, Arthur's son, and Arthur himself, who comes forward to weigh the claims of royal justice against blood vengeance.

Guenevere makes no attempt to deny responsibility. In fact, when Arthur summons their court into extraordinary session to judge her, she flings back the charges at all of them, in as remarkable defense as Morris's Guenevere makes to the charge of adultery. Murder? No, Guenevere responds,

Justice. Royal judgment that must be absolute and above question if there is to be any law at all. My lords, why should I dissemble? This was done by my will...and for reasons any one of you would approve. I begged the Emperor not to let this woman cross the wall. You saw her and her brood. Do you know there are two hundred more ready to follow after, to inhabit the land she demanded of our king?...My people...Have I not been a just queen, just and merciful, for many years? Does one of you think I had this woman killed for the foul personal insult she gave me? She had ambitions in Britain...aims that she didn't trouble to disguise, she was that sure of Arthur. He speaks of the war with Cerdic, a war to be fought for much the same reason. If Cerdic came into this hall now and demanded the same land, would our answer be any different?...Was it murder, then, or execution? (253)

For a complexity of reasons—not the least of which is the split her eloquence has caused among his advisors—Arthur imprisons her in irons in the bowels of Camelot, with more permanent disposition to await the final showdown with Cerdic's Saxons. The king is dismally aware that his queen will die before giving in and that either her death or her defiance could precipitate the civil war that has been simmering since before Vortigern, a conflict that could utterly unmake the kingdom they'd built.

In Morris's poem, in fact, in just about all of the variants of the story from Malory onwards, this would be Lancelot's cue to thunder to the succor of the brave but helpless queen. But not in *Firelord*; not to Godwin's Guenevere. Lancelot? Yes, he was at Guenevere's trial, and tried—ineffectively—to intervene. Yes, he had been the queen's lover years before, when she and the king had drifted apart. And yes, he challenges Arthur's right to her. And Arthur, far from being daunted or devastated, is wearily annoyed. He knows that whatever has jeopardized their marriage and their love, it is far more profound than the romantic vaporings of his quondam friend.

Neither Arthur nor Guenevere will ever meet an adversary as challenging and tendentious as they find in each other. That's one of the secrets of their love's endurance, as she acknowledges on the eve of her exile. "We're creatures of the same kind," she tells her husband, "Hatched from the same egg. That's why—funny, but after all the years and all the beds—you're the best friend I ever had" (311). But he is unyielding, she is unrepentant and so off she goes.

But not forever; in fact, not even for long. Guenevere has one more court card to play, Queen to King; or, rather, Queen and King have it to play together. And nowhere is their collective majesty as manifest as in their moment of confrontation and reconciliation. For Guenevere quickly connives her deliverance and rides north to Parisi country to re-establish her power base. Arthur pursues. The two meet, army to army, before her city, then person to person in the field fronting the walls. Arthur has a proposition ready: No reprisals against the insurgents, an official crown for Guenevere and formal acknowledgement as co-ruler and, most important, not only a total pardon for the queen, but a full and public apology as well. Guenevere ponders; then, to the unalloyed relief of almost everyone, she accepts. "Opposed, we were a threat to Britain," Arthur declares, "Together a fortress" (340).

After their reunion, of course, all else is anticlimactic, though there *are* sacrifices to be made. One of them is Morgana, or at least Arthur's public memory of her. Before the assembled armies, Arthur declares: "Since Guenevere has shown herself as wise and selfless a ruler as ever I hope to be, I give her full and unconditional pardon for the execution of Morgana, which was, but for my personal anger, an act seen by all as done for the good of Britain" (341).

On Guenevere's part there are her forlorn allies, Agravaine and Lancelot. When the former, aching for a fight, makes to charge Arthur and his escort, the queen physically interposes herself between the two bands, withers him with her scorn and dismisses him from her service. Then it is her turn to be publicly gracious:

All men have a piece of the truth, Agravaine no less than others. Arthur the king has made mistakes. Arthur the man has confessed them. Can I do less? We were both wrong. But his came out of love, while mine masked jealousy behind the good of Britain. But we have made composition, and there will be peace...A king asks forgiveness. A queen grants it...And Guenevere asks her husband for like grace. (344)

There remains Lancelot, and Guenevere dismisses him from her service as well, more gently than Agravaine, but no less inexorably. "Everything Agravaine said of me is true," she tells her former lover. "I use people. I know my price and I give nothing away without profit. I'm what he called me, a whore...The shoe fits...I was born to it, but at out rank they call us kings. Go home, Lancelot..." (347).

All this is, from both of them, shamelessly manipulative and cynical; it is also glorious and larger than life. Moments later, when they are alone, Guenevere asks the king: "When you and I go to hell, Arthur, will they please leave us together?" "I couldn't imagine them not," he tells the queen. "If they have any feel for government, they'll put us in charge" (347).

With these two huge, imperial personalities reunited, almost anything would seem possible: conquering or absorbing the Saxon federates, finally bringing the factious nobility to heel, forging an ordered and united kingdom for the ages. But unfortunately for their dreams, Modred is also possible, and on the eve of what looked to be their greatest triumphs as rulers and their greatest happiness as lovers, Arthur's son comes back from the savage lands to cut his father down. Thus, constrained alike by legend and history, Parke Godwin brings his Arthur to an end.

And so, it would inevitably seem, his Guenevere as well. For aggrandize her as he may as Arthur's consort and even equal, what life has tradition given Guenevere, *can* ever give her, after the king is dead? We remember how both Geoffrey and Malory diminish and then dismiss Guenevere. A burden to Arthur at the end of his life, she shrinks to a cloister-bound nonentity at the end of hers and at the end of their stories. "Ruat Artorius, ruat Britannia," and thus Arthur, Guenevere, and the legend all stop together.

This is not the nature of Parke Godwin's Guenevere, and this penitential durance was not to be her fate. Years after Arthur's death, looking back on an eventful widowhood and forward with gusto to even more life and adventure, she says of herself:

I'm self-sufficient, that's my hell, but I'll live with it or die guilty of it, whatever the rules say. I accept the way I was made...Come rack or angels, I'll make no excuses...The only tragedy would be Lancelot's kind of guilt. That would have made me pathetic. I've more style than that. (*Exile*, 261)

That style, with its manifestation in her transformation from Guenevere to Gwenda and back again, is the matter of *Beloved Exile*. In *Firelord*, Godwin has already given us a complex and memorable Guenevere fully capable of partnership with the splendid Arthur he fashioned. But in *Firelord* Arthur was Godwin's persona, and it was Arthur's voice who tells his story and Guenevere's. Now where legend ends, and with it both the support and the constraints of the traditional framework, Godwin creates rather than adapts, as Guenevere's voice takes up her own tale. She has yet several roles to play in her life— the first—most public and least worthy—is Queen of Britain, would-be sustainer of an order that was moribund as soon as her husband the King was no longer there to sustain it.

Guenevere is devastated by her loss, of course, and Arthur's memory will live bittersweet as long as there is life in her. But that memory is too precious to be trivialized by fruitless tears, and from the moment she receives the news, the queen throws her formidable person and powers into holding together the kingdom they built. This means that she must contrive to have herself anointed Arthur's legitimate successor, and retain or create the power to enforce that legitimacy, a dauntingly difficult task. Confronted by rebellious Britons to the West and entrenched Saxons to the East, with two inept but rapacious princelings challenging her succession, the queen widow can count only on the shaky support of Arthur's *combrogi*, who will back her now out of loyalty to their dead lord, but who are as suspicious of Guenevere's motives as they are dubious of her capacity.

These, however, are the sort of challenges that she faced with Arthur and with which, by temperament and training alike, she is equipped to deal. What she cannot face, and will toil for many years to come to terms with, is the concept which cornerstones *Beloved Exile*: that what remains of the world that has bred her, nurtured her and exalted her is not worth saving and—as long as maintaining it is her life's endeavour—neither is she.

Godwin underscores the magnitude of the lessons Guenevere must learn, and the depth of her incapacity for learning them, in a confrontation with Bedivere at the end of her first perilous year as Queen-Milite. Guenevere had never fully understood nor trusted this former stable boy, who had nothing but ability and integrity to recommend him to Arthur; consequently, when she and her dwindling party of retainers is betrayed, she fixes upon him as the turncoat and has him hauled before her in chains. In a scene significantly reminiscent of her own trial before Arthur, she hears Bedivere deny treachery but affirm his reluctance to serve her, as he denounces her will to power as no different from those from whom she would save Britain:

This country died with Artos, but you'll get your share of the guts and kill anyone who gets between you and the plate...You and Constantine and all the lord of your kind. Life or death, thumbs up or down, you're so used to power and your holy right to it, you've forgotten everything else....Don't come the country-lover to me. You didn't even know it when it reached out to you—just pushed it in the mud and walked away. (129)

Guenevere still doesn't understand. At this moment, prepared to condemn and sentence Bedivere on her unsubstantiated suspicions, she shouts about "my rights, my prerogatives. How else do you rule?" Scant hours later she's fleeing with a half dozen followers across the moors. And two days after this, stupid with fatigue and shock, she's chained in the hold of a Saxon slave ship, bound up the Humber to the slave market, deep in the old Federate territory. The seal on her slave collar is inscribed: GWENDA. PARS. F. c/CICAT./I/X: Gwenda, Parisi female with scar. Value, one pound ten. Not the oblivion of the nunnery, but effective oblivion nonetheless. For Guenevere, among the people she and Arthur fought, her anonymity is her safeguard; it would seem that she is doomed to end her life as a thrall (the word is new to her, but she grasps its meaning quickly enough) of the murderous pagans who had threatened for a century to engulf all that she held civilized. Her old life was over, and her new one seemed hardly worth the living.

Guenevere has always been a survivor and so will Gwenda be. But whereas Guenevere has always contrived to bend circumstances to her will, her new persona must reshape itself to yield to circumstances. Thus Gwenda contrives to submerge her imperious tendencies to her new self, to work hard, hold her tongue, listen and learn. She acquires a special friend, Raidda, self-renamed "Rat," former whore and thief from the stews of Londinium. It is Rat who, at the outset of their new life, encapsulates it for Gwenda with stark brevity. "Listen, Gwenda," she urges. "Yer gonner learn or yer gonner die...Yer been hitten all yer life, Gwenda. Ya never knew there was them what could hit back. Na yer one of us" (168). Gwenda accommodates herself to her "Saxon" master, to his wife and children and, most of all, to her real owner, Gunnar's termagant mother, Elfgifu.

In fashioning this neolegend, Parke Godwin intends neither a paean to royal martyrdom nor a cautionary parable on the Fall of the Mighty. The exertions of her new life agree with Gwenda; physically, she's healthier than she's been in twenty years. Nor does she sink into the self-protective stupor that can protect a slave from her memories. Resilient and inquisitive, she derives instructive amusement from seeing herself, Arthur and their knights through the eyes of their adversaries. To Gunnar, who with his freemen fought under Icel in the Badon campaign, Arthur's *combrogi* were superhuman, with Lancelot, Bedivere, Gareth and the others given places among the elves and demons of Teutonic folklore. Guenevere, Gwenda found, is most notorious with these family-oriented folk as a depraved wanton with an insatiable sexual appetite, whose reputed exploits were the subject of as much interest—and the object of as much awe— as the martial achievements of her consort.

She sees the battle of Badon itself from the other side too: how Gunnar and the others straggled back to Gunnarsburh, nursing the physical and psychological wounds that would keep them at bay for most of a generation. Most of all, she comes to know The Time of the Smoke, as the Iclingas called Arthur's scorched earth campaign of twenty years before. Eanbold, Elfgifu's husband and Gunnar's father, died then, as did their eldest son and his whole family. Elfgifu will never forget, and takes pains to insure that her "Welsh" slave won't either. "Did your man tell you about the Time of the Smoke, Gwenda?" she inquires. "The men left dead in their fields, the women on their hearths? The children cut apart and thrown into ditches? The years of hope and work wiped out in one summer? Did your drunken harpers make a song out of that?" (163).

Godwin does not, however, take the object lesson and Gwenda with it to the opposite extreme, portraying the Iclingas as naturally noble. Gunnarsburh and its inhabitants have their faults, blind spots, and shortcomings right enough. Indeed, as Godwin shows them to us, we see that they are of the same kind, of like magnitude, and are perpetrated by the same kinds of people as those she left behind in the crumbling society of Roman Britain. Guenevere hears Elfgifu's strident dream of rebuilding in England a Jutland that never was, and we remember Arthur's ruined grandmother, clinging to her ruined villa and shabby Latin as she yearns for the return of the phantom legions. And in the berserkers, the brutal anachronisms that still demand tribute from a society that has outgrown them, the queen-turned-slave remembers the homicidal xenophobia—disguised always as patriotic duty—that periodically infected Arthur's captains, and to which both she and Arthur were selectively blind.

Raymond Thompson has perceptively noted that

Just as Arthur had to come to terms with his Pictish side by living for a time with Morgana and her family, Guenevere, in an extended period of Saxon captivity, comes to value the qualities of a culture greater than her own...Godwin's deliberate romantic departures from the convention of the Arthurian legend are effective in that they permit the author to establish a parallel between Arthur and Guenevere—the "alien" experience that humanizes both. (*Encyclopedia* 203)

Yet there is a vital difference between the two experiences and their impacts both on the principals and their worlds. For all that Arthur loved Morgana, and cherished the life of the *Prydn*, he recognizes it as a dying life, and repudiates it tentatively when he chooses Guenevere, and absolutely at their final reconciliation. Guenevere's experience is the reverse. As she comes to know her new world, to measure its strengths with its weaknesses, balance its wisdom against its folly, she comes to realize that she is both observing and living the future of their land.

Most of all, she comes to understand, share, and revere their loving bond with the earth, so different from the British lord's claim over, and the British peasant's thraldom to, the land. It is a crucial and a lasting one, in which her allegiance is irrevocably given to her English masters. It begins when the lands around Gunnarsburgh are attacked by a band of marauders, who devastate the land with the same mindless ferocity that the *combrogi* did a generation before. As the irony of the situation strikes her, the old Guenevere arises briefly from limbo.

How does it feel [she asks Gunnar acidly] to have your own kind go for your throat? Is Port any different from your own day, when he carved a piece out of my country? Was Arthur any different from you in trying to hold it? To know history is no blessing, Gunnar; one laughs or goes mad. (227)

Yet Gwenda cannot remain ironically aloof. As she and the others watch Port's men burning the crops, and brace for his assault on the stockade, she recognizes in Port a part of her old self, and in a rush of self-realization repudiates both:

All because of you, you stupid, greedy old man. Because you don't think, only grab. Because taking and killing is somehow more honorable, and you can sit on your arrogant rump in a hall and listen to a wheezy skald drone out what a true son of the gods you are. That's the illusion, the tottering vanity that makes pride cheaper than common sense, speaking from some experience. I've been there, old man. I know the desperation you can't show and the determination you must, and how well or poorly you sleep at night. You can burn the earth, but you won't take it. You haven't sweated over it to make it yours. You haven't earned it. (236-37)

Gwenda *has* earned it however, in a bit of foolishness during the fighting that almost gets her killed. And later she confirms her stewardship during a killer drought which, near its searing end leaves only her and her lord-thegn to drag the plow over the parched fields. They join in their extremity to pray to the Goddess, by all the names—Freya, Epona, Mary, she is invoked, in a petition too elemental for distinctions. And to this moment she brings all that she had ever been, Queen and Lover, Wise Woman and Foolish, herself now doomed to die unmarked and mourned in any event, a victim, as was Arthur, of entities older than civilization.

Their prayer is answered, or their magic works, though with a final twist of divine or demonic humor. The rains do not come to the land of the Iclingas. But people do. Teutons, ethnic cousins, driven from their homes by pressure from the westering Geats, they come with Icel's blessing, well provisioned, but numerous and homeless. It is, all agree, an omen. It is time to go home; not to Jutland, not even for Elfgifu, but back to the Midlands, underpopulated and largely undefended as Constantine and Emrys bleed each other to death farther west. And it is a signal, as well, for the end of Gwenda. After being freed by Gunnar, and declining a place of honor on the trek west, the freedwoman who had been Guenevere and Gwenda sojourns into what is left of Britain, with no motive except a powerful sense that her time with the Iclingas is meant to be over, and no agenda except to see old acquaintances, and keep a promise to a dying friend.

Gwenda has no wish to resurrect herself as Queen Guenevere, even a Guenevere enlightened and transformed by her recent life, to lead a crusade for the peaceful and just establishment of a new order. Least of all does she wish to re-enter the contest for the throne. "If there was no hope of my regaining the crown," she reflects, "there was no desire for it either. Like my old kirtles it no longer fit...Britain had a spate of strong dogs; what they needed was a strong people. No, I'd go to Eburacum, keep my promise to Rat, perhaps say farewell to Emrys, pray once more at Arthur's tomb, and then..." (347).

Parke Godwin's Guenevere, however, is not destined to slip so modestly out of her story, for within that story the choice turns out not to be hers to make. At her return she was aghast at the deterioration Britain had suffered during her absence. It is the Britain that had been in the unmaking ten years before, had she eyes to see than how right Bedivere was. The people flood the roads, stripped of all they owned by claimants to this or that power, plodding along with resentment as dulled as hope; Guenevere falls in with a populist priest, who tries with her anonymous encouragement to shout and bully and pray into them some of the spirit Gwenda had so recently relished among the English. But to no avail. When Guenevere is at last recognized, and tries to add her voice to Father Coel's, all the people know to do is clamor for her to come back and rule them, tell them what to do, be their queen again, be their Goddess.

When inevitably she is recognized, and forcibly reunited with her former peers, she learns of the death of some, and finds the rest grown old, crippled, and embittered. "They clung to their faded finery," she reflects, "of a past they couldn't restore and wouldn't relinquish. They reminded me of myself once, painting myself with too much cosmetic at the first signs of age" (371). Her pleas for reform as the only prescription for survival are met with cynicism or outrage by the warring heirs presumptive, and she is soon a virtual prisoner. Her only ally is an unlikely one: Lucullus Aurelianus, ambassador plenipotentiary from the Court at Constantinople. This half-brother of the late Ambrosius is the last survivor from the expiring days of empire, and the link between Britain of Arthur's brief, golden interregnum and the days and powers to come. Now, he has come to bring the greetings of the Byzantine Emperor to the lords of the English. "All things change, Guenevere," he observes. "Thirty years ago we were all outraged at these pirates plundering a province of the empire. Now the gamesters give different odds. One must look to the future" (391).

Lucullus finagles for his old friend a safe conduct for her back to New Rome, in return for her relinquishing all claims to the throne. The queen, knowing how much their claim is worth under any conditions, cheerfully names each of the rival claimants as her heir and prepares to leave a land and a people she can no longer love.

Her departure, however, is more easily arranged than done. For on the eve of her embarkation, for auld lang syne, she decides to pay one last visit to her erstwhile lover Lancelot and his family. The court at Astolat, even more than the one at Caer Legis, vividly embodies all that has gone wrong and rotten in Roman Britain. Guenevere's former lover and the once-dashing captain of Arthur's cavalry is now as past his prime as the others she left behind her, vaguely loyal to Emrys, or the ghost of Arthur, or all three, or whomever his wife tells him. Galahalt has petrified into a pillar of aristocratic stupidity, convinced beyond arrogance of the rectitude of things as they are and as, under God, they will be, world without end.

But Eleyne is the worst. *Soi-disant* descendant of Joseph of Arimathea and anointed guardian of the Grail, she has been all her life a cast-iron bigot, who has forgiven Lancelot his fling with Guenevere with a pious implacability that has effectively unmanned him. But she has never forgiven Guenevere. To her horror, Guenevere finds herself a prisoner at Astolat, and realizes that Eleyne had been the instigator of all the betrayals that had dogged her after Arthur's death, and has even now sold her out to Constantine, All, of course, *ad maiorem gloriam Dei*, as Eleyne, with serene madness, proclaims the Divine Plan: her son to unite what was Caesar's and what is God's, and damnation for all and everyone else.

As she listens to Eleyne's ranting, the whole hopelessness and folly of what Britain has become is incarnated for Guenevere in her fellow British noble:

For her son and her warped dream of a Britain conjured from her unreal visions and fermented wrongs, she'd murdered the reality, sent men to their deaths as servants to a kitchen, torn open cities, sundered lives, turned out hundreds...to choke the roads. She never thought of the numbers or put faces or hope to any of them. That was beneath and beyond Eleyne. She'd fling to hell forever any hope of a Britain to stand in a real world. She was Elfgifu gone rotten—courage, determination, soured longing, insanity like encroaching mildew. (408)

This Eleyne that Parke Godwin has limned for us is hardly the Elaine of tradition. At first look, her portrayal might smack of a contorted plot maneuver, a conventionally unpleasant character tricked up as a narrative scapegoat by a writer who values ingenuity above integrity. There is, however, much more to his depiction than that. Throughout both novels, Eleyne is gradually but consistently revealed as the person Guenevere could have become, the extreme of what their whole class *was* becoming. And that has been Godwin's narrative substructure all along: the ruination of society brought on, not by conquest from without, but by rigidity of class, perversion of faith, and meagerness of vision within. It is poetic justice—not only for Eleyne but for Britain—that her machinations brought about the deaths of her husband and son, caught in mistaken ambush by Constantine's men, and poetic mercy, perhaps, that this tragedy permanently unmoors Eleyne's wits from the real world.

Guenevere's final confrontation with Britain takes place, fittingly, with the "other" king of Britain, Constantine, who arrives, in fulfillment of his bargain with Eleyne, to take her into custody. She knows the futility of even talking to Constantine, since she recognizes in him a distorted reflection of what she had been ten years before and what, in some degree, the rest still were. "We were," she reflects,

All ghosts now, walking old ramparts out of dull habit, reaching out of a reason only dimly remembered for a right we couldn't name. Ghosts. In the last days of my rule, I was no different, only more efficient, than the down-to-earth king hunched in his chair. And he could be me ten years ago, hunted out of Witrin, falling down to gasp for breath in the ruins of Aquae Sulis for one too-brief space before running on with the hounds at his heels. (417)

Guenevere's rescue—for rescued she must be, since she has survived to tell us her story—is a bit of eleventh-hour daring-do that Godwin makes plausible. First, in the nick of time, Emrys and his cavalry come pounding out of the forest, engaging Constantine and inadvertently almost killing the Queen, as she is bounced and dragged from one band to another like a rag football. Moments later, as Constantine is closing in to finish the job, a cloud of arrows falling between the warring bands heralds the arrival of Gunnar and his English infantry, come at Lucullus' bidding to claim their inheritance. It's all so supremely apt, at the end like this: the former of Queen of Britain, a future Thegn of Britain, and a Diplomat whose career has marked the fall of the Old Rome and the rise of the New, mediating the dispute between two starveling warbands fighting for the right to an empty title.

This is her finest hour, as she savors a triumph even sweeter than over Arthur at Eburacum, when she won for herself the powers and prerogatives that had then seemed so precious. After mockingly proclaiming both men heirs to a kingdom that has ceased to exist, she turns to the polyglot crowd—Constantines's Cornish, Emrys's northerners, the common Brits who followed her from Astolat, Gunnar and his freemen—and demands: "Who shall carry the sword of Britain?" And, in all the languages of England the reply comes: "Gwladys! Guenevere! Gunver! Gwenda!" (429). There was a time when she might have been tempted by this. No more. She has been all of these singly in her life; now, she is all of them together. And now it's time to go. With a valedication to Constantine, she gives her final bequest. "On to exile. It's all yours now, King-of-the-hill and ravening challenger. Fight over it, children, but do wait until I'm off the field. Mother wants to enjoy her obscurity" (430). She goes with Lucullus to take ship for the East, the beloved exile of the title. The last thing she sees and hears, as Bedivere, Gareth, and Bors fall in as her escort, is the two British bands flying at each other, with Gunnar watching from the hill of which he is now king.

A melodramatic denouement? Exuberantly and unashamedly so. And it works wonderfully because both the author and his persona revel in relating it and because, having come to know her so well, the reader would have found any other resolution quite out of character.

And character is, finally, what makes Parke Godwin's creation sublime. At the end, as his Guenevere connives for her life and bargains for the future of her land, we realize what Godwin has brought into being. The queen who had bargained with her consort for half a kingdom was admirable; now, as *quondam* queen who bargains away it all, then walks into exile from the field where Britain dies and England is born, she is awesome.

A quarter of a century later, well past eighty and almost blind, Guenevere returns home for the last time, to taste her country once again and then to be laid to rest beside Arthur. She bears an official letter of introduction from Justinian himself which contains, in a *sub-rosa* postscript, an unofficial tribute from one remarkable individual to another:

There is little about Guenevere that is not touched by the fabulous. Why, my grandmother remembered stories about her and her husband. Legends, actually. I don't believe the half of them. But I shall miss her. (435)

Guenevere's assessment of her likely place in history is much more modest and, as thing have turned out, more accurate. "They'll remember you as savior of Britain and the patron of the Grail," she whispers to the memory of Arthur, "while I'll be remembered as a rebellious whore" (7).

And so most of the singers *have* sung. Until Parke Godwin. But then, most of those others had little good to sing about the Saxons, and they were wrong about them. For they weren't all Saxons anyway. And they abided. And prevailed. And so had the last laugh. And, thanks to Parke Godwin, so—somewhere, somewhen—does Guenevere.

Works Cited

Godwin, Parke. *Beloved Exile*. New York: Bantam, 1984.
_____ *Firelord*. New York: Bantam, 1982.
Thompson, Raymond. *"Firelord* and *Beloved Exile"* by Parke Godwin. *Avalon to Camelot* I, 4 (1984) 13-14.
_____ "Parke Godwin." *The New Arthurian Encyclopedia.* Ed. Norris Lacy. New York: Garland, 1991.

Joseph Campbell
and the Power of Arthurian Myth

Mildred Leake Day

Joseph Campbell, interviewing with Bill Moyers in *The Power of Myth*, introduced comparative mythology to television viewers around the world. His six-part series attracted two and a half million viewers a week. In a second series, *Transformations of Myths Through Time: The World of Joseph Campbell*, Campbell described the great myths of the world in richer detail, culminating with the stories of Tristan and Parzival as the major myths of Western Civilization. Through television and videos—as well as the books written to accompany them— Campbell's scholarship in myth and the human spirit has become accessible to an audience far beyond his classes at Sarah Lawrence College. He has changed the ways we view the Arthurian legend.

"The Hero's Journey," the first episode of *Transformations*, is Campbell's own life story. Born in 1904, he was raised a Roman Catholic in New York, but even as a boy he was fascinated with the lore of the American Indians, spending hours in the Museum of Natural History. As an undergraduate at Columbia, he studied classical mythology and medieval literature. His master's thesis on *Le Morte Darthur* won him a traveling fellowship from Columbia. He studied the Arthurian Legend in Paris in 1927; and in 1928-29, philology and Sanskrit in Munich. But he did not finish his doctorate. Instead, with a small legacy as support, he spent the next five years reading.

Campbell's decision was not merely a reaction to the Depression and the difficulty of finding teaching positions. He describes an experience in the garden of Cluny in Paris:

It suddenly struck me: What in heaven's name am I doing? I don't even know how to eat a decent nourishing meal, and here I'm learning what happened to vulgar Latin when it passed into Portuguese and Spanish and French. So I dropped work on my Ph.D. On my return I found a place in upstate New York and read the classics for 12 hours a day. I was enjoying myself enormously, and realized I would never finish my degree because it would have required me to do things I had already outgrown. In Europe, the world had opened up: Joyce, Sanskrit, the Orient, and the relationship of all these to Psychology. I couldn't go back and finish up that Ph.D. thesis; besides, I didn't have the money. And that free-wheeling maverick life gave me a sense of the deep joy in doing something meaningful to me. (*An Open Life*, 125-6)

In 1934 he began teaching at Sarah Lawrence College, on his own terms. He remained on the faculty until his retirement in 1972. His publications include *The Hero With a Thousand Faces* (1949); editing the posthumous works of Heinrich Zimmer, *Philosophies of India* and *The Art of Indian Asia; The Flight of the Wild Gander* (1951); *The Masks of God* (Four volumes, 1959-68); *Myths to Live By* (1971); *The Mythic Image* (1975); *Historical Atlas of World Mythology* (Two volumes, 1983-88); and *The Inner Reaches of Outer Space: Metaphor as Myth and as Religion* (1981-84). The television series *Transformations of Myths Through Time* was taped from lectures at Sarah Lawrence College and elsewhere, delivered over several years. *The Power of Myth* with Bill Moyers was filmed in 1985-86. Campbell died in 1987 before the book to accompany the series was published.

The Hero's Journey, defined by Campbell, is the path a man or woman takes, risking everything to accomplish a special good. That risk can be in battle or childbirth; it can also be a spiritual quest for power or wisdom that will benefit one's people. The hero's path is one that goes and returns. Campbell's special phrase for the deliberate choice of the hero's role is "follow your bliss." Campbell deliberately followed the mythic path of the hero in his own life. He answered his own special call. He brought back the unique treasures of his scholarship and shared them. He was asked once whether—if he had his life to live over—he would make the same choice, and he answered that he would, that when he made his choice he did not know whether it was a good one, but that looking back, it was indeed the only choice for him. He had followed—and found—"his bliss."

The most memorable moment in *The Power of Myth* is seeing Campbell, scholar of ancient legends, talk about *Star Wars* as myth. George Lucas had read *The Hero With a Thousand Faces* and consciously shaped the quest of Luke Skywalker to follow the pattern of the hero's journey. Young Luke finds it difficult to follow the expected career of his foster parents. He discovers a mentor (or the mentor finds him). He must learn new skills and he must learn to ally himself with the Force (an acceptance of natural energy, not just technology). The fall into the garbage shoot is a mythical variation of being in the belly of the whale. And so the plot goes. But the theme that keeps repeating is that the dark power armed with technology (the modern black magic) is not the final answer: the natural, human spirit is what makes the difference. The Hero with a Thousand Faces is Luke, or Arthur retrieving the Sword from the Stone, or Gawain saving his shipmates from Greek Fire in *De ortu Waluuanii*— or characters beyond naming in the fiction currently being written by sword-and-sorcery authors like David Eddings (The Mallorean Series), Terry Brooks (The Scions of Shannara), or Dave Duncan (A Man of his Word).

But to Campbell, the Arthurian legend and the Holy Grail represent a re-telling of the ancient Hero's Journey by authors sensitive to the mythic power of the material. He goes even further, insisting that the story of Tristan and Isolde is the first evidence of the importance of the individual as himself and herself in Western culture. As Campbell explains, love as an intensely interpersonal experience is a relatively new phenomenon for men and women. There has always been *eros*, the natural lust that keeps the species going. The Church added *agape*, the love one ought to have for one's neighbor. Neither of these loves, however, is focused on a single unique individual. Campbell reminds us that the new way of love, *amor*, was first expressed in poetry by the troubadours of Provençal. As the troubadours portrayed it, the new love begins in the eyes and finds its home in the heart. The lovers must be worthy and gentle. It becomes an all-consuming passion sublimated in poetry and great exploits on the battlefield. *Amor* was a passion for noblemen and noblewomen only—and it was adulterous. Marriage, of course, was a political and economic linking of families, often arranged in childhood. A noble passion between individuals attracted to one another as persons was a concept that could shatter the accepted customs of the age.

The legend of Tristan and Isolde dramatizes how shattering such a love could be. Under ordinary circumstances, Tristan as a Knight of Cornwall would have never met a royal maiden as an individual. But Tristan, grievously wounded and set afloat, came ashore in Ireland. He was tended and nursed back to healty by Isolde and her mother the Queen. In the months of recuperation, Tristan had taught Isolde to play the harp. When he returned to Cornwall, his description of the Irish princess convinced his uncle King Mark to ally the two kingdoms, taking Isolde as his bride. This, of course, was the role for which Isolde was intended by birth and breeding. Tristan was sent back to Ireland to escort the King's bride to her wedding. The infamous love potion was merely the catalyst for the relationship between two young people that was blossoming naturally, not *eros* but *amor*. This personal love broke all the mores of feudal society—bonds between knight and lord, between kinsmen, between husband and wife, between the kingdoms that the marriage united.

Campbell describes the moment when Isolde's nurse discovers that they have drunk the potion:

...she goes to Tristan and says, 'You have drunk your death.' And Tristan says, 'By my death, do you mean this pain of love?'—because that was one of the main points, that one should feel the sickness of love. There's no possible fulfillment in this world of that identity one is experiencing. Tristan says, 'If by my death, you mean this agony of love, that is my life. If by my death, you mean the punishment that we are to suffer if discovered, I accept that. And if by my death, you mean eternal punishment in the fires of hell, I accept that, too.' Now that's big stuff. (*The Power of Myth*, 190)

Tristan and Isolde suffered all the punishments that King Mark and their culture could inflict. Yet as true heroes, they followed their bliss, and as culture heroes, brought back the treasure of love between two individuals. Western expectations of the possibilities of human love had changed.

Campbell sees even more profound changes in what Wolfram von Eschenbach created in the Hero's Journey of *Parzival*. Parzival has two paths of learning: the first is to learn how to be a knight; the second, how to be the Grail king. He must first learn to fit the culture into which he was born; then he must learn to surpass that culture by opening his heart to the natural and the supernatural. The Grail for Wolfram represents man's deepest aspirations. The quest is individual; the goal a numinous blending of the cultural with the natural.

The mythic material of the Grail is ancient: a life-restoring cauldron, a cornucopeia, the golden cup of Sovereignty, the sacramental bowl of the late Classical Orphic sect. Wolfram's Grail brings in much of these traditions, but the central object is a mystic stone, related to the Philosopher's Stone, but as a holy thing brought from heaven to earth by the angels, an echo of the Ka'aba as well.

The Grail, for him, was a cult-transcending talisman of cross-cultural associations, pointing to an image of man ('The Wish of Paradise') released from ecclesiastical authority, perfected in his nature through his own personal adventure, serving the world not through servitude but through mastery, and through love fulfilled.... (*The Flight of the Wild Gander*, 219)

Parzival fails in his first visit to the Grail Castle because he follows the instructions in proper behavior that he has received—and not the compassionate concern of his own heart. For this failure, he is told he will have no second chance. Yet because of his dedicated persistence, the rules are changed.

At the onset of the five years of wandering that follows his failure, he renounces God. When he finally surrenders his heart to God again, it is not to a God of the churchly theology of his mother but to God as the cosmic principle corresponding to the individual heart.

Yet the single most important action that Parzival accomplishes in his Quest is neither his determination to find the Grail nor his new theology. It is his love for his wife. Parzival and Condwiramurs have discovered *amor* for one another, not in adultery, but in freely entered, true marriage.

The Grail becomes symbolic of an authentic life that is lived in terms of its own volition, in terms of its own impulse system, that carries itself between the pairs of opposites of good and evil, light and dark. One writer of the Grail legend starts his long epic with a short poem saying, 'Every act has both good and evil results.' Every act in life yields pairs of opposites in its results. The best we can do is lean toward the light, toward the harmonious relationships that come from compassion with suffering, from understanding the other person. This is what the Grail is about. And this is what comes out in the romance. (*The Power of Myth*, 197)

Campbell was not merely a scholar of comparative mythology in the sense of being a cataloger of the myths of the world. He certainly was more than the "popularizer" that his critics call him. He was a man in search of symbols that still have mythic power in the modern world. His definition, repeated in his lectures, is that a symbol that is genuine does not have to be explained: a symbol that is genuine opens up to the transcendent and is beyond explanation. The Holy Grail was for him just such a symbol. Campbell teaches us to read the Arthurian legend as the central myth of modern Western culture, seeing in the Grail the point of unity between that culture and nature.

The continuing delight we have in reading our versions of the Arthurian romances shows the inexplicable power of stories of the quest. So do the stories and songs about love—the myth of Tristan and Isolde with only the names changed.

But Campbell does not limit the power of myth to fiction and music. Campbell ends the final lecture in *Transformations* by encouraging his listeners to discover their own individual hero paths, to live authentic lives that unite both nature and culture, and to follow their bliss. Campbell concludes with the challenge, "Go forth with joy into the sorrows of life."

Works Cited

Cashford, Jules. "Joseph Campbell and the Grail Myth." John Matthews, ed., *The Household of the Grail*, Wellingborough, England: Aquarian, 1990. 198-217.

Segal, Robert A. *Joseph Campbell: An Introduction.* New York: Garland, 1987; Rev. ed. New York: Mentor, 1990.

Selected works by Joseph Campbell

Creative Mythology. The Masks of God. London: Penguin, 1968.

The Flight of the Wild Gander: Explorations in the Mythological Dimension. 1951; rpt. New York: Harper Perennial, 1990.

The Hero with a Thousand Faces. Bollingen Series XVII. Princeton: Princeton UP, 1949.

An Open Life. In Conversation with Michael Toms (compilations on tapes of interviews from 1975-85). Larsons Publications, 1988.

The Power of Myth with Bill Moyers. PBS series filmed 1985-86. (BOMC offers recordings and compact discs, cassettes and records. Write BOMC, Camp Hill, PA 17012) Book: New York: Doubleday, 1988.

Transformations of Myth Through Time: The World of Joseph Campbell (Thirteen lectures on video and a book). Concord, MA: Home Vision, 1990.

Berger's Mythical *Arthur Rex*

Suzanne H. MacRae

Thomas Berger's mercurial voice, his Protean stylistic range, and his dazzling array of genres perplex the critics. His language runs the gamut from ribald to archaic, deadpan colloquial to elegantly philosophical. Since 1958 he has written sixteen novels using varied literary formats such as western picaresque in *Little Big Man* (1964), science fiction dystopia in *Regiment of Women* (1973), Kafkaesque nightmare in *The Neighbors* (1980), hardboiled detective in *Who is Teddy Villanova?* (1977) and chivalric romance in *Arthur Rex* (1978). Academics have not embraced Berger in the way they have Joyce, Borges, and Barth; neither has the wide audience for writers like Mailer, Heller and Steinbeck flocked to his books. Berger's biggest success has been *Little Big Man,* and that undoubtedly owes much to the popularity of the film version. The problem seems to be that people do not know exactly what to do with Berger, how to read him. His use of popular genres puts the elitists off the scent; his language pyrotechnics and subtle alterations of the literary prototypes estrange him from the mass audience.

Basic issues about his novels remain unsettled: tone, effectiveness, authorial intent, the presence or absence of satire. Judgments on *Arthur Rex* show a typical divergence of opinion. A *Time* magazine review deems it "haphazard parody" with an unsuccessful mishmash of medieval and modern styles (Atlas 107, 110). A *Christian Science Monitor* reviewer finds no virtues whatsoever in the book (Yohalem). The *New Republic* calls the novel fragmented and the villains limp, comparing it unfavorably with T. H. White's *Once and Future King* (Epps 35, 36). One defender of the book believes it is "funny, poignant, tragic" (Fuller 18). Malone and Schickel think *Arthur Rex* is serious comedy rather than satire ("American" 536; *NY Times Book Review* 1, 21, 22). John Romano praises Berger as a "first-rate literary wiseguy," judges the novel "the Arthur book of our time," and finds Berger a parodist who debunks myths (3, 62). Brooks Landon, the author of the only book-length study of Berger, asserts that Berger is the consummate artist for whom manipulation of style and language, not satire, is paramount.

Berger himself testifies in letters and interviews that he writes only for his own pleasure and detests the idea of publication (of course, he does publish and presumably gets paid). For him, writing creates an alternative to intolerable reality (Schickel, *NY Times* 22). Berger disallows any interest in satire, parody, spoof, or even social commentary (Malone, "American" 535). Social amelioration is neither possible nor desirable; he would not "walk across the street to save the world" because he "did not see it as a problem to which there was a solution.

"Existence seems...to be simply there" (Ghose 11). Berger's judgment cannot, of course, be swallowed whole; writers are often the most muddleheaded critics of their own work. Yet it is wise to keep his comments in mind.

The question of whether Berger is satirical is central to the entire debate about tone, intent, effectiveness. The difficulty of answering this question is compounded by the problem of precisely defining a term which stretches like the elastic of a girdle and covers as much terrain. Satire may or may not be humorous; it may or may not have a moral intent or effect. It could advocate social or individual reform, but it might not. Leonard Feinberg, in his *Introduction to Satire,* after affirming that no set definition is possible, provides one: "a playfully critical distortion of the familiar" (19). For him satire de-emphasizes plot in order to make its point through humor, unfairly distorting its subject matter and allowing the audience to vent its spleen from a superior position. Feinberg believes that satirists only pretend to high moral purpose while actually concentrating on the expression of anger and/or wit (4-12, 226-28).

Northrop Frye in *Anatomy of Criticism* offers the clearest and most workable definition of satire: wit, humor, fantasy, and the grotesque become instruments of attack and criticism of the subject. Even if satirical writers are not motivated by moral aims, they still hold an "implicit moral standard" against which the absurd is evaluated (223,224). Frye distinguishes between satire and irony, which are closely related: "Satire is militant irony; its moral norms are relatively clear, and it assumes standards against which the grotesque and absurd are measured" (223). In contrast, readers of ironic literature feel unsure about the author's attitude and what their own attitudes should be (223). Giving wide latitude for various styles of writing satire, Frye anchors his definition in the double view of norm and departure from it. His concepts provide the most practical benchmark for evaluating *Arthur Rex.*

The novel's *enfance* section, which narrates the begetting, youth, and early kingship of Arthur, offers a plausible case for satire. Persistent, irreverent humor leaves virtually no character or institution unscathed. Berger's verbal scalpel slices excess, self-delusion, naiveté, hypocrisy, self-indulgence. Yet a subtle undercurrent subverts any pure satire. Ygraine, Arthur's mother, for instance, combines the self-aggrandizement of the yuppie with the spiritual smorgasbord of the New Age advocate. In fits of boredom she resorts to religion but focuses on the social hierarchy of heaven and competition with her rival queen of Ireland for the seat nearest God in the paradisical feast. But when an aged prelate makes a pass at her, Ygraine deserts Christianity to dabble in Zoroastrianism, Judaism, Druidism, and finally the cult of Gluttony, where she finds fulfillment. Lying on her bed she appropriately resembles "a mounded white pudding with her eyes small as two currants" (22). Ygraine's faddishness is mocked, yet religion itself may sustain a blow, too, as the mainstream and the eccentric religions both fail to satisfy the needs of the seeker. The lustful cleric rightfully upsets the queen, yet he hardly represents real danger, and his actions do not necessarily discredit Christianity itself. But in a "California" culture would anyone deny Ygraine the privilege and indeed the sacred right to suit her own religious notions? In a supermarket of cultural choices, the shopper can afford to be omnivorous and choosy. Why shouldn't a queen find happiness as a pudding?

Arthur's father, Uther Pendragon, is derided by the very machismo standards he upholds. A coarse, womanizing warrior, he detests the pagan sodomite Anglo-Saxons (he calls them Germans) while insisting that British, Christian, heterosexual lechery marks the real man. He embarks on war just to bed the wife of his enemy and uses Merlin's magic to disguise himself as the husband and gain access to her. But then he finds that she is the one who has been seducing him all the time, having left her castle unguarded, the dogs kenneled, and an embroidered Cadwaller emblem of the Pendragons hanging on a door in her chamber. Uther has been known as the ravisher of a thousand females per year, but his sexual prowess wilts when he attains the longed for queen. He is also embarrassed to see that the sexual equipment of his rival, which he has temporarily highjacked, is much more richly endowed than his own. Yet the narrator later validates Uther's masculine credentials with this comment: "He killed many men and took many maidenheads wherever he went and was considered the greatest king of his time" (21). Logically the paratactic "and" before the third verb does not imply a cause-effect relationship. Rather it connotes grammatical equivalence with a non-specific connection among the verb phrases. Yet casual, especially oral, usage leads us to conclude that the killing and raping justified the political approval. Has Berger slyly coaxed us into a Freudian deduction? Or were sex and violence indeed legitimate criteria for fame and power in the Middle Ages? Are they still criteria today? Or are these political values being criticized? Do we respect Uther more, or less, because of his forcefulness? Is Uther's sexual vulnerability to Ygraine something we despise or find sympathetic? Berger makes us decide.

The characterization of Arthur bites more gently and subtly than the description of his parents. He is the rustic innocent who must adapt swiftly to his royal destiny. Reared in bucolic Wales with no knowledge of his biological family or his kingship to come, Arthur prefers leeks to dainty dishes and would rather sleep with his dogs than in a fine bed. He lacks knightly vocation and appears bumfuzzled by his seemingly accidental advancement when he removes the sword from the stone. Yet quickly Arthur slips unconsciously into the royal "we," and his first executive order demands that the London brothel be burned, its customers arrested, its professionals transferred to a convent. Without Merlin's political counsel Arthur would have executed the corrupt clergy instead of having the worst of them, the Archbishop, crown him. The danger of the country boy coming to town is that Arthur has power without sophistication; his naiveté glides easily into zealotry or pomposity. But, on the whole, Arthur is admirable— brave, kind, diligent in pursuing the welfare of his kingdom and its peace. And his innocence charms as well as appalls us.

The astute political advisor Merlin is, however, feckless as a magician whose power extends neither to nature nor women. He cannot provide the beardless Arthur any genuine chin whiskers before their time. Any and all females thwart his plots. His magic depends on mechanical legerdemain as he dabbles like Don Herbert's Mr. Wizard in anachronistic technology such as light bulbs, x-rays, and phonographs, none of which anyone else understands, appreciates, or uses. Nor does Merlin use his inventions himself, either for personal gain or powerful strategic destruction as Twain's Hank Morgan does. The kindly Merlin is a bit daft and at most times irrelevant to the action of the novel.

The humorous descriptions of these characters feed off eccentricity, excess, naiveté, self-indulgence. Yet they lack full satirical force for several reasons. The ridicule is diffused among the characters and the absurd values and institutions which guide them. Corruption and self-seeking seem themselves to be the norm; hence, it would be folly to go against the flow. Removing the characters' illusions would not only make them miserable and unable to cope but might also render them more dangerous. Berger makes it difficult to isolate a clear moral and social norm; placing blame becomes a slippery or ambiguous operation. And finally Berger seems to like his characters; his lighthearted irony—"what fools these mortals be"—expresses neither serious morality nor the expectation or desire for reform. Berger echoes this philosophy in a letter: "I couldn't myself survive in any society that eliminated its eccentrics, perverts, monsters, and madmen" (Ghose 12).

But the flippant good humor of the *enfance* section gives way to bittersweet elegy in Berger's narration of the love of Tristram and Isolde. The lovers' sad destiny is determined more by fate than choice. Tristram's symbolic name implies that he is constitutionally melancholy, and the events of his life fulfill his genetic propensity. The loss of his parents when he is an infant initiates the chain of sadness which culminates in the tragic love affair.

Tristram and Isolde fall in love before they drink the potion and before Mark has even heard of her, much less secured her as his bride. But the couple refuse to act on their erotic feelings until the love potion bonds them beyond choice and will. By this point Isolde is already betrothed to King Mark and the pair are sailing to Cornwall for the wedding. Caught in the classic medieval conflict of loyalties, Tristram and Isolde are doomed to hurt either themselves or the king no matter what they do. But they try to live discreetly, keep their passion secret, and steal their pleasures when they can. The intensity, generosity, sweetness and fidelity of their love contrasts sharply with the crassness of the other characters.

King Mark, for example, deludes himself into taking pride in his aging sexual prowess and finds delight in memories of erotic exploits which never happened but were produced by chemically induced fantasies. He alternates between belief in the innocence of his wife and suspicion of the lovers. He thinks that his nephew is effeminate because Tristram displays no open lechery, yet he plots with the vengeful dwarf Frocin to expose the adulterers. But a combination of fate, God, and the ingenuity of Isolde and Brangwain outwits the king time and again. And even Mark later forgives the lovers when he learns of the potion.

Berger eliminates much of the cruelty and sophistry of Gottfried von Strassbourg's heroine and validates the nobility of Tristram's love by showing that his affection increases after Isolde becomes prematurely aged and withered. He allows Isolde to regain her lost beauty when she is buried with Tristram in a single grave where they find peace at last. Berger omits the mystical and liturgical dimensions of the German poem and is content to tell the story on a simpler, more emotional plane. He sees Tristram and Isolde as emblematic of authentic feeling in a crass world. Their adultery merits an elegiac tear rather than criticism. And even Mark is described ironically more than satirically.

Elegy darkens into somber irony and then tragedy in Launcelot and Guinevere's love affair, which lacks both the zestful energy of Uther's sexual romps and the bittersweet affection of Tristram and Isolde. This love is rooted in the pathology of the characters rather than natural lechery or some external force. And the political destruction spreads much wider here than in the Cornwall scandal because this adultery prompts the collapse of the Round Table itself. Launcelot's entire life is enervated by melancholia, guilt, and asceticism. His invulnerability in battle renders warfare insipid to him, and he longs to fight a knight who can defeat him. Believing himself immune to sexual love, he drives Elaine to suicide by his unintended encouragement of her unrequited love. Life constantly reminds him of human wretchedness and his own failure, yet piety prevents him the release of his own suicide. When Bors urges him to use his God-given prowess, Launcelot replies,

"...I do not know that...I could exercise my gift at arms for ought but vanity on mine own part and envy on the part of others. Therefore, going into the world to fight against evil I should in a very real way but increase its sway." (144)

His spiritual sloth mutates into despair as the greatest knight of Arthur's court fights without desire or hope.

Guinevere languishes in her own brand of frustration and longing. More intelligent and politically adept than her husband, she must sit as mere consort rather than exert any genuine power. She romanticizes what she lacks, but the real Launcelot shatters her fantasized dream of him. Boredom, vanity, and self-defeat lead her to love him. Yet she despises his piety and duty and strives to corrupt his will, not being satisfied with just royal command of his services.

The couple's sexual initiation speaks a bitter prophecy. Launcelot keeps watch over the sleeping Guinevere during a bout of psychosomatic illness. She unconsciously takes his hand and places it on her breast but wakes to accuse him falsely of felonious assault. He clenches his teeth and bloodies his lips in trying to control his passion for her. She asks if he would comply with an order to love her; he answers,

"May God damn me, lady, if I do that not by your order, but by mine own need!" and he thrust his bloodied hand into her golden hair and cleansed it thereupon, saying, "Now we are both stained forever." (192)

From this point on they cannot or will not extricate themselves, no matter the spiritual or political consequences. Love torments them, but they remain locked in a struggle for mastery of the other. Their mutual addiction is fueled more by pride than lust. Only when faced with public exposure do they momentarily conquer their vanity and express genuine feeling. Guinevere admits to Launcelot, "...I can not live without thee...mine apparent disdain is merely the means by which I have endeavored to defend myself against becoming thy slave—and failed" (432).

But such honesty will not save them or the Round Table fellowship. Launcelot and Guinevere are doomed by both innate character and choice. Berger's novel has shifted from good natured mockery to elegy to full-blown tragedy.

With Camelot in tatters and Excalibur dulled, Arthur recoils in guilt from his duty to kill Mordred, his incestuously begotten son whom he has rejected both as offspring and heir. Arthur despairs over his life: "Perhaps there was some justice in the triumph of perfect evil over imperfect virtue, which is to say, of tragedy over comedy. For have I not been a buffoon?" (483). But Gawaine, now a ghost, comforts his uncle,

...we are all fools for we live but temporarily, and beneath our armor we wear human skin, which is to say, motley. But the difference between a great man and a mere entertainer is that the former doth seek to please no audience but God, and thus he goeth against the mean instincts of humanity....And though man be eternally contemptible, he should not be contemptuous of that which he can achieve. (483)

Gawaine praises the gallant Round Table knights who have neither sought nor won "easy victories" (484).

The Lady of the Lake corroborates Gawaine's judgment and says to Arthur: "Thou couldst not have done better than thou didst" (484). When Arthur chastises himself for sin in condoning by inaction the adultery of Launcelot and Guinevere, she rebukes him:

Address me not in Christian sentiments...the which I find too coarse for fine kings. Thine obligation was to maintain power in as decent a way as would be yet the most effective, and a Camelot without Guinevere, a Round Table without Launcelot, were inconceivable, as would be an Arthur who put to death his best friend and his queen. All human beings must perform according to their nature. (484)

Her choric words summarize the final perspective of *Arthur Rex*: as human knowledge, wisdom, and power are limited, so must human expectations be tempered with realism. The innate character of a person conditions his or her behavior; genes in a way are destiny. Yet, paradoxically, the struggle against the odds of nature and circumstance can produce heroic achievement.

Gawaine and the Lady of the Lake's comments indicate Berger's sympathy and at times admiration for his characters despite their intellectual and psychological warts. For example, Arthur's people praise his saintliness and his efforts to wrest peace and justice from an unruly society. Tristram, Launcelot, and Perceval all have integrity without malice. Merlin's practical political advice curbs Arthur's youthful ignorance and excess. Yet Gawaine comes closest to fulfilling the best of humanity. Without sentimental whitewash he becomes Berger's moral touchstone. His flaws—lechery, pride and anger—all can and do transform into virtues, just as the good traits of some characters become vices. Gawaine's seductions lack the egotism and manipulation of the typical rake; women love him because he exults in them and their sexuality. His usual invocation to sex is "Come, sweet chuck, let us have some sport" (181). His joy in natural carnal desire is infectious. And Gawaine matures sexually when he agrees to marry the ugly hag Dame Ragnell in order to save Arthur's life. When she asks him to choose if she should be beautiful by day or by night, he grants her sovereignty over her own life in a much more positive and moving fashion than does Allison of Bath's fifth husband, who does it out of guilt and fear. Gawaine replies to his ugly bride,

"...thou art not an object which I possess like unto a suit of armor. Thou art one of God's creatures, and in all fundamental matters thou must answer alone to him. This choice therefore must be thine alone." (325)

Gawaine's remarkable piety and humility merit him a wife beautiful *and* faithful both day and night. Happy marriage makes Gawaine a bit rotund, somewhat boring, and content to chat about children and gardens. The old insatiable appetite for women and adventure now appears to him juvenile.

But the old fire of vengeance and family pride flares again when Gawaine attacks Launcelot for inadvertently killing Gawaine's two innocent younger brothers. Gawaine's anger fuels the Camelot conflagration, and he and the Round Table die in the process. Yet death restores Gawaine's sanity, tolerance, and forgiveness. He has been caught like others in the unwinnable conflict of loyalties which tears Tristram and Launcelot and even Arthur apart. The narrator's eulogy rightfully praises him.

And Sir Gawaine, one of the very greatest knights who ever lived and the finest man of the company of the Round Table (for he had all the virtues and of the vices the most natural), was greatly mourned on earth by all the brave knights and all the beautiful ladies, whilst in Heaven the angels rejoiced to have him amongst them, with his great virile integrity. (466)

Yet despite such good men moral evil often triumphs in *Arthur Rex*. The cowardly Meliagrant prevails in battle "for evil is always more easily managed than virtue" (158). Evil frequently parasitizes good. When Meliagrant for once tries to be virtuous to impress Guinevere, his charity backfires: a beggar who receives gold from him first tries to eat the coin and, failing that, buys a crossbow to shoot his benefactor. Morgan la Fay relinquishes her campaign against Arthur's rule and converts to a nun, intending thus to wreak more havoc through piety than through mischief. The vile Mordred effectively preys on the guilt of his father Arthur, who has brooded over his secret sin of incest for years. Mordred convinces Arthur to abdicate the throne for him and place Excalibur on the ground, where Mordred picks it up and mortally wounds the king.

Good intentions regularly "gang a-gley." Pellinore's obsession with his noble quest blinds him to his daughter's needs, and she commits suicide. Perceval's innocence leads him to fornication, but he is chastized not for the sexual offense but for being ignorant of what he did. His naive piety elicits people's outrage, and many lesser knights challenge him in battle, only to die at his hand. Arthur's idealism, bruised by reality, transforms first into sanctimoniousness and then despair. Launcelot's piety saps him of martial vigor and of the ability to resist Guinevere's tyranny. Excessive or tunnel vision virtue turns destructive; innocence provokes catastrophe.

Berger tells us that, since good and evil often shade imperceptibly into each other, distinguishing one from the other is quite difficult. When Arthur asks Merlin for a scale to measure moral differences, the wizard admits,

"There is none ready to hand....Each king must fashion his own, and determine for himself where pride becomes mere vanity, where apparent generosity is real meanness, where justice is not held in equilibrium but is overweighted towards spite or cowardice." (39)

Launcelot, as he fights his final battle with Gawaine, realizes how ethically complex chivalry is and now revises his moral judgment of his entire life, condemning it as banal at best and "squalid" at worst (462).

When the best of secular warriors despairs and the most spiritual knight, Galahad, is sickly and dies young, desiring to leave a tawdry world, what hope can there be for ordinary mortals? God's perfection indicts all; time and circumstance damn all dreams. Yet Berger finds gold in the junkheap of life. Even though intractable reality cannot be changed, humans still can find worth and reduce the degree of the destruction they commit. The benchmarks for positive human values are the natural, the reasonable, the practical. Joy properly derives from things like food, sex and irony when they are motivated by pleasure rather than egotism and power lust. Rulers can avoid disaster when they accept the impossible burden of leadership but exercise their duty with courage, using imperfect people and institutions as instruments of peace to fend off chaos and stabilize a disorderly populace. Recognizing their human fallibility, people can exercise modesty and caution. Where possible they can transform weakness into strength. And finally, says Arthur, they must "...fail gloriously, and glory doth come only from a quest for that which is impossible of attainment" (97).

Berger's claim not to write spoof or parody is correct for the most part. The comic mockery that waxes strong in the first part of *Arthur Rex* is undercut by his tolerant amusement, by his diffusing of blame and blurring of moral norms, by his disinterest in amelioration. However, his disavowal of social commentary is compromised, as sly humor gives way to tragic pathos and irony. For Berger, like any writer worth his salt, does imply values; his pessimism is not nihilism. He believes that folly is what makes us mortal, interesting, and able to survive, sometimes achieve. He yearns for no Golden Age past since there was no such thing. Merlin sighs, "No man is free who needeth air to breathe" (78). The tears are Virgilian *lacrimae rerum*. He looks forward to no future Golden Age either and would not desire such even if he could have it. His philosophy is to enjoy living in an absurd world and try to make something of it, to find happiness in pushing Sisyphus's rock up the hill.

Berger has masqueraded as a satirist in the early part of *Arthur Rex* yet subverts pure satire through diffusing the blame, enjoying the folly of his characters more than criticizing it, confounding good and evil, and eschewing social reform. His real intentions become clearer as elegiac pity absolves Tristram and Isolde of blame in the suffering they experience and cause others. Berger reveals his true colors as tragic ironist as he tells the bitter love story of Launcelot and Guinevere, whose affair foreshadows and precipitates the collapse of the Round Table. Berger blames no one for simply being a fallible human and in fact praises those who find strength in the human condition and strive for the heroic deed even in the face of inevitable failure. Without passion, mistakes, ignorance, and courage there would be no human story and perhaps worst of all no human literature. Berger's heart, head, and pen find their happiness in the recreation of myth.

Berger's main concern is literature. He neither parodies nor spoofs his prototypes; he pays homage to his wide range of sources for *Arthur Rex*—Malory, Malory's chronicle and romance models, *Sir Gawain and the Green Knight*, the *Wedding of Sir Gawain and Dame Ragnell*, Gottfried's *Tristan*, Chaucer's *Wife of Bath's Tale*. He maintains a flavor of archaic language; he continues Malory's emphasis on narration and character more than description; he stresses the emotional impact of his narrative as Malory did; he organizes the huge, sprawling material into more or less separable tales as Malory did; he weeps Malorian tears at the loss of things worthy.

Yet Berger's homage is not slavish; to serve up the old tales cold on a dusty platter would not compliment Malory. A re-telling must speak from and to its own cultural context, and Berger impresses an idiosyncratic, contemporary stamp on the material. Whereas Malory's narrator remains almost invisible as an authorial voice, Berger's persona articulates a blatant, often jaundiced point of view as he lambasts foreigners, grovels in conventional piety, and fawns on authorities. Berger develops more fully than Malory many characters, especially female ones such as Margawse, Morgan la Fay, and even Guinevere, who now has an identity not completely leashed to Arthur and Launcelot. Berger is more persistently humorous than Malory and revels in puns, modern slang, and sexual angst. But most importantly, Berger saturates his adaptation with Twentieth-Century absurdity—pessimism about intellectual and moral certitude and resignation to the intractibility of existence and the fallibility of religion, science, politics, and social programs. Berger plays his modern anxiety in jester's motley but with Emmett Kelly's tear in his eye.

Berger does not debunk myth, as some commentators assert, but rather revitalizes it. The modern dress does not shroud the older form but testifies to its enduring power. Berger subtitles the book "A Legendary Novel" and means it. The narrator confesses in the last sentence that King Arthur was "never historical, but everything he did was true" (499). He believes that the Age of Chivalry was worthy "for all men of that time lived and died by legend (and without it the world hath become a mean place" (433). The mass audience may find *Arthur Rex* too ironic and disturbing for its literary easy chair; elitists may think it too accessible and plebeian. If so, both camps deny themselves a rare pleasure: a supple, sad, wise, and witty book which reincarnates the essential thing—the old story.

Works Cited

Atlas, James. "Chivalry Is Dead." Rev. of *Arthur Rex*, by Thomas Berger. *Time* 25 September 1978: 107, 110.

Berger, Thomas. *Arthur Rex: A Legendary Novel.* New York: Dell, 1978.

"Briefly Noted." Rev. of *Arthur Rex*, by Thomas Berger. *New Yorker* 6 November 1978: 216-17.

Epps, Garret. Rev. of *Arthur Rex*. *New Republic* 7 October 1978: 34-36.

Feinberg, Leonard. *Introduction to Satire*. Ames, Iowa: Iowa State UP, 1967.

Frye, Northrop. "The Myths of Winter: Irony and Satire." In *Anatomy of Criticism*. Princeton, N.J.: Princeton UP, 1957. 223-239.

Fuller, Edmund. Rev. of *Arthur Rex*. "An Enchanting Retelling of Arthurian Legend."*Wall St. Journal* 5 February 1979: 18.

Ghose, Zulfikar. "Observations from a Correspondence: From Thomas Berger's Letters." *Studies in American Humor* 2 (Spring 1983): 5-19.

Landon, Brooks. *Thomas Berger*. Boston: Twayne, 1989.

Malone, Michael. Rev. of *Neighbors*, by Thomas Berger. "American Literature's *Little Big Man*. *Nation* 3 May 1980: 535-37.

———"Berger, Burlesque, and the Yearning for Comedy." *Studies in American Humor* 2 (Spring 1983): 20-32.

Malory, Sir Thomas. *Works of Sir Thomas Malory*. Ed. Eugene Vinaver. 1954. London: Oxford UP, 1962.

Romano, John. Rev. of *Arthur Rex*. "Camelot and All That." *New York Times Book Review* 12 November 1978: 3, 62.

Schickel, Richard. Rev. of *Vital Parts*, by Thomas Berger. "Bitter Comedy." *Commentary* July 1970: 76-78, 80.

———"Interviewing Thomas Berger." *New York Times Book Review* 6 April 1980: 1, 21, 22.

Yohalem, John. Rev. of *Arthur Rex*. "Berger's Blights of the Round Table." *Christian Science Monitor* 24 January 1979: 19.

Works Consulted

Berger, Thomas. "I Am Not a Movie Person," *American Film* 7 (December 1981): 34-36.

——— *Little Big Man*. New York: Fawcett, 1964.

Cleary, Michael. "Finding the Center of the Earth: Satire, History, and Myth in *Little Big Man*." *Western American Literature* 15 (1980): 195-211.

Edwards, Thomas. "Domestic Guerrillas." Rev. of *Neighbors*, by Thomas Berger. *New York Times Book Review* 6 April 1980: 1,23.

Elliott, Robert C. *The Power of Satire: Magic, Ritual, Art*. Princeton, N.J.: Princeton UP, 1960.

Highet, Gilbert. *The Anatomy of Satire*. Princeton, N.J.: Princeton UP, 1962.

Kernan, Alvin B. "A Theory of Satire." In *The Cankered Muse: Satire of the English Renaissance*. New Haven: Yale UP. 1959. 1-36.

——— *The Plot of Satire*. New Haven: Yale UP. 1965.

Landon, Brooks. "The Radical Americanist." *Nation* 20-27 August 1977: 151-53.

Moore, Jean P. "Thomas Berger's 'Joyful Worship': A Study of Form and Parody." *Studies in American Humor* 2 (Spring 1983): 72-82.

——— "The Creative Function of the Popular Arts in the Novels of Thomas Berger." Diss. U. of Florida, 1981. *Diss. Abstracts* 42 (1981): 1636A.

Paulson, Ronald, comp. *Satire: Modern Essays in Criticism*. Englewood Cliffs, N.J.: Prentice-Hall, 1971.

Rowe, John Carlos. "Alien Encounter: Thomas Berger's *Neighbors* as a Critique of Existential Humanism." *Studies in American Humor* 2 (Spring 1983): 45-60.

Ruud, Jay. "Thomas Berger's *Arthur Rex*: Galahad and Earthly Power." *Critique: Studies in Modern Fiction* 25 (Winter 1984): 92-100.

Studies in American Humor 2.1,2 (Spring, Fall 1983). Devoted to Thomas Berger.

Thomas, Jimmie Elaine. "The Once and Present King: A Study of the World View Revealed in Contemporary Arthurian Adaptations." Diss. U. of Arkansas, 1982. *Diss. Abstracts* 43 (1982): 3316B.

Thompson, Raymond H. *The Return from Avalon: A Study of the Arthurian Legend in Modern Fiction.* Westport, Conn.: Greenwood, 1985.

Wallace, Jon. "The Implied Author as Protagonist: A Reading of *Little Big Man*." *Western American Literature* 22 (Winter 1988): 291-99.

Weber, Brom. "The Mode of Black Humor." In *The Comic Imagination in American Literature.* Louis D. Rubin, ed. New Brunswick, N.J.: Rutgers UP, 1973. 361-71.

Wilde, Alan. "Acts of Definition, or Who Is Thomas Berger?" *Arizona Quarterly* 39 (Winter 1983): 312-50.

Waxing Arthurian:
The Lyre of Orpheus and Cold Sassy Tree

Sally K. Slocum

The legend of King Arthur functions in a myriad of ways. We see that it has been an inspiration to artists of many genres, and even when the subject matter is not rooted to the traditional legendary framework, recognizable Arthurian elements may appear. The range of the legend's impact may vary from the governing framework for a work of art, to a subtle suggestion that nevertheless colors the work. Examples from each extreme will serve to verify that point. Robertson Davies' *The Lyre of Orpheus* has at least three identifiable, working Arthurian motifs; Olive Ann Burns' *Cold Sassy Tree* makes only two specific Arthurian references, but their effect is large. These novels, both published in 1988, provide interesting illustrations of the degrees of uses of the Arthurian tradition. Davies' novel is rich in the Arthurian mythos, knows it and blatantly develops many Arthurian and medieval themes in a fictional contemporary Toronto, Canada. The third novel in The Cornish Trilogy, following *The Rebel Angels* (1981), and *What's Bred in the Bone* (1985) the *Lyre* is the only Arthurian novel of the trilogy and discloses the legacy of Francis Cornish, who is dead before the *Lyre* begins. It is Francis Cornish's huge estate and the well-endowed Cornish Foundation that supports the artistic endeavors of the main plot.

Arthur Cornish, Francis' nephew, presides over the Cornish Foundation which is dedicated to scholarship and artistic endeavors, such as the project at hand: among the papers Francis Cornish had collected is a fragmentary manuscript by E.T.A. Hoffmann, left incomplete at his death. The manuscript contains the genesis of an opera entitled *Arthur of Britain or The Magnanimous Cuckold* which the Foundation wishes to have completed and performed. The opera, as it exists in manuscript, contains a few musical passages, and although there is no libretto, some correspondence between a possible librettist and the thoroughly disapproving Hoffmann remains. The novel concerns the efforts of the Cornish Foundation's central group—The Round Table—and its efforts to bring this project to fruition.

Robertson Davies knows many things: he knows rather a lot about staging 19th century operatic performances, about music and opera, about society, good eating and hard drinking, about outrageous oaths and insults ("I'd as soon go to bed with a bicycle"), and about art.

Ovid...says somewhere...that the great truths of life are the wax, and all we can do is to stamp it with different forms. But the wax is the same forever—

96

'I have it,' said Maria. 'He says that nothing keeps its own form, but Nature who is the great renewer is always making up new forms from old forms. Nothing perishes in the whole universe—it just varies and renews its form—'

'And that's the truth that underlies all myth,' shouted Darcourt, waving at her to be quiet. 'If we are true to the great myth, we can give it what form we choose. The myth—the wax—does not change.' (146)

Predictably, Arthur Cornish is the King Arthur figure, but he remains throughout the novel not much more than the noble holder of the purse strings, a shadowy figure who commands devotion. He is appreciated by the recipients of goods and tolerated by those who want independence to follow their own paths. Except for his support of the Hoffmann Opera project, the most notable things Arthur does are catch the mumps and be magnanimous.

Maria, his wife, is this novel's Guenevere. She is lovely and loved by everyone. She truly loves Arthur but her involvement with this Lancelot is by no means the intense, inescapable love affair that we have come to fear in its passion. In fact, she does not even love this Lancelot, nor does he much love her, certainly not with any overwhelming passion, for he reserves that for himself. He is her friend and he wants her sexually, but not immoderately.

Lancelot—Geraint Powell—is the director of the novel's opera, collaborator in the Cornish Foundation and handsome Welshman. He is, of course, the cuckolder of the main plot. But when Maria reveals the details of their only sexual encounter, she describes it as '"A mythical tale. Like a god descending on a mortal woman"' (247). She had gone to bed, expecting Arthur home later in the evening. Powell came to her bed, robed in the dressing gown she had given to her husband:

I had it made in King Arthur's colours and with King Arthur's device: a green dragon, crowned in red, on a gold shield. You couldn't mistake it. I could feel the embroidered dragon on the back. He slipped into my bed, opened the dressing-gown, and there we were. [They spoke not at all.] Did he smell like Arthur? Well—yes and no. (249)

That encounter is not consistent with modern notions of the medieval love-making between Lancelot and Guenevere, at least not Malorean suggestions of their unions. Rather, Powell's disguise smacks of Uther's coupling with Igerne, or even of the spell Dame Brusen casts on Lancelot for the begetting of Galahad. This was, to me, a satisfying twist of the wax. As the Merlin figure says to Maria: '"It's a story that roams back through the ages, and it's a story that doesn't grow old. It's the demon Lover"' (250).

Not to be confused with "The Best Knight in the World," Powell is a handsome, arrogant man but a gifted director. He does endure a sort of mad scene which he claims resulted from reading Malory, and he even quotes Malory: '"...he lepte oute at a baywyndow into a gardyne, and there wyth thornys he was all to-cracched of hys vysage and hys body, and so he ranne furth he knew not whothir, and was as wylde as ever man was" (267). But Powell's wildness was prompted by alcohol and his running was actually driving an automobile. The consequent crash and hospital stay are less than romantic.

His good looks and aloofness do, however, touch a romantic core in the young, unattractive doctoral student commissioned by the Foundation to write the music for Hoffmann's opera. Hulda Schnakenburg, a talented musician, begins her role in the *Lyre* an ill-kempt and pathetically socially inept young woman, suggesting Malory's Bewmaynes or La Cote Male Tayle. Shortly before the opera's debut performance, she attempts suicide, influenced no doubt by the stuff of the opera itself, because Powell doesn't give her the time of day, much less love her. Her attempt—"Nearly a hundred aspirin and half a bottle of gin"—fails (409). Powell endears himself to me when he tries to make Schnak see the difference between her artistic feelings and romantic feelings:

But if we were romantic lovers, the kind you're thinking of, do you suppose I'd hold your head while you puked, and mop your face, and try to make you see reason? The kind of love you're dreaming about takes place on mossy banks, amid the scent of flowers and the song of birds. (415)

Not exactly the Lancelot and Elaine story, and yet. . .

If there is a Modred figure, I suppose he's the dunce, the garage attendant Wally Crottel, the bastard, who claims to know who his father is because his mother said the man is the only guy who ever gave her an "organism." He tries to damage Arthur and Maria, but is caught selling dope to school children and arrested.

There are two possible Morgan Le Fays. One is Maria's mother, a Gypsy woman who early on deals a stunning Tarot hand that is also intriguing to any reader trying to figure out the counterparts to the Major Arcana turned up in the deal. Another possible Morgan is Dr. Gunilla Dahl-Soot, supervisor of the musical aspects of the opera. She is a kind of witch, she is a sorceress at conjuring music and she is called "the perfection of a fairy—or I suppose I should say lesbian—godmother" (470). Two Morgans is not too many, as everybody knows.

The Merlin figure, also the Fool figure of the Tarot hand, is the principle character. Simon Darcourt, Episcopal Priest, holds the Round Table together, is everybody's confidant, keeps the peace among the various participants in the opera, and solves the remaining puzzles about Francis Cornish. We see much of the novel through his understanding. Powell explains to him that he is the Merlin of this Round Table, and Darcourt is flattered exceedingly by the identification (112).

The single sexual union between Maria and Powell does produce issue, a baby boy. When Arthur learns Maria is pregnant, he is disconsolate and weeps profusely. The mumps, of course, rendered him sterile, not impotent. Thus when he learns of the pregnancy, he knows someone has done his office 'twixt his sheets. It is Merlin/Darcourt who presents Arthur with two options:

One: You beat up Powell, or perhaps kill him, and create misery that will last for several generations. Two: you take a hint from this opera that has brought about the whole thing, and decide to be the Magnanimous Cuckold. And what that may lead to, God only knows, but in the tale of Great Arthur of Britain it has led to something that has fed the best of mankind for centuries. (232)

The opera itself, is rather two operas. Before his death in 1822 Hoffmann had corresponded with Planché about the libretto. Planché had supplied only an absurd, low-romantic series of hunt scenes of the Arthurian Court, transferred to the Kingdom of Turkestan, surrounded by Titania and Oberon (fairy ballet), and the Seven Champions (played by women) under the counsel of Merlin and the fairy knight Pigwiggen (79-83). Among the dog-trot lyrics left by Planché:

> We all went out a-hunting
>   The break of day before,
> In hopes to stop the grunting
>   Of a most enormous boar! (84)

Clearly this sort of thing won't do! Further recounting of the bombast of Planché's stupid plot is not desirable here. This kind of insipid treatment was, however, popular with audiences in the early nineteenth century, and serves as a good example of how the wax of myth can be restamped to the tastes of time. *Camelot* and *Monty Python* are evoked in the novel as other examples of our time (87).

The opera that is performed, however, at the novel's end is more suited to our tastes and more in keeping with a plot woven together from Thomas Malory and Walter Scott, actual libretto by Merlin/Darcourt. Early plans for the opening go like this:

> ...we raise the curtain on a vision scene...the Magic Mere, and Arthur and Merlin on its shore. At a gesture from Merlin the great sword arises from the water, gripped in the hand of an unseen spirit, and Arthur seizes it. But as he is overcome with the grandeur of the moment, there arises from the Mere a vision of Guenevere...presenting the scabbard of Caliburn; Merlin bids Arthur accept the scabbard and makes Arthur understand...that the scabbard is even more important than the sword, because when the sword is in its scabbard there is peace, and peace must be his gift to his people. But...the visionary Guenevere shows by a gesture that the scabbard is herself, and that unless he knows her value and might, the sword will avail him nothing. (137-38)

That is decidedly more like it. One effective detail about the opera performance is that Merlin is sung by a falsetto. That sets him apart in an otherworldly way.

Thus Davies has woven three Arthurian plots in one novel—possibly not a record, but three is probably enough. As this opera and its complexities surround and influence the main Arthurian plot's unfoldings, there is no doubt that the wax of myth remains the same; only the form changes.

Arthurian legend has a very different function in Olive Ann Burns' *Cold Sassy Tree* even though it is not an Arthurian novel. Here the wax of Arthurian legend is applied for a surface shine. The characters do not parallel the Lancelot, Guenevere, Arthur triangle; there is no Modred figure, no Grail quest, no Merlin. But the novel does reflect, albeit vaguely, Arthurian ideals, and references to Arthur and knighthood inform us of a collective knowledge that is given in a small Southern village a half century after the Civil War. Burns is not heavy-handed with the allusions. The Arthurian mythos is so strong that to include it as a cultural influence only slight, subtle mention is necessary. A little dab'll do ya.

This is not a South of gone-with-the windy belles and happy darkies brought down by the Union army, but an always poor South of dirt farmers made poorer by the war, and finally on the mend, its people living as nobly as they can in frugality and traditions that evolved among country ways and the certainties of the Southern protestant churches.

In July of 1906, when the novel begins, in the village of Cold Sassy Tree, Georgia, the community standards of behavior are shattered when Rucker Blakeslee, a widower for only three weeks, marries again. Worse yet, he marries the milliner who works in his general store. Worse yet, his new wife, Love Honor Simpson, is a Northerner. Probably most shocking to his family, who never expected him to remarry, but certainly would have expected him to observe a traditional mourning period of at least a year, is the rationale that he offers them. Miss Mattie Lou, beloved by the community as a saint, says Mr. Blakeslee, "is as dead as she'll ever be" (5).

Will Tweedy, the fourteen-year-old whose account of the year's events make up the novel, learns from his Grandpa Blakeslee and Miss Love that nobility is not conferred by the community's approval, but arises from within. High standards of behavior, which mean conforming to the community's social traditions—like observing the caste system, attending church, and more or less keeping things as they have always been—dominate the village. In this milieu Will Tweedy operates, trying to be good yet true to himself.

To Will Tweedy King Arthur is an ideal, remote but real, who represents the very best person possible. Arthur is brought subtly into the novel as the polar opposite of Will's hated Aunt Loma, selfish, bossy, mean-spirited. To describe how much he hates Aunt Loma, Will presents a list of the three people he hates most with examples of why he hates them. Third in line is Mr. Tuttle who has caused Will to get more whippings than he could count.

Us boys were always trying to get back at him. Just for instance, one day we sneaked into his barn, just fooling around, and chanced to see a gallon of yellow paint that he put on the handles of all his farm tools so if somebody showed up with a yellow-handled hoe, everybody would know it was stolen from Mr. Tuttle.

Well, it was real cold the day we went in there, and his barn was full of mules, horses, and cows brought in from his farm; sharecropper tenants being bad to steal, if you live in town, it's the custom to bring in all of your animals, wagons, and farm tools for the winter. What we did, and it was my idea, we dipped every horse, mule, and cow tail in that yellow paint. When one flipped, good gosh it sent a spray of yellow all over the dern animal, the stalls, the hayracks, everything...

You never saw anybody as mad as Mr. Tuttle when he got home and he never doubted who'd done it. That night Mama didn't just ask me to be a better boy; she insisted on it.

If I had told her just how much I hated Mr. Tuttle, she wouldn't of believed it. But compared to the way I felt about Aunt Loma, he was like a favorite uncle. (106)

Another foe is a boy at school: "We were always fighting at recess. I really hated him, and the feeling was mutual. But compared to Aunt Loma, Hosie

Roach seemed like a best friend" (106). The most hated person on his list is his other grandfather, Grandpa Tweedy:

> I just couldn't hardly stand him. One time he was fussing about tenants stealing out of his woodpile, I watched while he drilled holes in several sticks of stovewood, filled the holes with gunpowder, sealed them over with candlewax, and put them on top of the woodpile. 'What if somebody gets kilt?' I asked him.
>
> I was just a little bitty boy, so I believed him when he said, 'Ain't go'n hurt nobody. Hit'll jest scare the livin daylights out of 'm.'
>
> Next morning at breakfast we heard a big WHOMP, BOOM from the tenant shack. A few minutes later, the cook rushed in and said, 'Mist' Tweedy, one them white-trash chillun's hand done got tore up, po li'l lamb, an dey stove's ruint.'
>
> Grandpa saucered his coffee and took a big slurp before he spoke. His voice was hard. 'Well, then I reckon they won't steal no more a-my f'ar wood.'
>
> You can see why I despised Grandpa Tweedy and didn't have a dab of respect for him. But compared to Aunt Loma, he was King Arthur and I was a Knight of the Round Table. (107-8)

Interesting in this escalating list of bad people and their relationships with Will is the judicial weight given each. Mr. Tuttle, the cranky tattletale, is the opposite of a favorite uncle. The schoolboy rival is the opposite of a best friend. But the mean and stingy Grandpa Tweedy, whose disregard for others' misery, by far the worst, is contrasted with King Arthur who evidently in Will's mind would never harm the innocent.

Will Tweedy thinks in a terminology of honor and knightly deeds despite his penchant for practical jokes. His attitude is decidedly chivalric. When he draws a bucket of fresh water from the well for Miss Love, he feels "gallant" (209). When he promises Miss Love that he will keep her secret a secret, she thanks him for his friendship and he reflects, "I felt so noble and generous" (157). And in a rare moment of kindness, Aunt Loma tells him that she has decided he should become a writer. "'Will, I want you to write plays.' She said it as solemn as if she was a queen knighting me with words" (213).

It could be argued that Will Tweedy's Arthurian tendencies are trite and ordinary, the common fantasy of school boy romanticism. But it seems significant that he maintains them without self-consciousness or bluster. The Arthurian mythos is simply natural to him, part of his center, and while not central to the novel, the Arthurian tradition enlarges the scope of the novel.

These characters are by no means bookish people, nor do any of them have pretense of education beyond community requirements. Yet the well-dressed drummers who peddle merchandise to Grandpa for sale in his general store he calls "Knights of the grip" (72). It is as if tales of King Arthur are as familiar to these people as are, say, the disciples or Santa Claus.

Such references clarify the characters and events not only for the reader, but for the characters themselves. In the strangely homogeneous protestant world of the novel, there are nevertheless strident differences among the creeds of Southern Presbyterian, Baptist and Methodist congregations. Allusion to the universals of Arthurian traditions suggests a unifying foundation to the general ideals of the community. For Arthur to be viewed as the paragon of goodness by a young boy may seem ordinary, but such a standard is acknowledged even by Miss Love. Raised in Baltimore and seeking relief from a broken heart she endured in Texas, Miss Love also reveres the excellence of Arthurian tradition.

> She said, 'I knew God didn't want me to marry a man like [Son Black]. He talks tough but inside he's just a little bitty boy, scared of his mama...' She was silent a minute, then laughed and made a joke. 'Reading King Arthur is what made me an old maid, Will. I kept holding out for a hero, a knight in shining armor. I really thought some rich, exciting man would come riding up on a white horse and rescue me from being poor and unhappy. After I fell in love with the man in Texas...Well, he was rich and had a white horse, but he was no knight. And neither is Son Black. He couldn't qualify as the hero in a cheap novel.' (134)

Though we never get to know much about Son Black, we know enough about him from the allusion to know Miss Love is better off with Rucker Blakeslee.

In fact, it is Grandpa Blakeslee who emerges as the hero of the novel. Although he is never specifically associated with King Arthur, he nevertheless embodies some Arthurian qualities in an unstudied way. Will Tweedy recognizes that Grandpa Blakeslee is admired by the community, not because he is a pillar— he is not by any conventional thought a model to be followed. But Will admires the public image of Grandpa because he follows his own wisdom, without caring what the town will think or say. Rucker has a reputation as a man who was able to win fights, even though he lost part of an arm in the Civil War (20-21). He is a champion of justice for the unfortunate. Once some old men of the village who were playing checkers outside the depot set fire to a mangy dog. Rucker pulled out his pistol, shot the dog to end its misery then shot the checker game "to kingdom come" (295). The suicide of Loma's ineffectual husband (who could blame him?) might have brought more shame to the family were it not for Grandpa's compassion. The previous suicide in Cold Sassy was scorned even at his own funeral. "The burial service was just one sentence. The preacher said, 'God won't forgive this awful thing he did'" (333). But Grandpa arranged a real funeral for Loma's poor husband Camp, shocking the town. "There were those who thought it was going too far to put somebody who was already halfway to Hell at the feet of a lady who'd been a saint on earth if ever there was one. But Grandpa didn't ask anybody's permission" (334). He claims a command, a kind of authority. "Grandpa had the manner of a king or duke: when he said do or don't do something, you said yessir before you thought" (20). Whether it was out of the townspeople's fear or love or uncertainty, Grandpa had his way: "Even grown people mind Mr. Blakeslee, Will, as if they had no choice" (330). All of this surrounds Grandpa Blakeslee with an Arthurian drape.

It would be saying too much to claim the spirit of Arthur permeates the novel, but references to King Arthur, as casual as they may be, nevertheless round out the rough edges that cling to a poor people in a poor area recovering from war. Vague notions of chivalry here do not seem connected to belles and beaux of the "Old South," yet there is nothing new or newly fashionable about them either. Arthurian ideals are merely a part of right thinking in this small town, and reference to Arthur is enough to make the perfect and heroic a part of the heart of Cold Sassy Tree, Georgia. Olive Ann Burns adds a tapestry of meaning with just two specific references to King Arthur. But the Arthurian story is so strong that maybe one would be enough.

The easily molded wax of Arthurian legend serves the artist's needs very well. These two novels, miles and years apart in plotlines, are formed and polished by strikingly different uses of the great myth that stamps them both old, both new.

Works Cited

Burns, Olive Ann. *Cold Sassy Tree*. New York: Dell, 1988.
Davies, Robertson. *The Lyre of Orpheus*. New York: Penguin, 1988.

The Matter of Britain
in British and American Popular Music
(1966-1990)

Michael P. Rewa

We are witnessing an assimilation of the Matter of Britain in American popular culture and its agencies equivalent to the Continentalization of the Matter in the high literary culture of the Middle Ages. Naively or calculatingly, businessmen and advertisers invoke Matter images because they immediately suggest high quality and value, something special and out of the ordinary; movie makers, because the adventure and pageantry perceived as central to the Matter appeal to audiences; biographers, essayists, journalists, because the Matter of Britain is an unfailing source of popular metaphorical reference and imaginative suggestion. Not to mention popular novelists, in the 70s particularly, who produced numerous Arthurian fictions. Or popular musicians. For all who use them, Arthurian references are an iconic shorthand capable of calling up opportune, medievally-grounded associations, all of which are invested with a charmed claim on our pocketbooks, eyes and ears.

In the early 60s, when the U.S. was still relatively untouched by the waves of British rock music that began to sweep over it in 1964, aspiring English groups talismanically gave themselves such Matter names as the Round Table Rockers; the Shades of Knight; the Singing, Rocking, Green, Blue, Silver Knights; Lancelot and the Gallants, Avalon, Camelot, the Galahads, Wizard Wrock, the Lancers, the Jousters, the Merlins and King Arthur Rock. English performers took names like David Galahad, Guinevere, Merlin and Lancelot. None of these local and largely unrecorded groups or performers (remembered only because my wife, an enthusiastic teenager living in Anglia in the Kennedy years, bothered to note them in her diary) had any lasting success—all of them whited-out by the stellar brightness of the Beatles' genius and popular authority.

In America such naming never occurred, not even as part of the Camelotting of Washington during the same period. To do so then would have been considered too decadent in a country different in historical premise and experience and inherently more disposed later to accept such phrases as "Blood, Sweat and Tears," "The Grateful Dead," "Big Brother and the Holding Company," "The Association," even "Buffalo Springfield" (the name of a tractor) or "Crosby, Stills & Nash" (sounds like a law firm) as icons of identification—with whatever degree of irony contained in the names. But in the late 60s, one kind of pop music in America became almost defensively lyrical, in response to the traumas of social and political awareness produced by assassinations, racial and military conflict. For it the Medieval world and especially the Matter of Britain provided an appealing and expressive context for mapping and peopling that psychic space filled with fantasy as well as social concern the public young of the mid-60s chose to live in, for a "Yes" kind of music that picked up where protest's "No" music ineffectively left off.

For its Romantic celebrations of love and aesthetic yearning, its music of social lament (if not protest), frustrated idealism, and apocalyptic hope, some of the culture's spokes-musicians found significant lyric inspiration in the Matter of Britain. For them, Camelot became an image of the world they would have grown up into were it not for authority's having forestalled that possibility by historical misadventures like the Viet Nam war, selfish ideas about the sanctity of private property and capital accumulation, discriminatory social and restrictive sexual attitudes.

The initial expression of this Modern imaginative impulse to *sing the Matter of Britain* is to be heard in British balladeer Donovan Leitch's 1966 "Guinevere." An "idyllic" Tennyson of lyricists, Donovan paints a verbal and melodic picture of an "indigo"-eyed Queen under "dark, foreboding skies o'er the royal domain." In 1969, in *On the Threshold of a Dream*, the English Moody Blues, the first to hint at a Merlin-musician connection, followed with their less problematical Merlin song "Are You Sitting Comfortably?":

> Glide along the winds of time
> And see where we have been
> The glorious Age of Camelot
> When Guinevere was Queen.
> It all unfolds before your eyes
> As Merlin casts his spell.

In the same year, the trans-Atlantic trio, Crosby, Stills & Nash, the first of the many Atlantic Bridge groups to follow, also gave us a "Guinevere"—who had "green eyes like yours, m'Lady, like yours"— about the problems of love: "Why can't she see me?" The moving title song of Neil Young's 1970 album *After the Gold Rush* is actually in the Medieval form of a Dream Vision, beginning with what can be nothing else but a Matter allusion. Dreaming in the present, he sees both the past and future: "Well, I dreamed I saw the knights in armor coming/Saying something about a Queen." Only one Queen in Western experience can come to mind: her name is Guinevere. These two and the following lines evoke a world of imaginative Medieval/Matter associations: pennants, archers, fanfares. The next stanza describes the inhumanity of modern urban experience, and the third contains a final vision of a spaceship "flying Mother Nature's silver seed/To a new home in the sun." Parenthetically, this concluding image may have spawned an entire sub-genre of sci-fi rock lyrics in works to come like Elton John's "Rocket Man" and David Bowie's "Space Oddity." Imaginatively challenging, musically superb, as the *a cappella* version by the group Prelude reminds one, the song moves from evocations of Arthurian Romance tinged with elegy to an Arthur Clarkean *2001*—or is it *Childhood's End?*—vision of humanity's rebirth—a transformation also to be nostalgically figured in the Camelot imagery of 70s music.

The more ample production of Arthurian songs in America in the 70s coincides with the production of no fewer than eighteen Matter-related novels or books in the seven years 1973-1980: four of them published in America's Bicentennial year 1976—H. W. Munn's *Merlin's Godson*; Douglas Carmichael's *Pendragon*; Victor Canning's *The Crimson Chalice*; John Steinbeck's *The Acts of King Arthur*. This increased use of Arthurian subject matter is anticipated musically in Englishman Rick Wakeman's 1975 concept-concert album *The Myths and Legends of King Arthur*. There are seven songs on the album, all with words by Wakeman: "Arthur," "Lady of the Lake," "Guinevere," "Sir Lancelot and the Black Knight," "Merlin the Magician," "Sir Galahad," and "The Last Battle." While musically and lyrically arid—Wakeman is not good enough a lyricist to be trusted with "translating" Malory—the phenomenon of the album's appearance at least bespeaks an effort to perform the Matter of Britain in a substantial way for a popular audience.

Matter Music of the 70s is heavily charged with a sense of loss and hope, of degeneration and aspiration. Camelot became not only the imaginative model of late Medieval architecture and landscaping but also the symbol of an ideal social place. It is both Edenic Garden and Apocalyptic City—an image of an Eden Civilized. Both Garden *and* City, it is to be gotten back to and lived in, numerously populated like Woodstock, yet harmoniously related in all its parts. In this "city built to music,/Therefore never built at all,/And therefore built forever"—to cite Tennyson's classically prescient image from his "Gareth and Lynette" *Idyll*—all can feel themselves part of a pre-Lapsarian whole. Jango Beck, a perceptive entrepreneur in Norman Spinrad's 1975 novel *Passing Through the Flame*, welcomes the audience to a mammoth Rock Music event in these nostalgic terms:

Welcome to the magic hour . . . Now a legend returns. . . . It's the Summer of Love . . . Hendrix and Joplin live, and Dylan rides again, and the Beatles are united. And here we go back to those Strawberry Fields, **back to Camelot** rising from the ashes, back to the Haight, back to ourselves again. (428)

Graham Bond's "Arthur," a traditionally structured Blues song from the album *Holy Magick* (c. 1970), had earlier bespoken the desirability of that Camelot, attainable with the return in the present of the King:

> Ah, come back, Arthur, now
> Come back, King Arthur.
> Your power changes you once again.
> You promised us—yeah, that you'd
> Come back to us again.

Come back, and free us from the frustrations and disappointments of contemporary existence. Return as Savior of a Secular Apocalypse and re-create our New Jerusalem, Camelot. In 1978 David Mallet, otherwise summarizing from T.H. White's *The Once and Future King*, sang of Arthur: "Arthur, where are you now, we need ya./We've been much too long without a leader. . . . I have seen the changing signs./Now's the time for your return." The group Wishbone

Ash included a generalized, optimistic "The King Will Come" on its first album *Argus* (1972).

In Matter songs of the 80s, Avalon and the Lancelot-Guinevere relationship became the prime referents. Richie Havens used Avalon as a lover's name, primarily, I think, because it is a lovely word in English, in his 1977 song "Avalon": "Oooh, Avalon, your beauty shines out every night, Avalon./I'll turn every night for Avalon." The English group Roxy Music produced an album *Avalon* in 1982 whose nostalgia was double-edged: an Arthurian cover contained a record which alludes to the distant romantic heyday of the Avalon ballroom. Though Irishman Van Morrison's 1989 album *Avalon Sunset* has an allusive landscape cover, there isn't a Matter-related song on it. In 1990, Morrison fulfilled the implicit promise of that title in the splendid "Avalon of the Heart" from *Enlightenment*:

> Oh down by Avalon
> Sweet Avalon of the heart
> Goin' down by Avalon
> Gonna make a brand new start.

For Irish transplant Maura O'Connell, in "Send this Whisper (To Avalon)" from her eponymous 1983 album, Avalon is a symbol of loving unity:

> Three more weeks and then it's Avalon
> Think of me and dream of sailing on
> Cross the water with my bridges gone,
> Back to you in Avalon.

For Kenny Loggins in "Back to Avalon," from the 1988 album of the same name, Avalon also figures the condition of being in love:

> Love is a lesson hard to learn,
> It's never as easy to return
> But if you're willing to go on
> We'll find a way back to Avalon.

Lancelot and Guinevere are used as subjects in Scots-Australian Eric Bogle's rather straightforward, middle-aged love ballad "Lancelot and Guinevere" from his *Singing the Spirit Back Home* (1987), and by American singers Buskin and Batteau in their poignantly perceptive "Lancelot's Song" (1989):

> All my honor and glory
> Will just be a story
> Of the fall of the crown.

Scots folk musician Jake Walton offered "The Wanderer" (subtitled "Merlin's Exile") in 1983. The song is a setting to music of verses from the Anglo-Saxon poem of the same name cited by Mary Stewart in her Merlin novel *The Crystal Cave* (1970). Crediting his source on liner notes, Walton adds: "Legend has it that Merlin...also played the Celtic harp and composed songs." On the

Association's album *Stonehenge* Merlin's legendary role in the building of the monument is recalled. Tyrannosaurus Rex (later T. Rex) on *Unicorn* has a "Stones for Avalon" song, also alluding to Merlin's stone-moving.

Social and political activism in the 60s were premised upon the idea that there was something ineffably powerful and valuable in young people—a kind of magic waiting to be set free (even if by drugs, as suggested by Donovan in "The Trip"). John Sebastian's Loving Spoonful had asked, "Do you believe in magic?...Believe in the magic of rock and roll,/Believe in the magic that can set you free?" The Matter of Britain provided a powerful image for this premise, literally in accord with the aim of the music itself. As Ralph Gleason reiterated in *Rolling Stone*, rock music ideally aspires "to set you free." Young persons would agree with someone's suggesting that they and their spirits were potentially powerful Merlins trapped in caves of authority and expediency. Ken Hensly of the group Uriah Heep explicitly articulate such an image in his song "Traveler in Time" on *Demons and Wizards* (1972):

> I have tried for so long to find
> Some way of helping mankind
> But first I must wait till I'm set free
> And I don't know how long that's gonna be.

In the 60s Guinevere and a romantically-backgrounded Camelot figured as subjects. In the 70s the emphasis shifted substantially to the Camelotian Ideal and Arthur's return. In the 80s Avalon and the love exemplified by Lancelot and Guinevere appealed most as subjects. Merlin appears when he will.

Popular music and The Matter of Britain have found each other in the last generation. The Matter finds another form of expression in popular music. The Matter becomes, as well, a *means* of expression through its use as a source of allusions in this music. For example, the group America refers to the "tropic of Sir Galahad" in its song "Tin Man"; John Lennon, to "the search for the Grail" in "Mind Games"; Harry Chapin, to his being a "sad-sack Galahad" in "Mary's Not Here." Joan Baez labels her brother-in-law "Sweet Sir Galahad," and Gordon Lightfoot sings of a coal-miner's daughter ironically named "Guinevere." Donovan's "Legend of the Girl-Child Linda" combines the Sleeping Beauty story with Arthurian legend, and contains the line "My sword it lies broken/And cast in the lake." In "Half a Chance to our Romance" Carly Simon reminds the listener that one can't pretend it's Camelot when love goes sour.

While limited by personal listening experience (as well as by sparse and even unavailable discographical information for albums prior to 1975), the number of songs and references in this admittedly accidental and partial catalogue and the listings in the appended discography, prompt one to wonder if any other national mythology, period of time, system of references, group of characters, or body of material (outside of contemporary Christian music's Biblically premised lyrics), is so frequently and familiarly alluded to in contemporary popular music as the Matter of Britain.

This familiarity carries over in the naming of songs, albums and groups which in substance have no specific Matter orientation. The Batteaux Brothers' "Lady of the Lake" is the image reflected by a lover's mirror. Starcastle and the Strawbs found similar romantic overtones in this "Lady" image. Is it not with deliberate irony that the Kinks called the main character "Arthur" in their 1969 TV musical (and soundtrack album) about a middle-class, middle-aged workman? In Scotland in 1986, the Medium Wave Band changed its name to Avalon for its second album. A 1990 American Bluegrass band calls itself Excalibur!

The Bardic notes of the Matters of Greece and Rome and the Courtly notes of the Matter of France can scarcely be recovered or recreated. But the Matter of Britain *can* be heard, not only in Henry Purcell's 17th-century opera *King Arthur* (with text by John Dryden), or in Wagner's *Tristan and Isolde* and *Parsifal*, or in any of those items listed in John Nevins' "Musical Arthuriana" in *Quondam et Futurus* (X.4. Summer 1990), but also in contemporary English and American pop music. Not always forcefully or that frequently, but recognizably. Over some five hundred years only two popular Arthurian ballads survived to be included in Francis Childs' collection: nos. 30 and 31, "King Arthur and King Cornwall" and "The Marriage of Sir Gawain" (in which the King forces Gawain to fulfill the King's own obligation to a knowledgeable Loathly Lady). In the last twenty-five years, over two dozen Matter-related songs have been composed and recorded. And that's to omit the songs of the musical *Camelot*.

The Matter of Britain has the power to *charm*, to engage affective interest immediately, whatever the degree of the listener's acquaintance with its details. Its use, as well, defines and celebrates a yearning in young and not-so-young audiences for something more attractive than contemporary reality. Arthur as Restorer, Camelot as Civilized Edenic Place, Lancelot and Guinevere as symbols of the joy and costs of love, Merlin as Musician: the power of these images continues to affect the Western imagination, and that imagination creates contemporary modes to express itself. The Matter of Britain, founded by oral poets and minstrels, "built to music," endures in contemporary popular music. What was once sung is now being sung again.

Working Discography

All songs composed by listed artist unless otherwise noted.

Bogle, Eric, "Lancelot and Guinevere," *Singing the Spirit Home* (1987), Flying Fish Records, FF447.

Bond, Graham, "Return of Arthur," *Holy Magick* (c. 1970), Mercury Records, SR61327.

Buskin, David and Robin Batteau, "Lancelot's Song," *Buskin & Batteau* (1988), Single Records, CD2012.

Crosby, Stills & Nash, "Guinevere" (wr. David Crosby), *Crosby, Stills & Nash* (1969), Atco Records, ATC SD19117.

Donovan [Leitch], "Guinevere," *Sunshine Superman* (1966), Epic Records, BN26217.

Loggins, Kenny (co-wrs. Peter Wolf and Nathan East), "Back to Avalon," *Back to Avalon* (1988), Columbia Records, 40535.

The McCalmans, "Avalon," *Ancestral Manoeuvres* (1984), MACS, 003.

Mallet, David, "Arthur," *David Mallet* (1978), New World, NWS042977.

Moody Blues, "Are You Sitting Comfortably?" (Justin Hayward & Ray Thomas), *On the Threshold of a Dream* (1969), Decca, DES18025.

Morrison, Van, "Avalon of the Heart," *Enlightenment* (1990), Polydor, 847 100.

O'Connell, Maura, "Send this Whisper (to Avalon)" (wrs. Thom Moore/Janie Cribbs), *Maura O'Connell* (1983), Ogham Records, BLB5007.

Pendragon, "Excalibur," *Fly High, Fall Far* (1984), EMI Records, ARRMP-001.

Uriah Heep, "The Wizard" & "Traveller in Time" (re: Merlin, wr. Ken Hensly), *Demons and Wizards* (1972), Mercury Records, SRM 1 630.

Wakeman, Rick, *The Myths and Legends of King Arthur and the Knights of the Round Table* (1975), A&M Records, SP4515.

Walton, Jake, "The Wanderer (Merlin's Exile)," *Sunlight and Shade* (1983), Folk Freak Records, FF4012.

Wishbone Ash, "The King Will Come," *Argus* (1972), Decca Records, DL7-5347.

Young, Neil, "After the Gold Rush," *After the Gold Rush* (1970), Reprise Records, 6383.

Works Cited

Pichaske, David. *A Generation in Motion: Popular Music and Culture in the Sixties.* Granite Falls, Minnesota: Ellis P, 1989.

Spinrad, Norman. *Passing Through the Flame.* New York: Berkley Publishing Co., 1975.

Tennyson, Alfred. *The Idylls of the King*, ed. J. M. Gray. New Haven: Yale UP, 1983.

Vivien, Elaine and the Model's Gaze: Cameron's Reading of *Idylls of the King*

Constance C. Relihan

In 1874 and 1875, Julia Margaret Cameron published two volumes which paired excerpts from Tennyson's *Idylls of the King* and other poems with examples of her own photographs. Begun at Tennyson's request, these volumes constitute an early example of the interrelation between written text and photographic image.[1] Tennyson's poetry had, of course, inspired considerable artistic production during the 1860s and 1870s, including works by both painters and photographers, but Cameron's attempt to produce a series of images that would represent the entire progress of Tennyson's *Idylls* was the first such full-scale photographic attempt of its kind.[2] Cameron's artistic intentions and methods for this project, influenced not only by Tennyson, but by G. F. Watts and the Pre-Raphaelites,[3] are summarized in the poem by Tennyson's brother, the Reverend Charles Tennyson Turner, included in the first volume of *Alfred Tennyson's Idylls of the King and Other Poems Illustrated by Julia Margaret Cameron* (1874). Turner stresses Cameron's devotion to "Modern Beauty" which is able "[t]o tell an Ancient Story," and exclaims to her that:

> Thou lov'st all loveliness! and many a face
> Is press'd and summon'd from the breezy shores
> On thine immortal charts to take its place
> While near at hand the jealous ocean roars
> His noblest Tritons would thy subjects be,
> And all his fairest Nereids sit to thee.[4]

Turner's poem makes explicit Cameron's attempts, like those of Watts and the adherents of the High Art tradition (Hopkinson 161), to idealize Beauty, not only in her Tennyson images, but in all her photographs—especially those of women. It also emphasizes the process by which models were recruited: "Many a face/ Is press'd and summon'd from the breezy shores" of the Isle of Wight, where Cameron resided, to act as Arthur, Elaine, Guinevere, Lancelot and her other Arthurian figures. Cameron's photographs show the results of pressing into service household members, neighbors and visitors as models to reflect the nuances of Tennyson's characters. The resulting images are charged interpretations of Tennyson's poems which seem to simultaneously present readings colored not only by Cameron's assessment of the *Idylls*, but also by the models' presence in and reactions to their position in Cameron's work. Further,

111

because Cameron emphasizes Tennyson's Arthurian women, it is primarily the female gaze that qualifies the photographer's readings of the poems with which she is engaged. Cameron's images demonstrate clearly the need for readers of literary photographs to reconsider the role of those models who inhabit them.

The two volumes that comprise *Idylls of the King and Other Poems* consist of excerpts from the poems in a facsimile of Cameron's handwriting—occasionally with words underlined for emphasis or ellipses indicating omitted lines—preceding the appropriate photograph. The juxtaposition focuses attention on the moment within the poem Cameron wishes to depict. Of the fifteen photographs Cameron created for the poems, the majority consider female subjects, either in isolation or in groups, whereas only two—both of Arthur—depict solitary male figures.[5] Cameron's work seems to stress clearly Tennyson's female characters and, in so doing, it frequently alters the written text to redefine them. More often than in Tennyson's poems, Cameron's images—in part because of the role of the models themselves and the nature of the photographic medium—seem to create an ideal of the female that diminishes its sexual passion and power, transforming even Tennyson's most vibrant women into either Victorian allegorical representations of female devotion and martyrdom, or into figures robbed of their strength. Her technique calls into question the very use of the term "illustration": Cameron's Arthurian women clearly respond to nonpoetic concerns even as they enact scenes from Tennyson's work.

I

Cameron, who had begun to experiment with photography only ten years before her Tennyson volumes, saw it as an artistic form related to the Pre-Raphaelite paintings she often attempted to emulate, and further, as an art form with a highly moral and allegorical potential. As she once wrote in a letter to her friend, the astronomer, Sir John Herschel:

My aspirations are to ennoble photography and to secure for it the character and uses of High Art by combining the real and the ideal and Sacrificing nothing of Truth by all devotion to Poetry and Beauty. (1864, Gernsheim 14)

Cameron's goals suited Tennyson's approach to Arthurian legend. About the *Idylls*, Tennyson told his son:

My meaning was spiritual. I only took the legendary stories of the Round Table as illustrations. Arthur was allegorical to me. I intended him to represent the Ideal in the Soul of Man coming into contact with the warring elements of the flesh. (Tennyson 258-59)

Cameron's and Tennyson's emphasis on the ideal and the allegorical were well-suited to stories of Camelot and to each other. In addition to their interest in the "Ideal," which we may define as that which embodies Truth, Poetry, and Beauty (to use Cameron's absolutes), Gerhard Joseph has suggested that Cameron and Tennyson found each other sympathetic because both believed that, while poetry extolled the ideal, it "had its source in something rough, unkempt, and disorderly" (46): both believed very much in the "real" level of artistic signification and the need to use that unkempt reality as a means to illustrate (to adapt Tennyson's terms) allegorical conflict between the Ideal and "the warring elements of the flesh." However, allegory poses special problems for Cameron, as her comments to Herschel acknowledge. The difficulty of combining the "real" and the "ideal" within visual images that attempt to represent isolated selections from the narratives of the characters they depict— moments frozen in time, encapsulations of "Truth," "Poetry," and "Beauty"— is a problem that Cameron seems to understand as central to an art relying as heavily on the "real" (i.e., the presence of living models in definable locations, and the gritty elements that assail the flesh) as it does on abstractions. Tennyson may focus much more fully on the non-representational, on the "spiritual" and the "Ideal in the Soul of Man": unlike Cameron, his art may diminish his readers' awareness of the real because he maintains greater control than a visual artist over what his readers may imagine. Tennyson may portray the growing anguish in Arthur's soul without worrying about how anachronistic or contrived his armor appears to a Victorian audience.

While Cameron does acknowledge a need for the "real" to exist within photography, she is clearly uncomfortable with this aspect of her art; she desires her viewers to interpret the narrative of the characters she depicts while ignoring that of the models themselves. As Michael Bartram has suggested, perhaps Cameron's reliance on soft focus techniques attempts to diminish the role of the models within her art (132). Gernsheim, critical of the *Idylls* photographs, has observed that Cameron's images "persist in producing a realistic effect which can only be termed incongruous" (81). He maintains that Cameron is unable to surpass the constraints of the "real" and that, consequently, viewers of the photographs are generally unable to reproduce for themselves the illustrative readings suggested by Tennyson's lines. Cameron's representations of *Idylls of the King* repeatedly demonstrate the difficulty of unpacking the image's narrative in order to observe the union of the "real" and "ideal," and this difficulty is especially clear in those photographs that interpret the nature of Tennyson's female characters.

The insistent presence of the models within Cameron's images seems to acknowledge the clash between the physical "real" and the non-representational "ideal" which is inescapable in photography. Typically, photography's strength has been seen to be its ability to be documentary, even if documentary reality is itself subject to "certain distortions and deficiencies for which there is no remedy" (59), as Lady Eastlake noted in 1857. Although these "distortions and deficiencies" are what enable photography to represent the nebulous "ideal" and gain status as an art, they do not overcome the problem that André Bazin noted in "The Ontology of the Photographic Image":

The photographic image is the object itself, the object freed from the conditions of time and space that govern it. No matter how fuzzy, distorted, or discolored, no matter how lacking in documentary value the image may be, it shares by virtue of the very process of its becoming, the being of the model of which it is a reproduction; it is the model. (241)

Bazin isolates the problem Cameron's work makes explicit. While the photographs problematize Tennyson's analysis of the female characters of Arthurian legend, they also explore the nature of the models themselves, of the women and men who were coerced and cajoled into posing for Cameron's photographs. Because the images we are asked to interpret fictionally are of "real" persons whose historical narratives we can research or imagine, these photographs always present *at least* a double reading of the characters and scenes Cameron represents. It is the conflict between what Cameron calls the "ideal" in her letter to Herschel (what I will call the literary level of the photographs) and the presence of the "real," historically recoverable persons who posed for her (the photographs' historical level of meaning) that creates Cameron's version of Tennyson's *Idylls*, a version that reduces the threat—and the power—of Tennyson's female characters.

During most of her career, Cameron drew her models from her household and neighborhood on the Isle of Wight. In general, she tended to select her husband, Charles Hay Cameron, and her friends, such as Henry Taylor and Henry James Stedman Cotton, to portray male figures in her allegorical and literary photographs. For female models, however, she tended to rely more heavily not on women from her own socio-economic class but on her servants and dependents, Mary Ryan and Mary Hillier.[6] These women, whose economic relation to Cameron cannot be overlooked, were frequently made to pose for periods that may have ranged from three to twenty minutes (Gernsheim 42; Cecil 4); and they were not in a position to complain about their treatment, as their male counterparts often did.[7] The economic disparity between Cameron's male and female models for the *Idylls* photographs is not, however, quite as great as is commonly true in Cameron's work as a whole: the individuals who consented to become Arthurians-for-a-day were carefully chosen, regardless of social class, because of their ability to represent the "ideal" essence of Tennyson's characters. Nonetheless, Cameron's treatment of her models suggests she perceived them, regardless of their social class, as easily manipulable, curiously dehumanized and strongly subordinated to her art.

Perhaps the most obvious example of the ways in which Cameron disregarded her models' individuality and rights was her treatment of Cyllene Wilson, one of her adopted children and a frequent model for her allegorical images. In order to produce an image titled *Despair* with a suitably forlorn model, Cameron locked up Wilson for two hours. The episode was, as Gernsheim writes, intolerable to Wilson, "who hated the intrusion on her freedom by fulfilling Mrs. Cameron's whims in the studio day in[,] day out." Wilson subsequently ran away from the Freshwater community on the Isle of Wight and became a stewardess on an ocean liner (Gernsheim 78).

The case of Cyllene Wilson is only the most notable example of Cameron's manipulation and objectification of her existing and potential models. Gernsheim describes the hubbub that surrounded Cameron's household and community while she sought models for her Arthurian photographs. He reports that she would peer out of her windows, scanning the road for interesting passers-by going down to the shore. When she espied a likely model, she would send one of the maids running after the stranger, begging him or her to come and sit for her. If they agreed, they would find themselves posing in strange costumes as Geraint or Enid, Lancelot or Guinevere. They did not, of course, realize what they had let themselves in for....(42)

Vacationers, laborers, neighbors and strangers all found themselves subject to recruitment. The most well-known conscription was that of William Warder, a porter from Yarmouth (Hill 123), to portray King Arthur. Cameron reportedly felt that his face was "mythological and spiritual in the highest degree" (Hill 123). Absent from her description is any sense of Warder as an individual with his own historical narrative.

Clearly, Cameron seems to have dehumanized her models. They function as parts of her scenery unable to contribute to the project any relevant analysis of the roles they were asked to portray: Cameron seems to have been able to erase the historical or "real" dynamic of her models' lives, assuming, as Joanne Lukitsh has suggested, that a "closed network of shared assumptions" (18) permitted the models to ignore their responses to their role in Cameron's work *or* to the literary level of the images they were asked to create. The untenable nature of Cameron's critical position is apparent if we consider the flight of Cyllene Wilson or the report of a female vacationer who was asked to pose as Vivien, the seductress who destroys Tennyson's Merlin. She "very much objected to this, because Vivien did not seem to me to be a very nice character to assume" (Gernsheim 43). In addition, she was asked to pose as the non-Arthurian Zenobia, a role to which she also objected: "I felt rather alarmed. I secretly objected to be taken in such a 'masculine' character, and it was only after much persuasion that Mrs. Cameron succeeded in overcoming my objections" (Gernsheim 43).

This model, who calls herself the "Lady Amateur" in her published account of her experience as Cameron's model,[8] insists that we not ignore her response to her position as a "real," historical participant in this series of literary interpretations, and that we acknowledge her own interpretation of the characters she portrays. Cameron is in both cases able to convince the "Lady Amateur" to subordinate her own reading of the characters she is to portray to Cameron's analysis of Tennyson's Arthurian women. The model acquiesces because of Cameron's reputation and the pleasure, we assume, of adding a stint as a photographer's model to her list of vacation activities.

Cameron's images attempt to deny the historical presence of her female models, much as Dante Gabriel Rossetti tried to erase the historical presence of Elizabeth Siddal in his portrait of Ophelia. Severed from Cameron's control, however, the models defy erasure. Like the unnamed woman discussed above, Cameron's models clearly embody their responses to the legendary characters and stories they are asked to represent, insisting that the photographer's readings of Tennyson's scenes be qualified to accommodate their responses.

These historical individuals become part of the interpretive process Cameron attempts to control. Her autocratic methods and strong artistic sense are undermined throughout her Tennyson images. Her analysis of the legends she depicts is simultaneously qualified, amended and subverted by the presence of historical individuals who are able to resent, for instance, being asked to portray characters they feel are morally reprehensible.[9] Although Amanda Hopkinson asserts that Cameron's female models were permitted "greater scope for individual expression" than Victorian culture permitted them (15-16), these female models are at least partially circumscribed by Cameron's interpretations in much the same way that they are by their society. Only subtly do their qualifications of Cameron's analyses emerge from her images, yet these subtle contributions suggest that any analysis of literary photography must assess the historical reality of those individuals who inhabit its images.

II

Cameron received her first camera in 1863, and she continued to practice her art until 1878. Illustrating the *Idylls* was the last large-scale project she undertook. Obviously, she was working during the early stages of photographic technology, when methods were imprecise. Her decision to use the wet collodion process and plates larger than those commonly used added to her technical difficulties (Scharf 81). Such a preface is necessary to explain the tendency of some of Cameron's plates to become scratched during the photographic process, and the fact that often the edges of her images become blurred. Her lengthy exposure times often produced sitters who looked less than comfortable. Cameron, however, seems to have cultivated some of what her detractors have called technical defects for the effects they could produce. She disapproved of retouching photographs[10] and sought the soft focus present in most of her best images (Powell 12).

Cameron's representations of female Arthurian characters demonstrate the inability of the literary level of signification to obliterate the historical level of meaning. Her images of the idylls of Vivien and Elaine are especially crucial to our understanding of the interrelation between the historical and literary levels of meaning since they comprise eight of the fifteen photographs that illustrate the poems.

Cameron photographed two moments from Tennyson's "Merlin and Vivien." The first (figure 1) depicts the two characters (portrayed by Cameron's husband, Charles Hay Cameron, and a female visitor to Freshwater, possibly the "Lady Amateur" [Harker 52]) soon after Vivien's decision to "set herself to gain" (356) Merlin instead of Arthur. The lines Cameron asks us to associate with her photograph are:

> . . . . he was mute:
> So dark a forethought roll'd about his brain,
> As on a dull day in an Ocean cave
> The blind wave feeling round his long sea-hall
> In silence: wherefore, when she lifted up
> A face of sad appeal, and spake and said,
> 'O Merlin, do you love me?' and again,
> 'O Merlin, do you love me?' and once more
> 'Great Master, do ye love me?' he was mute,
> And lissome Vivien, holding by his heel,
> Writhed toward him, slided up his knee and sat,
> Behind his ankle twined her hollow feet

Fig. 1. "Vivien and Merlin." Julia Margaret Cameron. *Idylls of the King and Other Poems Photographically Illustrated by Julia Margaret Cameron, Text by Alfred Lord Tennyson.* New York: Janet Lehr, 1985: 587.

> Together, curved an arm about his neck,
> Clung like a snake; and letting her left hand
> Droop from his mighty shoulder, as a leaf,
> Made with her right a comb of pearl to part
> The lists of such a beard as youth gone out
> Had left in ashes
>
> (11.227-44)[11]

That serpentine imagery is associated with Vivien has certainly been noticed by critics of the poem,[12] and Cameron has selected a passage which emphasizes the snake-like qualities of the seductive Vivien: she is "lissome," she writhes and slides, she twines her feet together, and she clings to Merlin "like a snake."

Depictions of female characters as Lamia figures were, as Nina Auerbach has thoroughly described, prevalent during the Victorian period. Cameron herself, imitating the work of the Pre-Raphaelites—especially that of Dante Gabriel Rossetti—elsewhere created images of the serpent-like, seductive female. This photograph, however, works against the reptilian description Tennyson creates.

Cameron's Vivien is at too great a distance from Merlin to be sitting on his lap, her ankles and "hollow feet" are not permitted to twine about him, and her arm does not seem to curve "about his neck." In fact, the only detail that seems to be literally portrayed in Cameron's photograph is the right hand which parts "the lists of such a beard as youth gone out/ Had left in ashes."

The overall effect of this image undermines the notion of literal "illustration." Rather than reflecting Tennyson's emphasis on the frightening nature of female sexuality, the photograph diminishes Vivien's sexual energy and replaces her power with a kind of serenity that—except for the hand in Merlin's beard—connects this photograph with one of Cameron's favorite genres: images that depict young women and older men in poses of what Richard Altick has called "domestic instruction" (328).[13] This image seems designed to recuperate Vivien and undermine Tennyson's depiction of her malicious sexual strength. This sense of Cameron's interpretation is furthered by the caption that appears beneath the photograph in some copies of the volume, titling the image "Vivien and Merlin" instead of "Merlin and Vivien." Cameron's reversal of the two names may be seen as suggestive of a desire to emphasize Vivien's character, a desire to minimize slightly a sense of the idyll as developing Merlin's tragedy. Cameron's reading of Vivien—as indicated by the quotation which accompanies the image—seems to have been undercut by the reading of the model, probably the woman who objected to portraying a character she describes as "not very nice" and "objectionable." Even the language with which the model describes Vivien defuses the enormous sexual power with which Tennyson endows her.

The second "Merlin and Vivien" image (figure 2) also lessens our sense of Vivien's supposed evil. Accompanying this photograph, which depicts Merlin trapped in the hollow tree at the end of the poem, Cameron provides these lines:

> For Merlin, overtalked and overworn,
> Had yielded, told her all the charm, and slept.
> Then, in one moment, she put forth the charm
> Of woven paces and of waving hands,
> And in the hollow oak he lay as dead,
> And lost to life and use and name and fame.
>
> (11.963-68)

Perhaps physical limitations within Cameron's studio create the lack of entrapment we perceive in this image: Merlin seems not in the tree but rather in front of it, using part of it as an arm rest. The "Lady Amateur" claims that during the creation of this photograph Charles Hay Cameron was struck by a fit of the giggles. "It was," she reports, "more than mortal could stand to see the oak beginning gently to vibrate, and know that the extraordinary phenomenon was produced by the suppressed chuckling of Merlin" (Gernsheim 43). Nonetheless, although Vivien does seem a more threatening figure here (seen in the slightly serpentine curve of her body and—more importantly in Cameron's work—the fact that she appears taller than Merlin),[14] she still merely points at Merlin instead of demonstrating the "woven paces and...waving hands."

Fig. 2. "Vivien and Merlin." Julia Margaret Cameron. *Idylls of the King and Other Poems Photographically Illustrated by Julia Margaret Cameron, Text by Alfred Lord Tennyson.* New York: Janet Lehr, 1985: 591.

Perhaps more significant for our reading of this text/image pair is what Cameron chooses to exclude from the accompanying passage. The final four lines of the idyll, immediately following the excerpt she provides, are:

> Then crying 'I have made his glory mine,'
> And shrieking out 'O fool!' the harlot leapt
> Adown the forest, and the thicket closed
> Behind her, and the forest echoed 'fool.'
> (11.969-72)

Cameron may have wanted to exclude the sense of movement her frozen narrative image could not hope to contain, and yet the abrupt ending of the passage so close to the idyll's end must be seen as significant: it prevents Vivien from shrieking her cry of triumph and from categorizing Merlin as a fool.[15] Moreover, it prevents the poem from labelling Vivien a "harlot," a term which would categorize her as "evil." The literary level of signification is prevented here from condemning Vivien as greatly as Tennyson does: her demonic power is diminished by the excluded lines and her relatively static pose. She seems to exist almost apart from Merlin, whose stiffness and physical enclosure separate him from her. The model's reluctance to pose with the chuckling Charles Hay Cameron may amplify the seeming isolation of the characters. Cameron's photographs depict a Vivien who has been deprived—by the artist and her model—of some of the power present in Tennyson's text. She is reduced from an unrelenting, subversive power to a woman who is "not very nice."

Joanne Lukitsh has suggested that Cameron wanted to shift the focus of the *Idylls* away from Vivien or the unfaithful Guinevere to the virtuous Elaine (34).[16] Cameron photographed this idyll more fully than any of the others, including two photographs depicting it in the first volume of her work, and another two in the second volume. Taken as a group, these images summarize Cameron's attempt to valorize representations of the "ideal" Victorian woman. Elaine may be seen, as Michael Bartram has suggested, not only as a key figure for Cameron, but as the Victorian age's "central symbol of selfless virgin love" (158).

The first two images of Elaine (figures 3 and 4) present a seated, isolated woman first with both Lancelot's shield and the case she has created for it, and, secondly, with the case alone. The corresponding passages Cameron provides are:

> Elaine the fair, Elaine the loveable,
> Elaine, the lily maid of Astolat,
> High in her chamber up a tower to the east
> Guarded the sacred shield of Lancelot;
> Which first she placed where morning's earliest ray
> Might strike it, and awake her with the gleam;
> Then fearing rust or soilure fashioned for it
> A case of silk, and braided thereupon
> All the devices blazon'd on the shield
> In their own tinct, and added, of her wit,
> A border fantasy of branch and flower,
> And yellow-throated nestling in the nest.
> (11.1-12)

and,

> So in her tower alone the maiden sat:
> His very shield was gone; only the case,
> Her own poor work, her empty labour, left.
> But still she heard him, still his picture formed
> And grew between her and the pictured wall.
> . . . .
> And in those days she made a little song,
> And call'd her song 'The Song of Death,'
> And sang it: sweetly could she make and sing.
>
> 'Sweet is true love though given in vain, in vain;
> And sweet is death who puts an end to pain;
> I know not which is sweeter, no, not I.

Fig. 3. "Elaine, the Lily Maid of Astolat." Julia Margaret Cameron. *Idylls of the King and Other Poems Photographically Illustrated by Julia Margaret Cameron, Text by Alfred Lord Tennyson*. New York: Janet Lehr, 1985: 591.

'Love art thou sweet? then bitter death must be:
Love thou art bitter; sweet is death to me.
O love, if death be sweeter, let me die.

'Sweet love, that seems not made to fade away,
Sweet death, that seems to make us loveless clay,
I know not which is sweeter, no, not I.

I fain would follow love, if that could be;
I needs must follow death, who calls for me;
Call and I follow, I follow! let me die!'

(11.982-86, 997-1011)

Fig. 4. "Elaine." Julia Margaret Cameron. *Idylls of the King and Other Poems Photographically Illustrated by Julia Margaret Cameron, Text by Alfred Lord Tennyson.* New York: Janet Lehr, 1985: 593.

Unlike the images of Vivien, the Elaine of these photographs does not seem to have been caught mid-movement. She seems pale, passive, and immobile although she may be extending a hand in the first image to protect or caress the shield of her beloved Lancelot. Her passivity and weakness seem further emphasized, in fact, by the faded and hazy quality of the bottom of the first of the two images. The second of these two photographs portrays even less activity than the first: here we see her in profile as she sits lamenting the shield's loss. It seems difficult to imagine the Elaine in this image singing her song of love and death—we are given no musical prop, for instance. It is clear, however, that Cameron has captured something of Elaine's resignation in the face of her unrequited love. Yet, in Elaine's immobility and resignation she attains both the strength and dignity typically associated with the passive, martyred woman.[17]

The second image, like the second version of "Merlin and Vivien," is also accompanied by a passage containing a significant omission. Cameron provides Tennyson's lines describing Elaine's solitude and sorrow at the shield's loss and then jumps ahead to the lyrics of "The Song of Love and Death" that amplify those emotions. What she has excluded is the following passage:

> Then came her father, saying in low tones,
> 'Have comfort,' whom she greeted quietly.
> Then came her brethren saying, 'Peace to thee,
> Sweet sister,' whom she answer'd with all calm.
> But when they left her to herself,
> Death, like a friend's voice from a distant field
> Approaching thro' the darkness, call'd; the owls
> Wailing had power upon her, and she mixt
> Her fancies with the sallow-rifted glooms
> Of evening, and the moanings of the wind.
>   (11.987-96)

By excluding these lines, Cameron isolates Elaine more fully than does Tennyson. Whereas the idyll's Elaine has a father and brothers whose comfort she will not accept, Cameron's Elaine is entirely bereft of solace except for the death she welcomes. This isolation further deprives her of active power, but increases her status as a symbol of selflessness.

While the literary meaning of these images is clear, the model is clearly identifiable as May Prinsep. Cameron provides ample props to diminish the "real" or historical reading of Prinsep's presence in the photographs, but she remains physically present, reminding readers of her non-legendary status and her physical presence in Cameron's household. The props, in fact, can be seen to call too much attention to Tennyson's literal text, causing the literary meaning of the passage to be undercut.[18]

The two images for "Lancelot and Elaine" published in the second of Cameron's volumes (figures 5 and 6) emphasize the tragic isolation of Elaine even further by depicting the final stages of her story. The first shows the dead Elaine with the "dumb old servitor" on the barge that carries her body to Camelot. The passage Cameron cites is lengthy: it begins with Tennyson's description of Elaine's desire to be sent after her death to deliver a letter to Lancelot, and it ends only after her lifeless body has been placed on the boat with the letter, a lily and the shield case. Elaine's whiteness against the dark surroundings seems to emphasize her martyrdom.[19] Two additional elements of the photograph also emphasize the persistent inability of the literary level to eradicate historical signification. While Cameron's literary reading of the poem attempts to ensure an interpretation of Elaine as the ideal typification of innocent womanly devotion and unrequited love and martyrdom, the exclusion of significant portions of the text and the presence of Charles Hay Cameron in a second fictional role subvert Cameron's analysis.

First, Cameron again excludes lines from her accompanying quotation. In this case, the omitted passage contains Elaine's request that she and her barge be decked "like the Queen" (1.1111). Cameron eliminates Elaine's desire to confront Guinevere and prevents our seeing Elaine in relation to any other female figure within the poem: she remains alone, aloof, and empowered by her martyrdom.

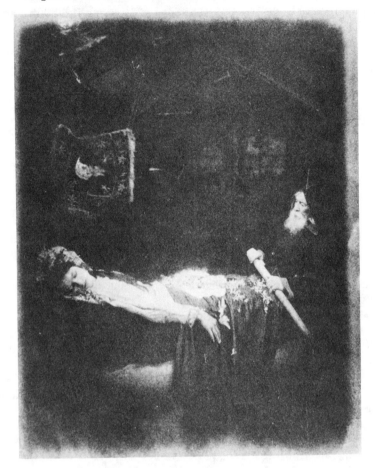

Fig. 5. "Elaine." Julia Margaret Cameron. *Idylls of the King and Other Poems Photographically Illustrated by Julia Margaret Cameron, Text by Alfred Lord Tennyson.* New York: Janet Lehr, 1985: 621.

The choice of model for the "dumb old servitor" who rows the barge to court also emphasizes a reading of Elaine as martyr, for the male model here is the photographer's husband, whom we saw earlier—and in essentially the same costume—as Merlin. Posing the magician at Elaine's feet, oar in hand, in a posture of either grief or rapt admiration, emphasizes the supernatural devotion of Elaine to the unfaithful Lancelot and further stresses Elaine's position as an embodiment of Tennyson's true feminine goodness, a quality seen even more fully in the final "Lancelot and Elaine" photograph. Simultaneously, however, the repetition of the same model as a new character prevents readers of the image from accepting its literary reading. While Merlin is an apt choice to emphasize Elaine's purity, that same presence assures the viewer of the limitations of Cameron's studio and resources, and of her difficulty in procuring suitable models. These factors undermine the literary signification of this image

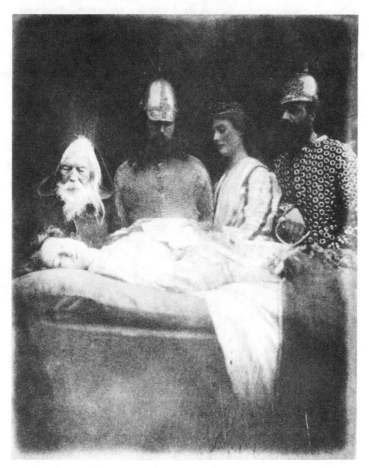

Fig. 6. "Elaine." Julia Margaret Cameron. *Idylls of the King and Other Poems Photographically Illustrated by Julia Margaret Cameron, Text by Alfred Lord Tennyson.* New York: Janet Lehr, 1985: 623.

and ensure that we fail to ignore the "real," historical dimension of the photograph.

In the final image illustrating "Lancelot and Elaine" (figure 6), Cameron cites the passage containing the contents of Elaine's letter as the porter/Merlin, Arthur, Guinevere and Lancelot look sorrowfully at the dead Elaine. While it is difficult to visualize the weeping Tennyson assures us greeted Elaine's words, one nonetheless senses that Cameron's Elaine—even more than Tennyson's— is to be seen as a tragic, isolated victim whose virtue becomes most apparent in the futility of her creative activity while alive (the fashioning of the quickly emptied shield case), and her willingness, in fact her eagerness, to undergo a martyr's death which her letter immortalizes.

Fig. 7. "The Parting of Sir Lancelot and Queen Guinevere." Julia Margaret
Cameron. *Idylls of the King and Other Poems Photographically Illustrated
by Julia Margaret Cameron, Text by Alfred Lord Tennyson.* New York:
Janet Lehr, 1985: 597. See Note 16.

Cameron attempts to emphasize Elaine's Victorian role as the ideal
representation of female virtue, virtue that is best demonstrated by inaction,
passivity, and, especially, death. Cameron's images of Vivien further stress this
relatively typical view of the Victorian feminine ideal through the ways in which
the literary and historical tensions present within the photographs diminish
Vivien's power. Female power, Cameron's images seem to suggest, comes not
from sexual, manipulative, or even the creative strength that permits Elaine to
embroider the shield case or write her own narrative; it comes from death.
Acceptance of Cameron's interpretation, however, insists that we eliminate the
historical level of signification from her images: the "ideal" level of her
photographs may require the death of Elaine, and the Victorian imagination
seems to have enjoyed such a fantasy, but viewers of Cameron's images are never
permitted to believe that May Prinsep has died. The Victorian myth is undercut
by the model herself, whose presence insists that we not ignore her historical
reality.

Fig. 8. "Guinevere and the Little Maid." Julia Margaret Cameron. *Idylls of the King and Other Poems Photographically Illustrated by Julia Margaret Cameron, Text by Alfred Lord Tennyson.* New York: Janet Lehr, 1985: 599. See Note 16.

Only by persistently acknowledging the historical presence of the model within the literary photograph can we hope to understand the intricate relation between image and text. Cameron, because of her medium and because of the people who inhabit her images, cannot "illustrate" Tennyson's *Idylls of the King.* Instead, as she strives to depict what she calls the "ideal," the interpretations of those whom she "press'd and summon'd from the breezy shores" (to return to Turner's poem) continually insert themselves into her reading, be it as actively as the Lady Amateur or merely by their physical presence as individuals who resist objectification.

Fig. 9. "Arthur." Julia Margaret Cameron. *Idylls of the King and Other Poems Photographically Illustrated by Julia Margaret Cameron, Text by Alfred Lord Tennyson.* New York: Janet Lehr, 1985: 601. See Note 16.

Notes

[1]These illustrations were originally intended to be used as woodcuts for an edition of Tennyson's poetry published by Henry S. King. However, Cameron's disappointment with the small and inexact renderings of her photographs prompted Tennyson to suggest she publish a volume of the photographs themselves (Gernsheim 44-5).

[2]Gustave Doré's engravings of the *Idylls* had been widely popular (Gernsheim 81). Charles W. Millard notes that two additional photographically illustrated editions of Tennyson's poetry were published shortly after Cameron's work. These editions (*Poetical Works of Alfred Tennyson* and *The Works of Alfred Tennyson, Poet Laureate, with Photographic Illustrations by Peter Jennings*) relied heavily upon landscape photography (Millard 199).

[3]See, for instance, the standard study of Cameron's work, Helmut Gernsheim's *Julia Margaret Cameron: Her Life and Photographic Work* (77-79); Amanda Hopkinson, *Julia Margaret Cameron* (58); and Michael Bartram, *The Pre-Raphaelite Camera* (129-32).

[4]From the microfilmed copy held by the George Eastman House Photography Collection. For a description of the various copies of Cameron's *Idylls*, see Charles W. Millard, "Julia Margaret Cameron and Tennyson's *Idylls of the King.*"

[5]The emphasis on female figures is typical of Cameron's photography as a whole. Hopkinson observes that, judging from her surviving work, Cameron used female models twice as often as either men or children (16).

[6]This gender and economic division is especially true for Cameron's illustrations of Shakespearean scenes. Because Cameron preferred to create female allegorical subjects, Mary Ryan and Mary Hillier were probably Cameron's most frequently photographed models. For additional information, see Gernsheim (31).

[7]Colin Ford cites an essay by Wilfred Ward to describe Cameron's treatment of Mary Hillier:

Mrs. Cameron...would show off to her friends the Mary who was called, from the shape of her face, 'Madonna,' using various devices to exhibit her to the best advantage. 'Mary, do stand on that chair and pull down that high curtain.' Then, turning to her friend, 'Isn't she perfect in that light, and in that profile as you see now?' (*The Dublin Review*, January 1912, qtd. Ford 130).

[8]"A Reminiscence of Mrs. Cameron" by a Lady Amateur, *The Photographic News*. London: January, 1886. (Quoted at length in Gernsheim 43).

[9]Even those sitters who were not treated as Cyllene Wilson was, or who did not object to the characters they were asked to portray, would find themselves bullied and subordinated to Cameron's concern that her "strength" and photographic materials not be wasted by their involuntary movement during the photographic process (Gernsheim 75).

[10]Cameron wrote in a letter to Sir Edward Ryan on December 8, 1874, regarding blemishes on her *Idylls* photographs: "...they must I think remain. I could have touched them out but I am *the only* photographer who always issues untouched photographs and artists for this reason amongst others value my photographs" (qtd. Gernsheim 47).

[11]Because of difficulties with both the Lehr and microfilmed copies of Cameron's edition, quotations to Tennyson's poems are to Christopher Ricks's *The Poems of Tennyson*, 3: 263-563.

[12]See, for instance, William E. Buckler, *Man and His Myths: Tennyson's Idylls of the King in Critical Context* (106-07); and Beverly Taylor and Elisabeth Brewer, *The Return of Arthur: British and American Arthurian Literature Since 1800* (105).

[13]See Hopkinson (17-18).

[14]Relative height of human figures is repeatedly used in Cameron's work to indicate dominance or submission. The scenes of "domestic instruction" clearly illustrate this power dynamic, as does the group composition, *King Lear allotting his Kingdom* (reproduced in Weaver 83), which subtly stresses Goneril's subversive power through her height.

[15]Taylor and Brewer, it should be noted, see the forest's echo as an indictment of Vivien herself, who has failed to learn from Merlin the value of the social order he represents (105).

[16]The decreasing sympathy Cameron and her models give Guinevere supports Lukitsh's assessment. Guinevere's adultery, too central to Arthurian legend to be softened as greatly as is Vivien's evil, is criticized by Cameron through the increasing stiffness in the images created for Guinevere's idyll. The three images Cameron creates for "Guinevere" (figures

7-9) gradually distance the reader from a sympathetic reading of the Queen, concluding, in fact, with a unique image of the solitary Arthur, thereby erasing the Queen completely from her idyll.

[17]These images support Lukitsh's argument that although Cameron's female characters are generally conventional, the figures depicted gain strength from their isolation from men and are, consequently, elevated from their "otherwise secondary status" (29).

[18]Bartram argues that the literalism in the first of these two images (which calls too much attention to Lancelot's shield and its case) is Cameron's response to the criticism Henry Peach Robinson had received for his photograph, *Elaine Watching the Shield of Lancelot* (1859). Critics had charged that in Robinson's image, "Lancelot's shield was not battered enough" to stir Elaine's emotions (166). Generally, states Bartram, "literalism is not a predominant feature of Cameron's art" (166).

[19]Elaine's virtue and martyrdom are further stressed, as Lukitsh has aptly observed, by the visual link Cameron creates between the dead Elaine and Arthur: both are depicted in death as being transported by boat to their resting places. This subtle bond colors our interpretation of the virtue of both figures. See *The Passing of Arthur* (Cameron 625).

Works Cited

Altick, Richard D. *Paintings from Books: Art and Literature in Britain, 1760-1900.* Columbus: Ohio UP, 1985.

Auerbach, Nina. *Woman and the Demon: The Life of a Victorian Myth.* Cambridge: Harvard UP, 1982.

Bartram, Michael. *The Pre-Raphaelite Camera: Aspects of Victorian Photography.* Boston: Little Brown, 1985.

Bazin, André. "The Ontology of the Photographic Image." Trans. Hugh Gray. *Classic Essays on Photography.* Ed. Alan Trachtenberg. New Haven: Leete's Island Books, 1980. 237-44.

Buckler, William E. *Man and His Myths: Tennyson's Idylls of the King in Critical Context.* New York: New York UP, 1984.

Cameron, Julia Margaret. *Idylls of the King and Other Poems Photographically Illustrated by Julia Margaret Cameron, Text by Alfred Lord Tennyson.* New York: Janet Lehr, 1985.

———*Illustrations to Tennyson's Idylls of the King and Other Poems.* 2 vols. London: Henry S. King, 1875. *History of Photography Monographs.* Microfilm Reel No. 299. Woodbridge, CT: Research Publications, Inc.

Cecil, David Lord. "Introductory Essay." *A Victorian Album: Julia Margaret Cameron and Her Circle.* Ed. Graham Ovenden. New York: Da Capo, 1975. 1-7.

Eastlake, Elizabeth Lady. "Photography." *Classic Essays on Photography.* Ed. Alan Trachtenberg. New Haven: Leete's Island Books, 1980. 39-68.

Ford, Colin. *The Cameron Collection: An Album of Photographs by Julia Margaret Cameron Presented to Sir John Herschel.* Wokingham: Van Nostrand Reinhold, 1975.

Gernsheim, Helmut. *Julia Margaret Cameron: Her Life and Photographic Work.* New York: Aperture, 1975.

Harker, Margaret. *Julia Margaret Cameron.* London: William Collins Sons and Company, 1983.

Hill, Brian. *Julia Margaret Cameron: A Victorian Family Portrait*. London: Peter Owen, 1973.

Hopkinson, Amanda. *Julia Margaret Cameron*. London: Virago, 1986.

Joseph, Gerhard. "Poetic and Photographic Frames: Tennyson and Julia Margaret Cameron," *The Tennyson Research Bulletin* 5,2 (November 1988): 43-8.

Lukitsh, Joanne. *Cameron: Her Work and Career*. Rochester, NY: International Museum of Photography at George Eastman House, 1986.

Millard, Charles W. "Julia Margaret Cameron and Tennyson's *Idylls of the King*," *Harvard Library Bulletin* 21,2 (April 1973): 187-201.

Powell, Tristram, ed. *Victorian Photographs of Famous Men and Fair Women*. Introductions by Virginia Woolf and Roger Fry. 1926. Rev. ed. Boston: David R. Godine, 1973.

Scharf, Aaron. *Pioneers of Photography: An Album of Pictures and Words*. New York: Harry H. Abrams, 1976.

Taylor, Beverly and Elisabeth Brewer. *The Return of Arthur: British and American Arthurian Literature Since 1800*. Totowa, NJ: Barnes and Noble, 1983.

Tennyson, Alfred Lord. *Idylls of the King*. Christopher Ricks, ed. *The Poems of Tennyson*. 3 vols. Harlow: Longman, 1987. 3: 263-563.

Weaver, Mike. *Julia Margaret Cameron, 1815-1879*. Southampton: The John Hansard Gallery, 1984.

Transforming the Myth:
The Use of Arthurian Material
in the Church Universal and Triumphant

Kathleen Ely

Life liveth but in Life and does not roam
To other realms if all be well at home.
James Thomson

The distinction between poet and prophet is not easily made. Both "art and religion share the characteristic of being imaginative creations of human beings subject to relatively few empirical tests," says cult geneticist William Bainbridge. "Each is free to postulate general explanations without much fear of factual contradiction" (182). It is part of our job, as scholars, to explore and understand these explanations. Looking at cults may be useful not only because they bridge the gulf between art and religion, but also because, as Bainbridge adds, "Cult is culture writ small" (157). He explains that cults are to culture as *E. coli* bacteria is to scientific research; concentrating on a cult provides an intense focus for the themes which run through our culture at large. Howard Rome notes that "cults and established religions use the same basic operative and manipulative techniques and procedures" (174), and that cults can offer "theoretical implications [about] the formation as well as of the history of social movements" (175). Cults can provide answers to how other movements in popular culture function. And as we move toward the year 2000, when millenial cults can be counted on to spring up, cults may provide valuable information on how our society will enter the next century. Cults readily change attractive elements of popular culture in the ways they will find most useful to sell their own programs.

The Arthurian legend has often been transformed and manipulated by the cultures which encounter it. In his breezy essay "Dreaming of the Middle Ages," Umberto Eco notes of the United States that "a country able to produce Dianetics can do a lot in terms of wash-and-wear sorcery and Holy Grail frappe" (62). A dramatic example of this cultural transformation is the Montana-based cult Church Universal and Triumphant [CUT], which describes itself as "the leader of a new age in consciousness, the Aquarian Age." Summit Lighthouse was founded in 1958 by Mark L. Prophet. In 1963 he became twenty-four-year old Elizabeth Clare Wulf's second husband. Since his death in 1973, when the group became known as the Church Universal and Triumphant, Elizabeth Clare Prophet has been the source of "dictations" offered by of a host of various characters throughout myth and history, including the major figures of Arthurian myth. By attaching herself to the Arthurian myth on a personal level, she garners the authority of its various texts for herself. The added authority of a variety of other texts is also used to support the teachings of the cult, including the Bible, Shakespeare, and works ranging from *The Story of Philosophy* by Will Durant to the more curious writings of Edgar Cayce. The emphasis in this paper will largely be on excerpts from Tennyson proffered in works by the cult, because the poet provides convenient loci for the themes of the Church Universal and Triumphant: persistent nostalgia, sexual anxiety, and an apocalyptic vision. Use of Arthurian materials will also be examined to highlight the capitalistic nature of cult formation.

Cults are big business—there are over 30,000 members of the Church Universal and Triumphant, most of whom give large portions of their income to it. In a March 1991 article in the Bozeman *Chronicle*, reporter Scott McMillion notes:

With its constantly mounting legal and environmental cleanup bills, the church [CUT] has responded in ways similar to that of any beleaguered corporation: trying to cut costs, recruit new followers and come up with some new products and marketing strategies. (5)

Like all good entrepreneurs, CUT must constantly update its product and provide packaging which will sell its product; it must achieve "product differentiation." The Arthurian myth sells: it sold America on the Kennedys with their evocation of Camelot, and a look through any city telephone book will garner a host of "Round Table Restaurants," "Merlin Cleaners" and "Camelot Courts." Prophet has used various elements of the Camelot legend to reinforce it in her followers' minds. For example, she uses the name of the mercantile village of Avalon—Glastonbury—for twenty-acre tracts available for homesteading near Emigrant, Montana, just north of church headquarters at the Royal Teton Ranch. The CUT community stresses self-sufficiency in almost feudal terms, with its own Montessori-based schools, gardens designed to provide for all needs of a macrobiotic diet, and cottage industries including a carrot-packing plant and as well as in-home clothing manufacture. Glastonbury is the ultimate company town. All activities in the tightly planned community have a purpose.

Another way for a cult to serve its purposes, is by the appropriation of texts, producing a pastiche familiar to those conversant with post-modernism. Bainbridge offers this analysis of the process:

Innovative cults offer new configurations of familiar elements taken piecemeal from other religious organizations, from secular institutions, and from the petty details of modern life. (171)

Eco anticipates more exactly the configuration of CUT, in one of his descriptions of the Ten Little Mediavelisms:

The Middle Ages of so-called Tradition, or of occult philosophy...[is] an eternal and rather eclectic ramshackle structure, swarming with Knights Templars, Rosicrucians, alchemists, Masononic initiates, neo-Kabbalists, drunk on reactionary poisons sipped from the Grail, ready to hail every neo-fascist Will to Power. (71)

They are the "Middle Ages of early Bergman...and Wagner's Ring...and Conan the Barbarian" (71). And that of the Church Universal and Triumphant.

To track the history of Mark and Elizabeth Clare Prophet is to see the variety of sources available to the cult. Bainbridge notes that "In modern society, cults are born out of older cults, and most of them are known to cluster in family lineages" (159). Born into a family of Christian fundamentalists, Mark Prophet had been an early member first of the *I AM* movement, which is echoed in his claim to speak for "those who have the seed of the name *I AM THAT I AM* within their hearts" (*SGOP* 39). "An individual may join one cult, learn some useful new culture, then defect to a second cult taking this cultural material with him" according to Bainbridge (169). Mark Prophet was next inducted as a member of one of the *I AM* spores, the right-wing, conservative Bridge to Freedom. Bainbridge observes:

Especially in the entrepreneur model of cult formation, but perhaps also in the psychopathology model as well, a single individual founds a new cult on the basis of prior apprenticeship in an existing cult. (161)

Mark Prophet, who had served his apprenticeship well, passed on those skills to his wife, Elizabeth Clare Prophet.

All these cults were derived from Madame Blavatsky's late-nineteenth century spiritualist movement, Theosophy, with its own unique blend of Eastern and Western thought. Bainbridge tells us that the process of:

Cult invention involves finding attractive elements in the cultural environment, adding them to an existing cultic core, subtracting parts that interfere with more valuable parts, and transforming elements to make them fit their place in the compensator package offered to the cult's members. (171)

These forerunners, then, are the "cultic core" of the Church Universal and Triumphant; one of the "transforming elements" is Arthurian legends.

Publishing, as CUT spokesman Murray Steinman has said, is the church's "bread and butter" and Arthurian materials have been commercially valuable to them. While the only publishing figures available are those offered by the cult itself, they claim an average printing of 100,000 copies. Use of Tennyson's poem *The Idylls of the King* is included in several books "by" the Prophets: *Saint Germain on Prophecy: Coming World Changes* (1986), *Lord of the Seven Rays* (1987) and *The Lost Teachings of Christ: Book 3, Masters and Disciples on the Path* (1986; 1988). Further references to Camelot appear in *The Lost Teachings of Christ: Book 4, Good and Evil: Atlantis Revisited* (1986; 1988). All are published by Summit Lighthouse on its own presses in an old Burlington Northern warehouse in Livingston, Montana. The books look like the thick bestsellers lined up at the checkout stand of any grocery store; the vivid colors of their slick covers reflect the "chakras" or "inner lights" they are meant to represent, usually violet or green. The first three texts include the exact same Arthurian materials, though somewhat rearranged; presumably, once you have read one you will not be eager to read another and thus will not notice the replication. Footnotes are included throughout the texts, making it easy to track most of the sources used by the Prophets.

How the CUT texts are actually constructed is problematic and hidden behind the veil of mystery in which CUT shrouds itself, making it difficult to piece together its history. *Saint Germain* is "Recorded by Elizabeth Clare Prophet," allegedly from "dictations" given her directly by St. Germain himself. The two volumes of the *Lost Teachings* have both Prophets listed as authors. According to the Foreword, *The Lost Teachings of Jesus: Book 4* "...consists of fourteen lectures delivered by Mark between 1965 and 1973, illuminated by the lessons Jesus has given us in dictations, sermons and letters over the past thirty years." While *Book 3* offers no clue as to its development, the first chapter, "The Ladder of Life," makes indeterminate the very process of writing:

...we ought to say a few words about the hand-me-down religions that have fallen in our laps. For if the Bible is the complete and unadulterated word of God—written by him and not by mere mortals (who most assuredly held the pen)—then we should believe every word literally interpreted for us by these well-meaning pastors who desire to save our souls. Yet in the Bible itself are written these words: "The letter killeth but the Spirit giveth life." (II Cor. 3:6)...If Jesus did not entrust our souls to the written word alone, then why should we? (*LTJ* 3-4)

It is as if they were out to deconstruct their work and deprive their own position of any objective validity. As Derrida tells us "there is an originary violence of writing because language is first...writing" (99). In this bold disclaimer, the Prophets both deny and confront that violence.

Lord of the Seven Rays has as its subtitle "Mirror of Consciousness." It is really two books: the first a collection of interwoven "histories" of the lives of the seven lords, the second "dictations" channeled through the person of Elizabeth Clare Prophet herself. In a rambling, often incoherent discourse Prophet herself claims to be a reincarnation of Guinevere (as well as Martha, the sister of Lazarus and Marie Antoinette). She also says her second husband, Mark Prophet, is the reincarnation of Lancelot and further asserts that her spiritual teacher, Eli Morya, was the reincarnation of Arthur. This immediately suggests the adulterous relationship we have come to associate with the Arthurian myth, but such an interpretation Prophet personally dismisses out of hand, saying it is designed to undercut the true nature of the relationship between Arthur, Guinevere and Lancelot; through centuries of reincarnation, this has been resolved.

As Mrs. Prophet explains:

Witchcraft, intrigue and treachery destroyed Camelot, not the love of Lancelot and Guinevere as Tom Malory's misogynistic depiction suggests. (*LSR*, 259)

The perception of "misogyny" here seems to be personal; Prophet, after all, is supposed to be Guinevere. Note here, too, the casual and informal tone of "Tom Mallory," who is usually referred to as Sir Thomas Malory, as if Prophet herself knew Malory in a past life. Prophet lays the blame for the destruction of Camelot clearly at the feet of those who plotted against Arthur and his kingdom, in a style which borders on the baroque:

'Twas the king's bastard son Modred by his half sister Margawse who, with Morgana le Fay and a circle of like sorceresses and black knights set out to steal the crown, imprison the queen and destroy for a time the bonds of a Love that such as these (of the left-handed path) had never known nor could— a Reality all of their willing, warring and enchantments could not touch. (*LSR*, 259)

Prophet's source for the information that Modred was Arthur's son is a popular biography made to capitalize on the current romantic ideas about Camelot, *King Arthur* by Norma Loore Goodrich. The novel takes much of its authority from the text of the "misognynistic" Sir Thomas Malory. For Prophet, sources are used in whatever manner is convenient, to make the point which she wants to make.

Sometimes the point Prophet is making is very abstract. The sole reference to Queen Guinevere in *Lord of the Seven Rays* is very curious. One of the many pictures which illustrate the text is a late Victorian illustration of "The Wedding of Arthur and Guinevere" by Howard Pyle (*LSR*, 50). It shows a demure Guinevere meekly giving her hand to Arthur. She is not yet the Queen; only Arthur is crowned. On the right the bishop is blessing the marriage as Merlin, an old man with a shepherd's crook, looks on. The ladies of the Court strew flowers at the couple's feet. While the picture is contemporary with the pre-Raphaelites, it veers away from that tradition into a more maudlin one that works to gain authority from the sanctifying presence of church officials. The print is sentimental and hints that perhaps the most significant aspect of Guinevere's relationship with Arthur was the act of marriage itself. Marriage, to the Church Universal and Triumphant is an essential concept. After all, it is by marriage that Elizabeth Clare Prophet acquired her "resounding name." Marriage also suggests unity and wholeness, an emblem of future happiness.

The text which accompanies the picture is from Alfred Lord Tennyson's "The Coming of Arthur."

> Then Arthur charged his warrior whom he loved.
> And honour'd most, Sir Lancelot, to ride forth.
> And bring the Queen...

Only Arthur himself has the authority to bring forth the Queen. In Prophet's hierarchy, since he speaks with the authority of the prophet El Morya, only he can command the Queen's presence. Here the text breaks and the following lines from Tennyson are left out, lines which suggest the danger presented when Arthur gives up his own hierarchical authority:

> ...and watch'd him from the gates:
> And Lancelot past away among the flowers,
> (For then was latter April) and return'd
> Among the flowers, in May with Guinevere.

This portion of Tennyson's poem, that tells how Lancelot whiled away the spring with Guinevere, is removed to avoid even a hint of sexual impropriety. The bowdlerized text continues with:

> To whom arrived, by Dubric the high saint
> Chief of the church in Britain, and before
> The stateliest of her alter-shrines, the King
> That morn was married, while in stainless white,
> The fair beginners of a nobler time,
> And glorying him in their vows and him, his knights
> Stood around him, and rejoicing in his joy...

Again the text breaks, and here it is crucial. What is excluded is a description of May followed by the awful words of the ill-fated King:

> And Arthur said, 'Behold, they doom is mine.
> Let chance what will, I love thee to the death!'
> To whom the Queen replied with drooping eyes,
> 'King and my lord, I love thee to the death!'

The words "to the death" echo the fatal challenge offered from knight to knight so often throughout the poem. In Prophet's manipulation, these words would be dangerous, marking the true fate of the nobility. She resumes only with the "good news":

> And bold Dubric spread his hands and spake,
> 'Reign ye, and live and love, and make the world
> Other, and may they be one with thee,
> And all this Order of thy Table Round
> Fulfil the boundless purpose of their King!

Oneness, order, purpose, authorized by all that is holy and spiritual: these are the elements essential to the myth being propagated by Prophet. A recent CUT conference in October of 1990 was billed as "A Vision of Wholeness for the New Age" and many of the pamphlets issued by the cult also refer to "oneness" or "wholeness." This sense of unity is characteristic of fascist ideology, as Wilhelm Reich tells us, which promises a world where chaos is dispelled and all are one.

A sense of ordered history was necessary for Tennyson because he felt himself left out of his own time; his *Idylls of the King* perfectly reflects his obsession with the past. Thomas Carlyle depicted him, some time after he had been honored by the laureateship and only a year after his marriage, as "sitting on a dung heap among innumerable dead dogs." Tennyson once wrote to his friend Emily Sellwood that

To me, the far-off world seems nearer than the present, for in the present is always something unreal and indistinct, but the other seems a good solid planet, rolling round its green hills and paradises to the harmony of more steadfast laws. (171)

This persistent nostalgia can also be seen in CUT, which is constantly referring itself back to historical events, most already very mythologized and therefore romantic, to appeal to the reader of its text. Simply by tracking the history of the various characters who "dictate" through the Prophets reveals a great nostalgia for the past, while at the same time garnering the luster of the past's glory.

To fully understand the extent which Prophet uses the Arthurian myth requires a look at the genealogy of various reincarnates in her heirarchy. One of these characters is El Morya, the Lord of the First Ray, who has gifts of "faith in God's will" and "the word of Wisdom"; he is the "Initiator of the Throat Chakra." Beginning as the Hebrew prophet, Abraham, El Morya went on to be one of the Three Kings, Melchoir.

In the fifth century, El Morya reappeared as King Arthur, who is described as:

...warrior and guru of the mystery school at Camelot,...[who] guarded the flame of the inner teachings, instilling the quest for the Holy Grail by triumph over tyrants and the greatest tyrant of them all: that idolatrous carnal mind. (*LSR*, 92)

Fear of carnal sexuality is also often brought out in Prophet's material. She uses the seduction of Merlin to point out the dangers of sexuality, again using an excerpt of text from Tennyson:

> And in the hollow oak he [Merlin] lay as dead,
> And lost to life and use and name and fame.
> Then crying, 'I have made his glory mine,'
> And shrieking out, 'O, fool!' the harlot leapt
> Adown the forest, and the thicket closed
> Behind her, and the forest echo'd 'fool.' (*KSR* 121)

The hollow oak connotes Merlin's sexual depletion; in it he lies "as dead." Sex, for Prophet, is a kind of death, which leaves the participant "lost to life and use and name and fame." As Wilhelm Reich points out, "the anchoring of sexual inhibition and sexual anxiety" is necessary for the formation of the authoritarian structure." Prophet uses sexual repression in many forms, controlling the lives of her converts and their minds through the use of such "authoritarian" tests, reinforcing the need for sexual repression. All may be a reflection of her own psychopathology, as described in an article in Maclean's:

Prophet's former secretary, Susan Modenhauer, who was thrown out of the church for having a man in her room, says that her boss had a particular obsession about oral sex. 'That got you the second death,' she explained, 'in which the guilty party is consigned to '50,000 years in outer darkness.' (35)

The resultant problem of succession is often a subtext in Prophet's materials, if not quite as it was for Tennyson who dedicates the *The Idylls of the King* to Prince Albert, the consort of Queen Victoria who had died in 1861. His dedication asks, "Or how should England dream of his sons/Hope more for these than some inheritance/Of such a life, a heart, a mind as thine?" As a cult leader, descending from other cults, Prophet needs to assert the clarity of her own succession. She writes that

...these keepers of the flame of Camelot endured tasks and tests which included exorcising dragons, giants and demons and battling wicked kings, bastards and female enchantresses.

She is concerned with the danger of "bastards and female enchantresses," presuming her own exclusion of the latter category. Bastards are equivalent to "wicked kings" and remote from El Morya's next incarnation as "Akbar, greatest of the Mogul emperors." His further incarnations included Thomas Beckett and Thomas More—who with "the soul of Arthur...with tender words and gifts of love...[More] touched the heart of a world forever." As Master M., he sponsors the Theosophical Society. Later, through Lanto, another voice of Mark Prophet, he announces:

Beloved ones, I am here...here in Darjeeling, here at Camelot...in the fullness of the Light of the will of God; though others determine to remove that Light, it is invincible in heaven and on earth. (*LSR*, 379)

For Prophet, Camelot is a transitory place, existing wherever St. Morya exists. Camelot is the name of several retreats that have been owned by the Church Universal and Triumphant, including the original in the Santa Monica Mountains, near Malibu, California, and a second in Maui, Hawaii. Wherever it is found, Camelot seems to be a very nice place.

Another reincarnate is Saint Germain, the Lord of the Seventh Ray, who has the gifts of prophecy and works miracles; he is the "Initiator of the Seat-of-the-Soul Chakra." According to Prophet's schemata, Saint Germain first appeared fifty thousand years ago as the ruler of a "golden-age civilization [which] thrived in a fertile country with a semitropical climate where the Sahara Desert now is" (*SGOP* 3). Unlike Saddam Hussein, Saint Germain renounced his throne to avoid a bloody battle by a conquering king. Saint Germain then appeared as "the High Priest of the Violet Flame Temple on the mainland of Atlantis thirteen thousand years ago." He then became the Old Testament prophet, Samuel (c. 1050 B.C.), "dubbed Uncle Sam by his people" (*SGOP*, 39). He also appeared as Saint Joseph (1st century A.D.), father of Christ; Saint Alban (3rd century), the first martyr of the British isles; and the Greek philosopher Proclus (c. 410-485 A.D.).

Prophet declares first that "Saint Germain was Merlin," then that "Saint Germain *is* Merlin" (*SGOP*, 12-13). Her sources on Merlin are from a variety of tertiary materials. She quotes from Geoffrey of Monmouth's text *Vita Merlini*, but found in Nikolai Tolstoy's *The Quest*, to provide us with Merlin's own words:

'I was taken out of my true self,' he said. 'I was as a spirit and knew the history of people long past and could foretell the future. I knew then the secrets of nature, bird, flight, star wanderings, and the way fish glide'. (*SGOP*, 13-14)

He lends authority to Prophet's visions and understanding of history and reincarnation. She describes him as:

...the 'old' man who knows the secrets of youth and alchemy, who charted the stars at Stonehenge, and moved a stone or two, so they say by his magical powers—who would astonish no one if he suddenly appeared on a Broadway stage or in the forests of the Yellowstone or at one's side on any highway anywhere. (*SGOP*, 12)

In this odd collection of images, Prophet calls forth—in one breathless sentence— the authority of ancient (and pagan) Stonehenge, the popular stage version of "Camelot," her own religious community based on the Yellowstone River in Paradise Valley, Montana, and her version of Everyman, on a "highway anywhere," if presumably in America. Recruiting and seducing a cult member, then, involves recalling the past with a catchy tune to remind him or her of the idyllic world to which one can aspire, if only one will take to the road.

She also quotes from a *Time-Life* popularization of Arthurian myths, *The Enchanted World: Wizards and Witches*, in support of Merlin's "pervasiveness- ...recalled in an early Celtic name for Britain, 'Clas Myrddin,' which means 'Merlin's Enclosure' " (*SGOP*, 14). *Time-Life* offers its own special brand of authority based on its popular news magazines, which have their own "pervasiveness," being on every newsstand in America. After Merlin, St. Germain himself is eventually an American. Before the transition is made, he becomes the philosopher and Franciscan monk Roger Bacon (c. 1214-1294), the "discoverer" of America, Christopher Columbus (1451-1506), and Francis Bacon (1561-1626)—who, according to Prophet, was the lawful son of Elizabeth I and Robert Dudley and also, the true author of the Shakespearean works.

From 1710 to 1822 he appeared as 40-year-old Count Germain—mentioned in the letters of "Fredrick the Great, Voltaire, Horace Walpole and Casanova" (*SGOP*, 30) and thereafter, as an Ascended Master. As such, he "stood by George Washington throughout the Revolution and...at Valley Forge" and "called for the signing of the Declaration of Independence, directed the writing of the Constitution and anointed Washington first President of the United States."

America has a special place in CUT's cosmology. As J. Gordon Melton points out, CUT considers the United States:

a country with a cosmic role, as it was prepared by the hierarchy for the individualization of God-awareness in the sons and daughters of God. It is the land in which the final release of light from the Great White Brotherhood will be made. The recent economic and social upheavals are the symbols of endtime and a cataclysm which America will go through before being resurrected into the Golden Age. To prepare for this transition, a program of survival that includes the storing of bar silver and of the necessities of life is being pursued by the...members. (161)

Not surprisingly, the politics of the Church Universal and Triumphant have been insistently reactionary, with a strong, right-wing conservative bent. According to *Time*, the cult has appealed largely to "upper middle class whites, most of them from California." All members of good standing are offered classes which instruct them in being Keepers of the Flame, an organization alleged to have been founded by its Knight commander, St. Germain. When Prophet describes the Keepers of the Flame in *Lord of the Seven Rays* the language harks back to Camelot, where:

...under King Arthur the chivalry of knighthood, side by side with fair maidenhood to Motherhood, portrayed the ideals of twin flames united in Love for the defense of Truth. (*LSR*, 92)

She is once again evoking herself by the reference to motherhood. Her followers call her "Guru Ma," "(the teacher who is mother) but more often 'Mother' because of her devotion to the flame of God as Mother." In his analysis of Nazi ideology, Wilhelm Reich notes that:

The subjective emotional core of the ideas of homeland and nation are ideas of mother and family. The mother is the homeland of the child, as the family is its 'nation in miniature'...The psychic contents of religion stem from the infantile family situation. (48)

To align oneself with Guru Ma is to come home to mother, denying that we can never go home again.

The rhetoric of the Keepers of the Flame Fraternity may seem relatively harmless until we learn that it:

...is a fraternal, outer order of the Great White Brotherhood whose members have vowed to keep the flame of Life blazing upon the hearts' altar of all mankind, *to be their brother's keepers* and to keep constantly in mind and heart all that the Father...has already given into mind, heart and hand for his glory and the speedy externalization of his kingdom upon earth [emphasis added]. (*LSR*, 197)

The Dutch Reformed Church of South Africa and the propaganda of Nazi Germany have justified oppression with this same deadly and deadening rhetoric. An inner group—which has access to a higher power—is responsible for others, *to be their brother's keeper*, others who might not be privy to the same exclusive information and would therefore, by implication, not be capable of controlling their own destiny. It is easy to see the appeal of such a message to a white middle class that feels threatened by a non-Great, not-White Brotherhood.

In the early summer of 1989, during the recent rapprochement in U.S.-Soviet relations, Prophet told *Time* that "It is all a trick. They are simply waiting for the right moment to strike. Because the United States has not even seen fit to install a single ABM system we will be in danger of attack during October of this year" (67). In anticipation of that attack, bomb shelters were built for 756 people on the Royal Teton Ranch and over 2,000 people at Glastonbury to provide for the survival of Prophet's adepts after the nuclear holocaust. Umberto Eco describes another form of the Middle Ages as:

Last, very last, but not least, the expectation of the Millennium. These Middle Ages which have haunted every sect fired by enthusiasm still accompany us and will continue to do so, until midnight of the Day After. Source of many insanities, they remain however as a permanent warning. Sometimes it is not so medieval to think that perhaps the end is coming and the Antichrist, in plainclothes, is knocking at the door. (88)

Indeed, the plainclothesmen did come knocking at the door of the Church Universal and Triumphant in September of 1989, when one of the members of Prophet's "Cosmic Honor Guard" was arrested for illegal possession of firearms. He was found to have large sums of cash and enough weapons for a small army. Investigation by the Federal Bureau of Alchohol, Tobacco and Firemarms led to the implication and ultimately, the conviction of Prophet's current husband, Ed Francis, on similar charges. Tennyson's Lancelot might well have suggested to his modern-day predecessor '. . . ye were not once so wise. . .' (92).

While this apocalypse has been late in coming, there have been a series of environmental crises for CUT, including leaking fuel tanks which spilled over 31,000 gallons of gasoline and diesel fuel, an Environmental Protection Agency review of the bomb shelters, and concerns by Yellowstone Park officials over CUT's proposed use of sensitive geothermal resources and treatment of buffalo which ranged out of the Park. So many state and federal agencies have requested information about CUT, Montana Representative Pat Williams formed a task force to help coordinate the various investigations of the state of Montana, the Federal Bureau of Investigation, the Immigration and Naturalization Service, the Bureau of Alcohol, Tobacco and Firearms and the Internal Revenue Service. These efforts rocked the Montana community of the Church Universal and Triumphant, resulting in the exodus of nearly a quarter of the five thousand followers who had settled in the Livingston/Bozeman area by 1989. In discussing Merlin's faults, Prophet unconsciously and ironically foretells what seems to be happening to the carefully redacted Church Universal Triumphant:

Aye, to err is human but to pine for the twin flame that is not there is the lot of many an errant knight or king or lonely prophet who perhaps should have disappeared into the mists rather than suffer sad ignominy for his people. (*SGOP*, 15)

Works Cited

Bainbridge, William Sims. "Cultural Genetics." *Psychiatric Annals*. April 1990.

Dawson, Patrick. "Prophet or Profit?" *Time*. 22 August 1988.

———— Personal interview. 4 April 1991.

Eco, Umberto. *Travels in Hyperreality*. New York: Harcourt-Brace, 1983.

Geoffrey of Monmouth. "Vita Merlini," in *The Quest for Merlin* by Nikolai Tolstoy. Boston: Little Brown & Co., 1985.

Jensen, Holger. "Trouble in Paradise; A doomsday prophet wears out her welcome." *Maclean's*. 7 May 1990.

McMillan, Scott. "Church regroups after turbulent year; Year later, 'life goes on'." Bozeman *Chronicle*. March 1991.

Melton, J. Gordon, ed. *Encyclopedia of American Religions*. Wilmington, NC: McGrath Publishing Co., 1976.

Prophet, Mark L. and Elizabeth Clare Prophet. *Lord of the Seven Rays*. Livingston, MT: Summit UP, 1987.

_____ *The Lost Teachings of Christ: Book 3, Masters and Disciples on the Path.* Livingston, MT: Summit UP, 1986, 1988.

_____ *The Lost Teachings of Christ: Book 4, Good and Evil: Atlantis Revisited.* Livingston, MT: Summit UP, 1986, 1988.

_____ *Saint Germain on Prophecy: Coming World Changes.* Livingston, MT: Summit UP, 1986.

Reich, Wilhelm. *The Mass Psychology of Fascism.* New York: Orgone Institute, 1946.

Rome, Howard P. "Personal Reflections: Cults." *Psychiatric Annals.* April 1990.

Tennyson, Alfred Lord. *Idylls of the King.* Middlesex, England: Penguin Books, Ltd., 1983.

Tennnyson, Hallam Lord. *Alfred Lord Tennyson, A Memoir.* 2 vols. London, 1897.

Variations on Arthurian Legend in
Lancelot du Lac and *Excalibur*

Richard C. Bartone

The parameters of interpretation surrounding Arthurian legend expands as scholars, novelists, poets, musicians and artists incorporate themes from primary sources of medieval times. The voluminous body of secondary sources range from historical, cultural and mythological criticism to poems, novels, plays, paintings, music and films. Arthurian study is enhanced and enriched when a work from a specific medium either broadens the interpretive framework that has circumscribed Arthurian legend or offers an interpretive perspective unique to the expressive resources of the medium being employed. Cinema's channels of articulation, or the aesthetic characteristics of the medium, permits another means to transfigure Arthurian legend. Channels of articulation are the resources available to the filmmaker, including photography (lenses), composition (shot length and framing), editing, camera movement, lighting, color, sound, performance and setting. When these channels of articulation, some inherent to film, produce a thematic investigation of Arthurian legend, the cinematic text contributes a unique interpretive perspective to Arthurian scholarship. Unfortunately, film audiences primarily perceive narrative progression and plot elements, overlooking how other aesthetic characteristics of the medium converge with narrative to interpret myth and history. This essay aims to illustrate cinema's ability to enrich discourse on Arthurian legend.

Lancelot du Lac (1974), written and directed by the French filmmaker Robert Bresson, and *Excalibur* (1981), produced and directed by British filmmaker John Boorman from Sir Thomas Malory's *Le Morte D'Arthur*, take distinctive formal or stylistic approaches to Arthurian legend. The films' formalistic strategies enhance their thematic concerns. The concept of channels of articulation is not unique to cinema. A poet's placement of words on a page is one possible channel of articulation that correlates to theme. The playwright has theatrical devices and stylized patterns of speech to articulate a vision. Each mode of transmitting any aspect of Arthurian legend is circumscribed and defined by the formal or structural tools of the teller, be it artist or scholar. Certain channels of articulation are inherent to a medium, such as editing for film, while other channels are available to different media. Although a channel of articulation may not be inherent to one medium, when it's combined with the inherent aesthetic resources of that medium the complete text (film, novel, criticism, painting, musical composition) exhibits a distinctive production of meaning and interpretive strategy. Cinema's ability to thematically reveal Arthurian legend depends upon the viewer's ability to understand that the various channels of articulation converge and contribute to rigorous discourse.

Internationally, approximately thirty-five films exist under the loose rubric of "Arthurian." The representation of Arthurian legend in film covers a wide range of genres, including comedy, musical, drama, experimental, documentary, non-fiction, romance and action/adventure. Cinema is one conduit for popular culture. But contrary to the beliefs of scholars from established, traditional disciplines, cinema's capacity to produce popular culture does not invalidate its ability to elaborate on Arthurian legend or cultivate Arthurian studies. Films on Arthurian legend have exposed the public to mythology, romance, topography, archaeology, religion, history and a system of values and beliefs rooted in medieval times. *Monty Python and the Holy Grail* (1975) as a comic repudiation of underlying assumptions of Grail mythology causes an uncomfortable recognition of the importance of Arthurian legend in our culture. The popularity of *Indiana Jones and the Last Crusade* (1989) proves the longevity of certain themes in Arthurian legend. Combining puppetry, newsreel footage and filmed theatre, Hans-Jürgen Syberberg employs Wagner's music in *Parsifal* (1982) to examine the influence of mythology on German culture from World War II. The film industry has embraced Arthurian legend and cinematically translated it into many narrative and non-narrative forms. Even in its most popular adaptations, cinema has forced open another path of introspection on Arthurian studies.

Lancelot du Lac, an historical drama, opened in two United States cities and closed after a few weeks, even though it received international acclaim for its uncompromising and imaginative vision. *Excalibur*, an action/adventure, historical drama, opened to mixed reviews, a wide U.S. release, a relatively long run in movie theatres and, now, a new life on videocassette and premium cable channels. The films represent the visions of the filmmakers, unmediated by contracts with a film studio or aggressive producers. *Excalibur* came out of a Hollywood studio arrangement, a joint venture of Columbia-EMI-Warner, but Boorman produced the film and co-wrote the script with Rospo Pallenberg.

Lancelot du Lac: MINIMALISM AND FORMAL CONSTRICTION

Bresson avoids acknowledging any literary sources influential to his original script. But based on Bresson's meticulous post-production process, his stated attraction to the mythological basis of Arthurian legend and a long-standing desire to direct the film, one can infer that Bresson's script arose from an assimilation and synthesis of primary literary documents. Bresson acknowledges one central idea that shaped the film and his vision of medieval times: "A situation in which the knights return to Arthur's castle without the Grail, that is to say the absolute God."[1]

Bresson cinematically structures *Lancelot du Lac* according to dominant thematic preoccupations. Two interrelated themes prevail: first, the failure of the quest for the Holy Grail signals a crisis in faith, leading to medieval society's disintegration; second, the decline of chivalry. *Lancelot du Lac* presents a bleak vision: man does not realize that the antiquated codes of chivalry and the impossible quest signals his own destruction.[2]

Lancelot du Lac begins with Arthur's remaining knights returning, divided and internally menaced after the failed quest for the Grail. Committed to a world permeated by spirituality and loyalty, Lancelot misreads this sign of failure, perceiving his love for Guinevere and deceit of Arthur as causing society's disruption and chaos. Lancelot's crisis is one of faith. He has made an allegiance to Guinevere, or carnal and physical love, and an oath to theistic love. Lancelot demands Guinevere rescind his oath of love, "to conjure fate, and turn away menace."[3] Guinevere's statement to Lancelot articulates Bresson's position on medieval society's illogical allegiance to symbolic theism:

It's not the grail you want to bring home, but God. God is not a trophy to bring home. You were all relentless. Killed, plundered, burned, turned on each other like madmen. And you accuse our love for this disaster.

The impossibility and presumptuousness of the quest for God leads to the destruction of medieval society. The failed quest and an absence of spirituality splinters the faithful and collapses the formal structure of medieval society. Now a fear of unseen, sinister forces, or an evil presence envelops the minds of Lancelot and Arthur's knights.

Lancelot confronts two conflicts: first, an internal crisis of faith and, second, the opposition between loyalty to King and loyalty to an oath (Guinevere). Lancelot's code of loyalty and, consequently, his dichotomy hold no validity in a crumbling medieval society. After almost dying in a jousting match, Lancelot returns to Guinevere, duty bound to his oath. Guinevere, a candid voice for Bresson's vision of medieval society, states that living strictly by a code of loyalty whether to the King or her will hasten an already crumbling world: "Poor, mad Lancelot, trying to stand firm in a shrunken world." Guinevere convinces Lancelot that under the law of the land it's his duty as a knight to return her to Arthur, who decries she is innocent of adultery. Lancelot agrees it's the law but not "justice." Guinevere responding to Lancelot's internal stasis states, "Forget justice." (Bresson's sparse dialogue evokes the essence of a conflict that destroyed medieval society.) After surrendering Guinevere, Lancelot takes the side of Arthur against the rebellious Modred. The film concludes with Lancelot falling into a pile of knights, uttering the word "Guinevere."

Eighty-four minutes of a minimal narrative constructs the framework for a rigorous formalistic interpretation of Arthurian themes. In *Lancelot du Lac* Bresson forwards a contemplative and unified vision of Arthurian legend through extreme formalization. Bresson cinematically transfigures the thematic through heightened attention to the film frame, composition, editing, sound, movement and acting.

According to Bresson, "A film is not a spectacle, it is in the first place a style" (qtd in Armes 91). In *Lancelot du Lac* shot-composition precludes spectacle. We never see groups of knights fighting or action on a battlefield. When two knights fight we see parts of each knight in separate shots (usually medium close-ups): a sword, a helmet, an arm, a torso. Negating narrative exposition and tension, such as knights preparing to attack, also precludes spectacle. Clashes between knights start with their conclusion or immediate defeat. Knights are often concealed by visors, obscuring their identity and viewer involvement with a camp. Bresson reveals only a small section of the Round Table. Unlike most narrative films that start a scene with an establishing shot, we never see the total courtyard and castle, just one exterior castle wall and the windows of Guinevere's room. A jousting match is represented through a series of close-ups and medium shots, restricting a sense of a tournament atmosphere. At the tournament we rarely see two opponents in the same shot. The camera never pulls back and remains stationary to let the tension build as the knights approach impact. Instead, the jousting match is a series of close-ups of lances, helmets and shields, or the feet, belly and tail of a horse. A joust concludes with close-ups of a lance striking a torso or a knight smashing against the earth. A tournament flag rising represents a castle, a close-up of bagpipes represents the knights approaching the gate and a medium shot of the spectators represents the crowd.

Minimizing visual information has expressive ramifications. Bresson sets up compositional constraints, breaking the flow of action through elliptical editing and denying spectacle dominance over a formal contemplative vision. Composition conveys themes. The medieval world is divided and fragmented. In a crisis of spiritual abandonment confusion reigns. Knights do not stand in community with other knights; consequently, jousting matches do not represent a camp, but an individual we cannot identify. The Round Table has no physical continuity and the castle no spacial continuity to bring the knights together as a community.

Bresson uses sound to articulate themes within a narrative framework. At the film's start, an old lady of the forest tells a child: "The knight's whose footsteps you will hear will die in a year." They are Lancelot's footsteps. Announcing Lancelot's inability to change the course of his life also negates suspense for the audience. Sound articulates Bresson's perspectives on knighthood and chivalry. Foreboding is constant in sounds: the neighing of horses signals unrest among the knights, a sense of tension and anxiety. The sound of horses and the close-up of their roving eyes reinforce the theme of a crisis of faith and an unseen presence, or sinister force. For Bresson animals are more perceptive than humans. They see and hear what humans cannot, and they watch with horror the carnage humans inflict upon others.

Sound pushes the viewer to a constitutive, interpretive position. Bresson foregrounds the sound of blood spurting and spilling on the earth. These sounds are amplified, while the action is minimal or partly seen in the frame. The spectacle of war and battle has been transformed into the isolation of sound and the physical draining of the individual. Courage and nobility are reduced to the sounds of steel armor clashing and blood splashing on the earth. These foreboding sounds convey the darker human side of the end of the age of chivalry.

Lancelot du Lac associates the passing of chivalry with physical weightiness. Attention is called to the physical nature of knights, emphasizing men straining to help others onto their horses. The film accentuates the physical falling of knights from their horses. The sound of armor hitting the ground suggests the cumbersome nature of a giant, not the gallantry of knighthood. During the jousting match Bresson pays more attention to the belly and legs of the horse straining to carry the knight in competition, rather than the grace of knights in competition.

Chivalry implies self-discipline and restraint. Bresson literally restrains the knights. Their armor is cumbersome and restrains movement. Chivalry suggests a pattern of behavior that is deemed correct. Bresson's editing repeats patterns of behavior: three shots of men mounting horses, three shots of hands closing visors on helmets, three shots of arms grasping lances. The intensity of restraint and discipline builds in repetition of movements in medium close-ups. Bresson's consistent use of close-ups and medium close-ups resonates on several thematic levels, including chivalry as constraint and a world entrapping the knights. They are repeating noble motions in a world where those motions no longer have consequences.

The slow, cumbersome movement of the knights corresponds to the theme of a society halting, weighed down by its own codes. The majority of shots of knights walking are from the waist down, which also suggests separation from a community of knights. At the jousting match we repeatedly see or hear the fierce impact of knights striking the earth. If the viewer does not derive the theme from formalization, Bresson does permit the dialogue once to imply the condition. Gawain looks at the clouds moving over the sun and states "the clouds are strangling it. We will stifle if we don't strike free." The compositional representation of the knights will not permit freedom.

Bresson does not use professional actors and rejects the codes of a psychological acting style. For psychology and passion Bresson substitutes behavior patterns and types of movement (Sitney 191). Avoiding expressiveness in psychological characterization, actors speak in monotones, clipped clauses, falling inflections and with neutral facial expressions and minimal gestures. The interactions of Lancelot and Guinevere are void of emotions. But each character has a unique absence of expressiveness that sets them apart (Sitney 192). Lancelot touching the Queen's hand in close-up directs viewer attention to the suppression of emotions, the restraint of a loyal, noble knight. "The detachment and retarding of emotions through the consciousness of form makes them far stronger and more intense in the end" (Sontag 181). According to Susan Sontag, "There is art that detaches, that provokes reflection" (177). Bresson substitutes patterns of form and movement for passion in his characters. "What I am seeking is not so much expression by means of gesture, speech, mimicry, but expression by means of the rhythm and combination of images, by position, relation and number" (qtd. in Armes 94).

Characters are passionate and enraged but never express it in a psychological acting style. Bresson's expressive decision on acting style suggests that the discipline of knights accords with the idea of self-discipline. The restraints placed on actors also correlates with chivalry as self-restraint. Bresson alleviates the psychological dimension of actors interpreting characters. Passion and nobility are replaced by the formalization of movement in the frame and intensified through a pattern of editing that repeats movement. But Bresson subverts the concept of nobility by having knights conceal themselves behind helmets. Lack of recognition is a means to subvert nobility and honor.

Formalization in *Lancelot du Lac* internalizes conflict. Bresson perceives chivalry and the absence of spirituality as suffocating knights through stricture, just as religion suffocates through stricture. The characters of *Lancelot du Lac* are trapped in their existence and the formal parameters of Bresson's cinema.

Bresson's uncompromising cinematic style transfigures his subject matter.[4] The expressive ramifications of cinema's channels of articulation and the constraints Bresson imposes on cinema establishes a unified vision of medieval times. *Lancelot du Lac* reveals a perfection of a minimalist style. Through composition, sound and elliptical editing the world portrayed in *Lancelot du Lac* is static, repetitive and void of meaningful action. A crisis of faith is strangling the sacred codes of the medieval world. After Lancelot is shot by arrows he stumbles slowly into the middle of a pile of dead knights. He falls, and the sound of steel permeates the forest. Before dying, Lancelot's body shifts causing one last sound. All that is left of the medieval world is the sound of steel hitting steel, with an empty echo.

Excalibur: FILM FORM AS DREAM

In theme and structure *Excalibur* is diametrically opposed to *Lancelot du Lac*. Although Boorman credits Thomas Malory's *Le Morte D'Arthur*, the film is a complex, creative and imaginative synthesis of characters, symbols and myths from several primary sources.[5] Boorman's film is mythopoetic, and the condensation of numerous sources supports the intensity of Boorman's mythopoetic ambitions. *Excalibur*'s theme is redemption for mankind through an imaginative, internal quest to constitute myth by transcending nature. Merlin and Arthur self-consciously confront their myth-making responsibilities in medieval times. *Excalibur* depicts the internal romantic quest and journey of King Arthur as redeemer.

Why does "Arthurian legend possess such perennial fascination" (Ashe 26) in modern poetry, plays, novels and films? Modern interpretations of Arthurian legend contain misery, struggle, failed quests and shattered romance, but are "endowed...with an aspect of grandeur" and a hope that the "golden age" of Arthurian legend, long lost, is somehow "recoverable" (Ashe 26). *Excalibur* aims to reconstitute the mythical elements of Arthurian legend as accessible to the human imagination and as a tangible dimension of modern dreams for a better self.

In three stunning scenes Boorman acknowledges hope through myth and dream. By the film's final act, Arthur recognizes his existence as vital to myth-making. After drinking from the Grail, brought by Perceval, Arthur affirms faith in himself (and individualism): "I lived through others for too long. Lancelot carried my honor. Guinevere my guilt. Modred my sins. My knights fought my battles. Now...I shall be King."[6] As Arthur and his knights rush on horseback to Guinevere, flowers, plants and trees miraculously blossom and brighten. We are in the world of dream. With heroic prophecy and romantic self-consciousness, Arthur proclaims to Guinevere:

I was not born to live a man's life, but to be the stuff of future memory. The fellowship was a brief beginning that cannot be forgotten because it will not be forgotten, and that fair time may come again. Now I must ride with my knights to defend what was and the dream of what could be.

Arthur places himself in the romantic movement "to the imagination's freedom" (Bloom 6). Romantic freedom, according to Harold Bloom, is "frequently puritanical, redemptive in direction..." (6). Arthur acknowledges that this internal quest to find "paradises within a renovated man" will result in an expanded consciousness and an "acute preoccupation with the self" (Bloom 6). Before Arthur leaves Guinevere in the nunnery, he articulates the precise journey of romantic self-consciousness: "I often thought in the hereafter of life, when I owe no more to the future, I can be just a man. If we meet you will come to me and claim me yours and know that I am your husband. It's a dream that I have."

Thematically, *Excalibur* proclaims Arthurian legend as necessary for human hope today and future aspirations. The three statements above are central thematic pronouncements of Arthur overcoming the "recalcitrance in the self," or the "unwilling dross that checks the spirit's flight" (Bloom 11) that permeated the Round Table until Arthur drank from the Grail. Before drinking from the Grail Arthur is immobile, noting, "I cannot die and I cannot live." Arthur finally achieves the romantic preoccupation with self, a self-consciousness that will permit imaginative quest, and the closure to the myth.

Excalibur constitutes the medieval world as dream. From dreams flow myth, and Arthur initially struggles to create mythical form from a dream world. Arthur must transcend nature through imagination. "Romantic or internalized romance, especially in its purest vision of the quest form, tends to see the content of nature as a trap for the mature imagination" (Bloom 10). When Arthur asks Merlin what it means to be King, he responds, "You will be the land and the land will be you." This statement condenses the most important underlying concept in *Excalibur*, and the interpretive key to its narrative form. Merlin perceives nature, the land, as imagination or myth. Romantic quest is against the imagination's containment by forms of external reality, or nature. An imaginative vision, myth-making, is a difficult and terrifying internal quest, where "the power of the mind over outward sense is so great that the ordinary forms of nature seem to have withdrawn" (Bloom 21). When Merlin notices Arthur's fright at the sights and sounds of night he proceeds to ominously tell Arthur, "what is out there: the dragon. The heart of such power that if you were to see it whole and all complete in a single glance it would burn you to cinders." Merlin's dragon is imagination, "which is everywhere and everything." Arthur fears the romantic terror of imagination transcending nature. Appropriately, Merlin's metaphoric portrait of the dragon captures the startling power of a visionary state to negate nature's constraints on perception. Merlin's advice to young Arthur is, "Be still. Sleep. Rest in the arms of the dragon. Dream." At *Excalibur*'s conclusion Arthur is a visionary and the land is dream, the imagination or romantic self-consciousness.

Boorman configures the medieval world as a dream and, consequently, formalistically structures *Excalibur* as a dream work. When Freud analyzed dreams he described their workings in terms of condensation, displacement, representability and dramatization (Freud, *Interpretation* 83, 311-385). Freud went on to investigate the structural and psychological correlations between dreams (latent and manifest content) and works of art exhibiting formal characteristics of dreams (Freud, *On Creativity*). Since *Excalibur* is the representation of a dream world, on a literal level the four concepts above apply to Boorman's visual and structural approach.

Dramatization, the easiest concept to grasp, states that latent thoughts (the unconscious) become manifest in the work of art through the narrative. For Freud dreams are narrative "picture puzzles" derived from the "unfolding dramas of the mind" (Spector 88, 93). These narratives are subject to the unpredictable, illogical working of the mind. *Excalibur*'s structure, its narrative turns, come from the mind of Merlin. Merlin's sudden appearances, decisions and actions conjure up the central plot elements and twists. Joseph Campbell's words are appropriate for the narrative structure of *Excalibur*: "Merlin was the great 'guru' of the Arthurian world. He had the whole program in his mind" (*Transformations* 214). Merlin invokes the dragon's breath for Uther to ride over water, reach Igrayne and satisfy his lust. Merlin saves Lancelot's life knowing Lancelot will sleep with Guinevere, advancing the myth. At the film's conclusion Arthur requests Merlin's magic. Tired, Merlin says to Arthur, "Your love brought me back to where you are now, in the land of dreams." Merlin then writes the future plot elements, defeating Morgana and creating the fog for Arthur's victory, to complete the mythopoetic scenario.

Excalibur has a frenetic, elliptical pace in scene progression. After Arthur and Lancelot's confrontation on the bridge, and the Lady of the Lake mending the shattered tip of Excalibur, Boorman cuts to the triumphant conclusion of the wars and then Lancelot escorting Guinevere to Arthur. The narrative Merlin weaves is, at times, intentionally puzzling, supporting Freud's notion of the mind's drama. The coils of the dragon, or the underground ice cave where Merlin takes Morgana to reveal the sacred charm of making, becomes a narrative puzzle as Boorman cuts between the cave, Guinevere and Lancelot's encounter in the woods, and Arthur discovering them. After this extended scene, three rapid scenes follow: Morgana, transformed into Guinevere, seduces Arthur; Morgana gives birth to Modred; and Arthur is struck by lightning at a ceremony requesting God's protection against Morgana. Boorman's narrative sweeps through myth, presenting fragments of myth, and suggests myth is as much puzzlement as it is substance. The narrative rhythm precludes assimilation and comprehension of the many fragmentary references to Arthurian legend.

Condensation, displacement and representability are intertwined concepts that explain the representational nature of dreams. In condensation many latent ideas, concepts and narratives are collapsed and condensed into specific film scenes or images. In addition, only certain latent elements appear in the manifest dream work, or the film. In displacement one latent idea is replaced "by something more remote" or obscure (Freud, *General Introduction* 182). You invest your emotions and energy in one direction, which serves as a displacement for confronting the real issue. Freud characterizes "the transformation of thoughts into visual images" (*General Introduction* 183) as representability, or the task of interpreting images. The difficulty with interpreting a dream, or film as a dream work, is that a symbol or image can be ambiguous and contain multiple meanings.

Condensation is abundant in *Excalibur*, and this abundance is one characteristic of the film's form as dream. Condensation implies that what we see is a "brief, meager" (*Interpretation* 313) form of a larger narrative or conceptual frame. But by only presenting a small fragment of that concept, or indirect references to a story or image, *Excalibur* is like a dream. The viewer must work to "disentangle meaning" (*Interpretation* 311) from fragments, always remaining uncertain of interpretation from what appears, or the manifest content. Three specific examples will establish the basic nature of condensation. The Lady of the Lake appears in three scenes: to give Arthur the sword, to hold and mend the broken sword and, finally, to receive the sword. Only in the second scene do we see the complete figure of the Lady of the Lake, and we must infer her role as guardian, ever present in nature, with powers superior enough to mend what Merlin says cannot be broken. After the birth of Modred and Arthur's incapacitation, the waste land spreads. Boorman introduces a complex concept, the waste land as a result of moral deprivation. But later in the film, Lancelot, now a beggar in the waste land, says, "They made themselves Gods and Christ has abandoned us." In both examples, the Lady of the Lake and the waste land, what is manifest or introduced in the film presents threads to a hidden or latent content that could offer deeper insights when intellectually mined, or disentangled by the viewer. The Holy Grail, *Excalibur*'s largest condensation, or omission, serves several functions. But its primary condensed function is narrative, a quest for the knights, because only it "can restore leaf and flower." Boorman resists interpretation of the Holy Grail's source of power or its religious implications.

Condensation's complexity enters when we realize that what is presented in collapsed form can possibly be explained through displacement. The quest for the Grail is Arthur's means to deny the consequences of placing the knights' code of honor over love for Guinevere, his wife. Arthur drove Guinevere into the arms of Lancelot when Arthur placed law above wife. By embedding Excalibur into the rock between Lancelot and Guinevere, Arthur relinquishes a symbol of his power as King, and the waste land appears. The quest for the Grail displaces Arthur's refusal to recognize and renounce his mistake. When Arthur announces that the knights must find what was lost, Arthur is refusing to look into his own heart for the cause of the crisis.

Words can function as displacement. Merlin's stated position throughout the film displaces his true intentions: to control myth-making. At the film's start Merlin allows Uther to satisfy his lust, producing Arthur, and proclaims: "The future has taken root in the present. It's done." After this Merlin periodically repeats the same concept: "My days are ending. The gods are going forever. This is a time for men. This world is done with me." Merlin does not believe this, nor does he want to vanish from the land. Merlin is pleased when Arthur's love breaks Morgana's spell and brings him back to the land of dreams. When Arthur finds out that Guinevere is with Lancelot he asks Merlin for advice: "I can tell you nothing. My days are ending. This is the moment you must face, at last to be King." Following their exchange we see Merlin's proud face as he states with determination, "That's it." Merlin relishes his role in the mythopoetic in writing the scenario, and his statements only serve to displace his true intentions.

Excalibur announces itself as a dream by employing dreams as a form of exposition. This strategy foregrounds the problem of representability, or the interpretation of dream images to reveal latent content. Lancelot's intense passion for Guinevere but equally intense desire to crush that passion is conveyed in a dream where Lancelot's armor attacks the naked Lancelot, piercing his side with a lance. The dream sequences central to the themes of *Excalibur* involve Perceval's search for the Grail. Perceval, lured by Modred into Morgana's lair, hangs from a tree with the decayed bodies of other knights. Dangling, Perceval dreams of the Grail: a draw bridge opens and reveals a large chalice suspended in air. Perceval, frightened by an omnipotent voice asking, "What is the secret of the Grail?" and "Who does it serve?" runs as the draw bridge closes. As he hangs on to the bridge Boorman cross-cuts to his boot's rowel cutting the rope from the tree. Perceval falls from the tree, denouncing his failure to procure the Grail. A few scenes later the people, disenchanted with Arthur's abandonment of them, beat Perceval into a stream. Submerged, Perceval sheds his clothes and rises up to enter the Grail Castle. To the question "Who am I?" Perceval responds, "Arthur, the King." To the question "Have you found the secret that I have lost?" Perceval answers, "You and the land are one." He reaches for the Chalice, turns and presents it to Arthur with the words, "Drink from the Chalice and you will be reborn, and the land with you."

Boorman conceives of the Holy Grail as an object of Perceval's dream, and Perceval's Grail quest as Arthur's dream. In *Excalibur* this elaborate dream forces a repressed concept into Arthur's consciousness: Arthur has blocked the power of the imaginative self to forge a vision for the future. Audience puzzlement over the intangible nature of the Grail, Perceval's sudden appearance next to Arthur with the Grail, and Arthur's sudden recognition is not unfounded. But if we understand these images and dreams, the external quest itself, as latent manifestations of Arthur's internal quest, *Excalibur* regains coherency. Coherency does not imply clarity in dream images or symbols. The sacred charm of making, possessed by Merlin, can be imagination, consciousness or myth itself. Boorman associates Excalibur with Arthur's visionary quest, and specifically, the tool to transform the land into imagination or legend. When Arthur forces the sword into stone between Lancelot and Guinevere, Lancelot proclaims: "The King without a sword, the land without a King." At the moment the sword enters the stone it also pierces Merlin. The sword impaling Merlin facilitates the viewer to construct the possible symbolic meanings of Excalibur. On a literal level, Arthur's action puts a stop to the mythopoetic scenario. The most incomprehensible aspect of *Excalibur* is how Guinevere obtained the sword, which she gives to Arthur at the nunnery. Boorman is not interested in logic, but in dreams. Arthur comes to Guinevere and announces his imaginative quest, the dream about to unfold. Presenting Arthur with Excalibur is Guinevere's gesture of love. Love and hope for a future reunion start Arthur's final journey. When we realize that lust, engineered by Merlin, starts the narrative, Guinevere's action resonates with meaning.

Conclusion: A CONTRAST IN VISIONS

The final battle scene of *Lancelot du Lac* includes the following images: arrows striking a knight on a horse, arrows striking a tree, a riderless horse gallops through the forest, arrows strike a tree, another riderless horse, a close-up of an arrow in the head of Lancelot's horse, Lancelot gets up and falls into a pile of dead knights. The scene's two dominant colors are dark brown and a dull green. It would take two pages to describe the choreographed violence on the massive battlefield that ends *Excalibur*. After the major battle, Arthur and Modred impale each other with lances. On a battlefield cluttered with dead bodies and blood, a blazing, setting sun provides a dream-like backlight to the two bodies propped up by lances. *Excalibur* ends with the image of Arthur's body on a ship, surrounded by maidens, going out to sea. Boorman's cinematic landscape ensures that the myth Arthur constructed will stay embedded in the imagination. Bresson leaves the viewer with an eerie sense of isolation and silence, as if the world of Arthur has disappeared from history and memory. Boorman's world, like dreams, are cluttered, frenetic and mystifying, evoking an enchanting fascination with the journey for salvation by men determined to regain honor and a place in history. Bresson's world is still and sparse, the individual unrecognizable, and viewer reflection on the value or purpose of the age of chivalry constrained by Bresson's formal rigidness. In both narratives cinema's aesthetic characteristics have expanded the parameters of introspection on Arthurian legend.

Notes

[1]This statement released in 1974 under the heading "Robert Bresson on *Lancelot of the Lake*" appears in the publicity packet distributed by New Yorker Films, 16 West 61st Street, New York, NY 10023. Since Bresson rarely gives interviews, he possibly prepared a statement for informational packets distributed at film festivals.

[2]I am indebted to Noel Carroll, Cornell University, for the methodological approach to analyzing Bresson's film form in *Lancelot Du Lac*.

[3]All dialogue is taken from the 16mm subtitled version provided by New Yorker Films. *Lancelot Du Lac*, dir. Robert Bresson, with Luc Simon, Laura Duke Condominas, Humbert Balsan, and Vladimir Antolek-Oresek. Photo. Pasqualino de Santis, ed. Germaine Lamy. Mara Films, ORTF, Laser Productions, Jerico Sound, 84 minutes, 1974.

[4]Bresson has detailed his philosophy of cinema in the following book: Robert Bresson, *Notes on Cinematography* (Massachusetts: Salem House Books, 1989).

[5]Wolfram von Eschenbach, *Parzival* (New York: Random House, 1961). Chretien de Troyes, *Arthurian Romances* (London: J.M. Dent & Sons, 1914). *The Romance of Tristan and Isolt*, Trans. Norman B. Spector. (Evanston: Northwestern UP, 1973). Geoffrey of Monmouth, *Histories of the Kings of Britain* (New York: E.P. Dutton, 1912).

[6]All dialogue comes from the videocassette version distributed by Warner Brothers. *Excalibur*, dir. and prod. John Boorman, with Nigel Terry, Nicol Williamson, Nicholas Clay, Helen Mirren, Cheri Lunghi and Paul Geoffrey. Photo. Alex Thomson, ed. John Merritt, mus. Trevor Jones. Warner Bros., 140 minutes, 1981.

Works Cited

Armes, Roy. "Robert Bresson." *Great Film Directors: A Critical Anthology*. Ed. Leo Braudy and Morris Dickstein. New York. Oxford UP, 1978.

Ashe, Geoffrey. "The Convergence of Arthurian Studies." *The Arthurian Tradition: Essays in Convergence*. Ed. Mary Flowers Braswell and John Bugge. Tuscaloosa: U of Alabama P, 1988.

Bloom, Harold. "The Internalization of Quest Romance." *Romanticism and Consciousness: Essays in Criticism.* Ed. Harold Bloom. New York: Norton & Company, 1970.

Campbell, Joseph. *Transformations of Myth Through Time.* New York: Harper & Row, 1990.

Freud, Sigmund. *The Interpretation of Dreams.* Ed. and trans. James Strachey. New York: Avon, 1965.

———— *A General Introduction to Psychoanalysis.* Trans. Joan Riviere. New York: Pocket Books, 1953.

———— *On Creativity and the Unconscious.* Ed. Ernest Jones. Trans. Joan Riviere. New York: Harper Colophon Books, 1958.

Mallory, Sir Thomas. *Le Morte D'Arthur.* Ed. Janet Cowen. 2 vols. New York: Penguin Classics, 1969.

Sitney, Adams P. "The Rhetoric of Robert Bresson." *The Essential Cinema.* Ed. P. Adams Sitney. New York: New York UP, 1975.

Sontag, Susan. *Against Interpretation.* New York: Dell, 1966.

Spector, Jack J. *The Aesthetics of Freud: A Study in Psychoanalysis and Art.* New York: Praeger, 1972.

Hollywood's Myopic Medievalism:
Ecalibur and Malory's *Morte d'Arthur*

Liam O. Purdon and Robert Blanch

Hollywood's most ambitious rendition of Malory's *Morte d'Arthur* is John Boorman's 1981 box-office disaster, *Excalibur*. Unlike other films treating Arthurian characters or subjects, films such as *Prince Valiant* (1954: directed by Henry Hathaway), *Monty Python and the Holy Grail* (1975: directed by Terry Gilliam and Terry Jones), or even the more recent *Sword of the Valiant* (1984: Directed by Stephen Weeks), Boorman and Rospo Pallenberg's screenplay version of Malory's *Morte d'Arthur* attempts to capture the full sweep of the legend of Arthur.

In order to achieve this goal, Boorman and Pallenberg, like Malory before them, labor to thin the romantic forest. While they enter the literary woods, lopping off the "Tale of Sir Gareth," the "Tale of Sir Tristram," and the "Tale of Arthur and Emperor Lucius," the full effect of their pruning is not as drastic as might be expected when more than half of an original work is eliminated. They do preserve, for example, part of the "Tale of King Arthur," sections of the "Tale of Lancelot du Lake," the "Tale of the Sankgreal," the "Book of Lancelot and Queen Guenevere," and the "Tale of Morte Arthur Saunz Guerdon." In addition, while retaining and transforming other minor parts of the cut narrative, Boorman and Pallenberg, unlike Malory, add to the miraculous.

It is unclear whether the screenwriters' preoccupation with miracles or marvels bears the imprint of T.H. White's *Once and Future King*, Tennyson's *Idylls of the King*, or both works. What is certain, however, is that this thematic strategy paradoxically unifies and weakens the film, thereby revealing a myopic historical view of the Middle Ages and Malory's medievalism. One obvious way this ahistorical reliance on or use of the miraculous is revealed in the film can be seen in Boorman and Pallenberg's treatment of Excalibur. This essay will examine that emphasis and consider how it departs from Malory's conception of feudal custom and practice as a unifying social and political strategy.

The film alerts the audience to the sword even before the film begins, for Boorman and Pallenberg introduce, in what might be termed a cinematographic prologue, the three major thematic concerns of their version of the *Morte d'Arthur*. Out of the dark suddenly flash the following lines:

> Out of those lost centuries
> Rose a legend...
> Of a sorcerer, Merlin...

Of the coming of a king...
Of the sword of power...
Excalibur

This prologue certainly pales when compared with other introductory statements like "Of Man's first disobedience, and the fruit/Of that forbidden tree...." But the intended effect is the same. As Milton completes the description of his epic's scope by acknowledging our restoration by means of "one Greater Man," Boorman and Pallenberg identify the principal focus of their work by acknowledging the legend of Excalibur last. Their use of the initial phrase "Out of those lost centuries" signalizes perhaps their limited historical perspective and knowledge of medieval literature. This feature of the introduction, however, is quickly forgotten when, immediately following the word "power," the word "Excalibur" itself appears, glowing with almost a phosphorescent green and resounding with a metallic clank, like a sword being beaten on an anvil.

Thus developing the emphasis on Excalibur established by the film's prologue, Boorman and Pallenberg treat the sword as the principal means by which order and peace are brought to the beleaguered peoples of Britain. At the beginning of the film, for example, Uther wants the sword because this powerful weapon will enable him to defeat the petty kings and dukes against whom he fights. Later, after Merlin has given him the sword and convinced him that the sword should be used "to heal rather than hack," the sword is employed to forge an alliance between Cornwall's men and Uther's band. In this particular scene Merlin unveils the sword's significance before the two armies standing in a meadow. After instructing Uther to show the sword, still aglow with a slightly green phosphorescence, Merlin says: "Behold the sword of power, forged when the world was yet young," etc. Following these words, Merlin asks Uther to raise the sword and to utter the socio-political concept of "One land, one king," a notion which assures Cornwall that his fief will remain intact. For Boorman and Pallenberg, then, the sword functions initially as a magical or miraculous symbol around which even adversaries may unite.

When war breaks out shortly afterward—a war sparked in part by Igrayne's dirty dancing and by Uther's mead-induced, unbridled lust—Boorman and Pallenberg reintroduce the film's principal motif, the idea of the sword as the only means of bringing peace to the land. This time, however, the restorative power of the sword is more real than symbolic, though something of the symbolic survives.

Once he is ambushed by Cornwall's men while attempting to retrieve his recently born son, Arthur, from Merlin, Uther thrusts Excalibur into a stone and dies. After a grown-up Arthur, a squire to Kay, pulls the sword out of the stone, those witnessing the miracle wish to proclaim Arthur their king, for the prophecy has been fulfilled. However, as soon as Arthur journeys to the forest to ask Merlin about the meaning of kingship, Arthur is thrust suddenly in the midst of a medieval combat where Excalibur as an actual tool for forging peace must be used. Sallying forth to the uplifting, driving rhythm of Carl Orff's *Carmina Burana*, Arthur, who has already pronounced himself king, brandishes green-glowing Excalibur and leads his rag-tag forces into battle.

With Excalibur (and with a little help from Merlin), Arthur nearly defeats single-handedly the whole baronial host laying siege to king Lodegreauns' castle. Excalibur of course cuts through everything and gives off such a light that even greenclad Guenevere notices the young king coming to her rescue. What is significant, however, is that the true miraculous power of the sword brings the struggle to an end.

Additional episodes in *Excalibur* call attention to the miraculous force of the sword. In Arthur's battle with Uriens, for instance, the power of Excalibur compels the recalcitrant baron to dub Arthur a knight. Several scenes later, when Arthur encounters Lancelot at the bridge, the king strikes down Lancelot and breaks the sword. Mortified by his unchivalric behavior (pride), Arthur then casts the broken weapon into the lake. The miraculous potency of Excalibur, however, is revealed when the Linda Evans look-alike Lady of the Lake floats to the surface of the water and returns the sword intact. At the conclusion of the film, the mortally wounded Arthur implores Perceval, not Bedivere, to throw Excalibur in the lake. After one feigned attempt, Perceval obeys his king and hurls the weapon far out into the water. Then, just before it hits the water's surface, the sword is grasped by the hand of the lake and is submerged until Arthur or one like him should return to rule the kingdom.

In general, Boorman and Pallenberg's treatment of the sword as the unifying motif in *Excalibur* causes this version of Malory to deviate from the original in many ways. Uther, for example, neither wants nor possesses Excalibur in the *Morte d'Arthur*. Furthermore, the miracle of Arthur's pulling the sword out of the stone is not set in a primeval forest before knights and garrulous peasants, but rather in front of St. Paul's, before baronial knights and commons. While Arthur uses Excalibur to fight the baronial wars in Malory's version, he actually loses the sword in his encounter with Pellinor, not with Lancelot. In addition, while Excalibur shines with the glow of twenty lamps (300 watts), the sword's scabbard, not the sword, is invested with magical powers. Even more importantly, in Malory's version, the miraculous force of Excalibur fails to unite the land; a renewed understanding and shrewd appropriation of the rite of vassalic obligation, including enfeoffment, however, does bring peace to the realm.

When Uther dies in Malory's *Morte d'Arthur*, a feudal upheaval occurs. As petty kings and barons vie for power, Merlin—a Machiavellian diplomatic figure—attempts to bring order by assembling all the barons of the realm to witness a Yuletide miracle. Although Arthur pulls the sword out of the stone, he is not recognized as king since he is not a feudal noble. Finally, under pressure from the commons or burgess class, not from tattered peasants and members of the Society for Creative Anachronism who appear in the film, Arthur is chosen king. To generate stability, however, Arthur does not raise Excalibur and go to war. Instead, he is dubbed knight by the "best man that was there," not by Uriens. After he has been crowned king, Arthur urges his knights to do homage and to swear fealty to him. In turn, Arthur renews feudal law and custom, including the review of property disputes and the return of fiefs to their rightful lords:

Also thenne he made alle lordes that helde of the croune to come in and to do servyce as they oughte to doo. And many complayntes were made unto sir Arthur of grete wronges that were done syn dethe of kyng Uther...; wherfor Kynge Arthur maade the londes to be yeven ageyne unto them that oughte hem. (11)

Arthur himself soon underscores the importance and implicit efficacy of this feudal means of establishing order. When rebuked by kings and knights after inviting them to a great feast, Arthur reiterates his concern with homage and fealty, for he asserts boldly he will "make them to bowe" (13). Thus Arthur forces the knights to submit to his lordship and to do homage, especially since bowing represents part of the actual rite of vassalage.[1] Accordingly, when Arthur has finally won, he turns again to feudal custom and practice to confirm the peace. While many lords do homage to Arthur after battle, a woman, Lyonors, also appears among them to participate in the rite:

Than in the meanewhyle there com a damesell that was an erlis doughter; hys name was Sanam and hir name was Lyonors, a passynge fayre damesell. And so she cam thidir fo to do omage as other lordis ded after that grete batayle. (30)

The inclusion of Lyonors in this feudal ritual is not particularly unusual, for numerous women in the age of Malory had inherited substantial fiefs under Anglo-Norman law. However, Lyonors' act of homage, Malory reveals, is not as important as her ability to conceive a son, an event triggered by her encounter with Arthur.

As "North Walis" and "Irelonde," the last parts of the British Isles to remain defiant, refuse to be subdued by Arthur's forces, Malory retraces the significance of feudal rite and custom as the pathways to peace and order. King Roynes of North Wales, for example, informs Arthur that he has consolidated his forces by defeating eleven kings, monarchs who have been forced to do homage to Roynes. Arthur, however, responds brusquely to this pronouncement of feudal solidarity by dismissing any need for homage to the Welsh king. Furthermore, he asserts to Roynes' messenger that Roynes should become an Arthurian vassal:

But telle thou thy kynge thus, that I owghe hym [none homage] ne none of myne elders; but or hit be longe to, he shall do me omage on bothe his knees, other ellis he shall lese hys hede, by the fayth of my body! For thys ys the moste shamefullyste message that ever y herde speke off. I have aspyed thy kynge never yette mette with worshipfull man. But telle hym I woll have hys hede withoute he do me omage. (43-44)

Somewhat later, when Balyn and Balan defeat Roynes' guard and subdue the king, they spare the monarch's life provided that he go with them to Arthur's court and do service unto the king. Malory uses this incident to demonstrate how a knight who has fallen out of favor with his lord may reclaim his right as a trustworthy vassal through an homage of atonement. When Arthur discovers who has sent King Roynes to him, Arthur predictably laments his previous expulsion of Balyn from the court. Guided by Merlin's advice, Arthur recants his former decision regarding Balyn and prepares for battle against King Roynes' brother, Nero. Once Roynes declares his fidelity to Arthur, he is included in the feudal order of Arthur's kingdom. Furthermore, Roynes' rite of homage generates other possibilities—subinfeudation and liege homage, especially since Roynes, as his messenger previously noted, had received homage from eleven kings.

To demonstrate the importance of homage and fealty, Malory also introduces the idea of specific or individual homage. When Arthur is about to marry Guenevere in the "Torre and Pellinor" episode of the "Tale of King Arthur," Merlin, still more of a diplomat than a necromancer, insists that each of the 28 knights of the Round Table do homage to the king in order to benefit from the king's maintenance:

Fayre sirres, ye muste all aryse and come to Kynge Arthure for to do hym omage; he woll the better be in wylle to mayntayne you. (73)

At the end of the same episode, Malory depicts Arthur as completing the stabilization of the realm through the establishment of feudal tenures. This part of "Torre and Pellinor" has often been identified as the focal point wherein the code of knightly conduct is both defined and affirmed by the knights of the Round Table. It should be noted, however, that the so-called Pentecostal Oath follows Arthur's enfeoffment of his knights, the completion of a military homage under militant kingship:[2]

...than the kynge stablysshed all the knightes and gaff them rychesse and londys; and charged them never to do outerage nothir morthir, and allwayes to fle treson, and to gyff mercy unto hym that askith mercy, uppon payne of forfiture [of their] worship and lordship of kynge Arthure for evirmore.... (91)

Once Malory establishes homage, fealty, and enfeoffment as the means by which the kingdoms and principalities of the realm are to be woven together in a larger political order, he explores the complications fueled by such feudal custom and practice. Two examples may clearly illustrate this point. The first of these involves the encounter between Arthur and Accolon. Morgan le Fay's craft nearly results in the death of her brother, Arthur. Yet when Accolon and Arthur identify themselves, the audience's attention shifts abruptly from Morgan and her wiles to the concept of fidelity and true kingship, for Accolon repents his treason and acknowledges that Arthur is his liege lord:

A Lordis! This kynght that I have foughten withall is the moste man of prouesse and of worship in the worlde, for hit is hymself Kynge Arthure, oure all lyege lorde, and with myssehappe and myssadventure have I done this batayle with the lorde and kynge that I am withholden withall. (107)

The second example involves Arthur's subsequent judgment of Sir Damas. This introduces the subject of aids and incidents, emphasizing the latter in the judicial decision Arthur makes regarding tangible income. Arthur declares that, because Damas is guilty of excessive pride and villainy, Damas must give his entire "manner with the apportenaunce" to his brother, Outelake, in return for a yearly tribute of "a palfrey to ryde uppon" since he is not worthy of a courser.

In conclusion, scholars have often demonstrated how the themes of love, disguise, and loyalty unify the entire *Morte d'Arthur*. Likewise, scholars have shown how Malory systematically reduces the miraculous in his sources in order to revalorize the concept. While the miraculous plays an important role in the *Morte*, Malory realistically sketches the unification of a feudal kingdom by emphasizing inevitable feudal warfare and practical feudal custom and practice. However, Boorman and Pallenberg, like other contemporary screenwriters, exploit warfare and the miraculous in *Excalibur*, but their apparent ignorance of real feudal custom and practice makes their treatment of feudal warfare ahistorical and their view of feudal life trivial. Since people of the twentieth century reflect the intense medieval interests in wealth and property, it should seem likely that film producers would create films that emphasize the customs of mutual obligation and land tenure in the Middle Ages. But, then, a film title like *Feudal Land Tenures in Frensham, Farnham, Surrey: 1200-1460* would no doubt attract even fewer customers than did *Excalibur*.

Notes

[1] See, for example, Galbert of Bruges, *The Murder of Charles the Good*, trans, and ed. James Bruce Ross (Toronto: U of Toronto P, 1982), 206-207.

[2] For a discussion of specific homage under militant kingship, see Thomas N. Bisson, "The Problem of Feudal Monarchy: Aragón, Catalonia, and France," *Speculum* 53 (1978): 468-478.

Works Cited

Bisson, Thomas N. "The Problem of Feudal Monarchy: Aragón, Catalonia, and France," *Speculum* 53 (1978): 460-478.

Excalibur, dir. John Boorman, screenplay, Rospo Pallenberg, Orion, 1981.

Galbert of Bruges. *The Murder of Charles the Good*. Trans. and ed. James Bruce Ross. Toronto: The U of Toronto P, 1982.

Sir Thomas Malory, *Works*. Ed. Eugéne Vinaver. London and New York: Oxford UP, 1966.

Acting Out an Old Story:
Twentieth-Century Tristan Plays

Alan Lupack

In the history of Arthurian literature there have been times when one genre or another has been dominant. For example, the Arthurian legend was most likely to be treated in a poem during the Victorian period, a novel in the latter half of the twentieth century and most recently in a trilogy of novels (as the completed or projected works of such writers as Mary Stewart, Gillian Bradshaw, Richard Monaco, Vera Chapman, Sharan Newman, Stephen Lawhead, Fay Sampson and Persia Woolley suggest). In the period from 1895 to about 1930, the most popular form was the play. About sixty-five Arthurian plays were written in these years.

The quantity of Arthurian drama in this period was probably due largely to the popularity of the 1895 production of J. Comyns Carr's spectacular *King Arthur*, starring Ellen Terry as Guinevere and Henry Irving as Arthur. Adding to the allure of the romantic theme and the famous actors were set and costume designs by Burne-Jones and music by Sir Arthur Sullivan (of Gilbert and Sullivan fame); *King Arthur* thus had all the makings of a memorable theatrical event with lasting influence.

Among the many English and American Arthurian plays following this production, a large number, seventeen in fact written between 1900 and 1930, focus on the legend of Tristan and Isolt. One might expect plays dealing with a similar theme to be tediously alike and depressingly derivative. After all, the legend demands certain things, and straying too far from the pattern of the received story invites criticism for tampering with the traditional. Yet there is surprising variety among these plays, and several even chart with great success the dangerous waters between the Scylla of obsequious subservience to the medieval stories and the Charybdis of overly clever invention.

Of course, not all are so successful. The first of the Tristan plays to be published in the twentieth century, *Isolt* by Antonia R. Williams (1900), is, as its subtitle "A New Telling" implies, an obvious and deliberate departure from the medieval traditions. Williams' attempt at newness takes the form of turning the play into a rather heavy-handed allegory of "Two Ideas in Conflict: Love and Fear" and of giving the tragic story a happy ending. The fact that this ending seems artificial—a distortion of the tradition rather than an addition to it—demonstrates the difficulty of using a well-known story in an original way. In the balance between tradition and originality, Williams puts too much weight on originality. Led astray by her allegory, she has undervalued the story and even the characters. And yet the attempt to make something new of the old tale is the same approach used in various ways and with varying degrees of success in the Tristan plays that follow.

At the opposite extreme is a play by Maurice Baring, which tries too hard to retell the medieval story without sufficient originality to create a sense of newness. In a note to his *Tristram and Iseult: A Play in Five Acts* (1911), Baring says that the subject matter of his play is almost entirely taken from Bédier's compilation of the Tristram legends (89). But what works in Bédier's leisurely prose narrative does not work in a relatively short play.

Baring is a good example of a writer overburdened by the weight of tradition, a writer who might have benefited from a balance between his own approach and that of Antonia Williams. He seems so anxious to include motifs and elements of plot from his source that he pays little attention to dramatic development, motivation or even plausibility. For example, in Act I, Scene iv, Tristram and Iseult, seeing Mark's shadow as they are about to meet for a lover's assignation, speak in such a way as to convince Mark that they are guiltless. The scene closes with Mark's statement: "Oh! blessed be this hour! Praise be to God! Tristram, my son, why did I doubt of you?" (108). In the next scene, after an exchange between Tristram and Iseult, Mark and Andret enter; and the first words the king utters since his joy in Scene iv are "Tristram, to-morrow you shall die..." (114). Almost all the scenes in the play are brief, and this example is typical of the way the action leaps from one traditional event or motif to another with little regard for dramatic structure. In short, there seems no point to Baring's reworking of the legend but to rehash traditional motifs.

A similar flaw mars *Tristram and Iseult* (1930) by Amory Hare (pseudonym of [Mary] Amory Hare Hutchinson). In an author's note, Hare suggests that Masefield (and Edwin Arlington Robinson, whose poem *Tristram* appeared in the same year as Masefield's play) "departed considerably from the traditions of the old manuscripts" (8) and that she owes "the greater portion of my play" to Bédier's rendition and to other medieval sources—except that she has omitted "the supernatural elements" (8-9). Unfortunately, as with Maurice Baring's play, which also claimed to use Bédier as its source, Hare's play is too derivative and unfocused. Her notion of character creating destiny seems to be an afterthought rather than a determining force or an essential element in the development of the play. As a result, her creation is not nearly so interesting as those she criticizes.

A number of authors, however, achieve a better balance between authority and imagination. Some of them use original structural devices to reshape the story. Louis Anspacher, for example, in *Tristan and Isolde: A Tragedy* (1904) tries to present the elements of the tragedy in the space of one day. The first act begins in "late afternoon," and the fifth and last act takes place at "twilight of the next day." This structure, of course, demands a good deal of exposition to reveal the generally familiar events that have led up to the tragic moment. Anspacher also uses a subplot in which Isabel, Isolde's maid, is wooed by two lovers. Neither of these devices is totally successful; the attempt at a unity of time leads to much more talk than action and the subplot lacks the relevance that those of Shakespeare achieve. But at least there is a sense that a new version of the story is being told and not just a watered down version of the old story.

This sense is intensified by the depiction of Mark as a good person who is not the agent of Tristan's death and who, in fact, becomes the tragic hero.

The treatment of the tragedy is much different in the *Tristram and Isoult* of Martha W. Austin (1905), who comments in her foreword on Anspacher's play. She notes that she saw a notice of the publication of his work when hers was already finished and delayed reading his play for six months because she feared it would make her own treatment "superfluous." But upon reading it she found that "there was still a place for my own version, as the two differed almost as much as it was possible for any two treatments of the same theme to differ" (5). She observes that while Anspacher based his play on the German tradition that Wagner followed, she uses Malory, especially in the crucial instance of Mark's character.

Though Austin does not achieve quite the success that a later play (Martha Kinross's *Tristram and Isoult*) does in using Malory's conception of the characters and his contrast of the Tristram-Isoult-Mark triangle with that of Lancelot, Guinevere and Arthur, she does handle well those elements of the play where she avails herself of the poetic license she claims, "the privilege of each to draw the thing as he sees it" (6). Particularly interesting is the general lack of guilt that Tristram feels. In a blending of legends, he goes so far as to compare the cup from which he drank the love potion to the Grail. He says, "I have found my Grail; the cup from Brangwane's breast / We took upon the ship..." (18). And later in the play he compares Isoult to the "angel of the Grail" (48).

Though Austin comments on the character of Mark, it is really Tristram who is most interesting in her play and who has the most potential. However, as is the case in a number of the Tristan plays, none of the characters, including Tristram, is developed fully enough to make the reader experience the tragedy as something personal yet legendary.

J. Comyns Carr's *Tristram and Iseult* (1906) is another play which achieves a considerable degree of originality, even though it also exhibits some structural weakness because Carr attempts to cover too much dramatic ground in too short a space. One must wonder, for instance, why he introduces Palomide, the Saracen knight. It is true that the tournament in which Palomide fights for and nearly wins the hand of Iseult provides the means by which Tristram wins her for Mark; yet anyone familiar with the Arthurian legends expects a continuing conflict between the Saracen and Tristram, an expectation that is frustrated when Palomide, having served as a means of forwarding the plot, is not heard from again.

Nevertheless, Carr, who must have pondered an even more serious problem of excessive material for the dramatic structure in his *King Arthur*, finds an original and dramatically effective means of abridgement of some of the major elements of his sources. For example, instead of trying to incorporate Tristram's marriage to Iseult of the White Hands, Carr presents her in the second of his four acts as a spectral figure who utters an ominous prediction about the future of the lovers. In the last scene, the vision appears again, stretching her white hands over the dying lovers. We realize with Iseult that the white hands represent death and yet "those white hands have brought me healing too" since, as Tristram says in his final words, "For all Love's wounds there is no cure but Death" (71).

Another author is innovative in the use of dramatic spectacle. Published the same year as Maurice Baring's *Tristram and Iseult* was a piece called *The Tragedy of Pardon* by Michael Field (a pseudonym for Katherine Harris Bradley and Edith Emma Cooper). The play begins on a promising note with a prologue which is one of the most original scenes in all the Tristan plays. It presents Queen Iseult of Ireland in a laboratory preparing the love potion, which is empowered by "star-rays" that "fall on the alembic and ignite it" (3). This visual symbol of the power of the potion and, by extension, the love it produces could, with proper staging, be a dramatically compelling opening.

Unfortunately, the promise of the prologue is not totally fulfilled by the play itself. There is a good deal of action throughout: Tristan shoots the spying Marjodo with an arrow and Melot buries the body; Iseult undergoes the ordeal of the hot iron to prove her innocence; Tristan and Iseult are discovered by Mark in their forest cave; etc. But the episodes lack unity, especially the kind that could be imparted by the consistent development of character.

The pseudonymous Field has a talent for dramatic spectacle, as the prologue, the cave scene, the ordeal and even the ending—in which Iseult uses not a black or white sail but a golden one to announce her presence—demonstrate. And some small touches are nicely crafted: as Iseult dies over the dying Tristan, her hair fans out and he sees it as a golden sail, a sign of the spatial and temporal confusion of the dying man.

This is the kind of play that could be extremely entertaining to witness. One could easily be caught up in the spectacle and forget the thematic weakness. It is good theater, but it falls short of being a great play.

Another Tristan play has less flair for spectacle but is thematically stronger and better unified. Arthur Symons' play *Tristan and Iseult: A Play in Four Acts* (1917) has been called by Nathan Comfort Starr (in *King Arthur Today*, 52) "one of the two or three most compelling versions of the story in our day." Yet it is structurally flawed in a manner that undermines the effectiveness of the drama. Trying to include all the elements of the traditional story, Symons presents a large cast of characters in action which is at times so diffuse that it does not allow for real development of those characters.

Mark is a case in point. He does very little in the play except to banish Tristan after learning of his love for Iseult and to arrive in Brittany in time only to forgive the dead lovers and command a royal funeral for them. Giving Mark such a minor role would not in itself constitute a flaw (though it is a break with tradition) if another conflict were developed to support the weight of the tragedy. But this is not done. Meriadoc, who loves Iseult himself and who ultimately gives Tristan his fatal wound, is almost as weakly drawn as Mark. He begins by hating Tristan, the slayer of his father Morholt; then he is reconciled with Tristan for no particular reason except that Iseult now looks with favor on Tristan. Finally, but without any real explanation of the reversion to hatred, Meriadoc stabs Tristan with a poisoned knife.

In Gottfried's *Tristan* the shift in Marjodoc's feelings from friendship to hatred for Tristan is explained in some detail. Marjodoc is upset to learn that his friend has been having an affair without telling him—and this disgruntlement intensifies to hatred when he discovers that Tristan's beloved is Isolde whom he (Marjodoc) also loves (see Gottfried von Strassburg, *Tristan*, 219-21). Thus the motivation is clear; but Symons, who asks his audience to accept two changes in affection, gives virtually no explanation.

Such superficial treatment of characters results from an over-reliance on the traditional elements of the story to support the action of the play. Where Symons is original, however, is in his use of the theme of honor as a focus for the events of the play. "Honor" serves to define a code which governs action. The Queen of Ireland forgives the slayer of her brother because he is a guest and the laws of hospitality demand that he be treated well. Before they fall in love, Tristan tells Iseult that if peace is not possible between them, one thing is: "Honour" (46). He also tells her that he serves his king and will also serve her as queen "in all things honourable" (46). After drinking the love potion, he observes that it "has withered honour in my heart" (54). When Mark first hears of the love between his nephew and his queen, he says that if it is true, "these two have done dishonour on their souls" (65). Though Tristan still feels that "Love is not love unless it honour honour / Above all mortal things," Iseult believes that "Love is not love / Unless it root up honour like a weed" (72).

In the final analysis, the play becomes a very modern comment on the triumph of the real emotions of love (and hatred) over some artificial code. Iseult of Brittany, jealous about being deceived by Tristan, who told her he was sending to Italy for a famous physician and not to Cornwall for the other Iseult, lies to him about the color of the sail and causes his death. Even Mark's regretful "Had I but known" and his assertion that had Tristan "but had faith in me...then had I given / Iseult...to be his wife" (109) rings hollow in the face of the tragedy. Perhaps he would have, but it is impossible to know if his honor or his real emotions would have won out.

The originality in Thomas Hardy's *The Famous Tragedy of the Queen of Cornwall at Tintagel in Lyonnesse* (1923) is in the extension of the action beyond the point at which it usually ends. Typically, when Iseult of Brittany lies about the color of the sail, Tristram dies, as does Iseult of Cornwall upon learning of his death. But Hardy arranges the action so that Tristram and Iseult do not die at this point. Iseult of Brittany rushes to the pier before the Queen of Cornwall can disembark and tells her rival, falsely, that Tristram is dead. After Queen Iseult has returned to Cornwall, Tristram, followed shortly by his wife, shows up at Mark's court, where Mark kills Tristram in jealous rage and then is slain by his queen. After stabbing Mark with the same knife he used to slay Tristram, she leaps to her death.

Perhaps the most interesting thing about Hardy's play is that the action which seems so familiar is actually quite original. The sense of familiarity comes from the results, the inevitable death of Tristram and Iseult. And so does the sense of fate. In the end, fate is as unavoidable for the principal characters as their deaths are for an author who reworks this material. (Of all the playwrights who treat this theme, only Antonia Williams allows Tristram and Iseult to live; and that outcome seems too untrue to the tradition to be taken seriously.)

The inevitable tragedy coupled with the twist that Hardy gives to the traditional story emphasizes his point, a point made specific in the words of Iseult of Brittany, or Iseult the Whitehanded, as Hardy calls her. Upon learning of the deaths of Tristram, Iseult and Mark, she observes that "even had I not come / Across the southern water recklessly / This would have shaped the same—the very same" (74-75). The interesting word "shaped" is clearly used in the sense of the *OED* definition (v. 21): "Of God, fate, fortune, etc.: To destine, decree." Iseult realizes that there is a force working to shape her destiny and the destinies of the others and that her actions had little effect on the ultimate outcome.

The short play *Tristram and Iseult: A Dramatic Poem* by An Pilibin (pseudonym of John Hackett Pollock) (1924) is a masterpiece of mood. A stage direction at the beginning of the piece indicates that "The players throughout, move and speak with marked slowness and precision" (7). The motion matches the setting: high summer on a ship becalmed at sea. But the calm is about to be broken by a fierce storm.

Myriads of swallows, sensing the coming tempest, roost on "every spar and shroud" of the ship. Iseult, young and innocent, asks after one white bird that used to "house above / My casement" (28-29). After the storm, a symbol of the tempest that foreshadows, in Shakespearean fashion, the coming tempest in the lives of Tristram and Iseult, Tristram is seen holding the white swallow—now dead. Tristram's apostrophe to the dead bird is the thematic center of the play:

Oh little life, Oh, fragile, piteous life!
As perishable as an autumn leaf
Whom the wind ravishes—how poor a thing
For Death to prey upon! yet he confers
Upon this tiny body dignity—
Since men, and gods, and planets likewise die. (37)

The dead bird represents at the same time Iseult's dead innocence—moments later she and Tristram drink the love potion—and the tragic nobility of the death that will come to them.

But that death is not portrayed here. After the lovers drink the potion, they "speak and move in a sonambulistic [sic] fashion" which reflects the calm that they achieve when they realize their place and purpose in the universe. In her final words, Iseult bids Tristram "let the stars, who, with benignant eyes, / Beheld the first espousals of our race, / Look upon this—the sweetest, and the last!" (45). This cosmic perspective links them, like the dead bird, to a larger scheme in which the impending tragedy is overshadowed by their triumph, a triumph reflected in the "Recitative" which closes the play:

The gods, in bitter wisdom, brought
The subtle plans man set above
Their will eternal, down to naught:
Natheless, in high compassionate thought,
To grant one sweet of life they sought—
And, taking all things, left them love.

And when, in sea-washed Brittany,
As vapour, breathéd on a glass,
These, Love's poor pensioners, must die,
The gods, in divine equity,

Shall touch with immortality
Their names, that these may nowise pass. (47)

Perhaps the best of the Tristan and Isolt plays are those which do the most original things with character. And the character who allows for the most original development is Isolt.

One of the most interesting of all these plays is Martha Kinross's *Tristram & Isoult* (1913). It is fascinating largely because of its depiction of Isoult and its focus on her, a focus sharpened by contrast to Guinevere. Whereas Malory highlighted the tragedy of Arthur by contrasting his nobility to Mark's mean-spiritedness and cowardice, Kinross makes Guinevere a foil by means of which Isolt's independence, courage and strength can be clearly seen.

Early in the play, Guinevere says: "Isoult the fearless, I have envied thee / Thy Joyous Gard, and the avowéd years / Lived open to King Mark and to the world" (6). This openness, coupled with a strength rare—or at least rarely emphasized—in the typical portrayal of Isoult, makes Kinross's heroine a compelling character. Isoult's fearlessness, from which her strength derives, is dramatically depicted when Mark confronts her in a tower at Tintagil. After she tells him that "I never fear," Mark says "almost I believe thy vaunt" (35) and then recounts an incident in which Isoult gave the death blow to a stag that, having been brought to bay, was slashing her hunting hounds with its horns.

The emphasis on Isoult and her confrontation with Mark suggests that the play has fairly obvious feminist overtones that are unusual for its time and that makes it a forerunner of the tendency towards giving female characters central roles in much recent Arthurian literature. In one scene, Mark declares that it is "the end I set my life" to "make thee fear" (36). Forcing her towards a broken parapet, Mark tries to break her spirit. But Isoult proclaims herself "undizzied" and then draws a dagger and orders him to "take off thy hands" (36-37). Isoult's open confrontation with Mark extends to an admission of her love for Tristram and even to contemptuous insult. She compares him to a dog that sniffs "at the thresholds / Of doors are shut to thee" (38).

Though Isoult does express "fear" that Tristram will forget her, her use of the word prompts him to comment that it is the first time he has heard it from her (58). And, to be sure, this is not the fear of a damsel in distress. The scene in the tower shows that she does not fit this stereotype. Rather, it is a fear that grows from a passion as strong as Isoult's character.

Her passion and her strength last to the end of the play when, with Tristram dead, she drinks a poisoned cup, which she refers to as "the Grail upraised." This image demonstrates her independence from conventional moral standards and is, ironically, an assertion that she will decide her own faith and her own fate. Her inversion of the traditional life-giving and religious associations of the Grail suggests that Isolt defines her own values and determines her own life and her own death.

Two other exceptional plays, one by John Masefield and the other by American author Don Marquis, both appeared in 1927 (a year which saw the publication of a total of four plays on the theme and of Robinson's *Tristram*).

Masefield's version, *Tristan and Isolt: A Play in Verse* (1927), attempts to give new life to the legend by combining elements from various sources. As he does in his collection of Arthurian poetry, *Midsummer Night and Other Tales in Verse,* Masefield tries to get close to the historical origins of his subject at the same time that he acknowledges the medieval tradition.

Perhaps the most obvious difference between Masefield's play and almost all the other retellings of the Tristan story is that he devotes a major portion of his work to re-creating an event described in one of the Welsh *Triads,* which tells about "Three Powerful Swineherds of the Island of Britain." The first is "Drystan son of Tallwch, who guarded the swine of March son of Meirchiawn, while the swineherd went to ask Essyllt to come to a meeting with him. And Arthur was seeking (to obtain) one pig from among them, either by deceit or by force, but he did not get it" (*Trioedd Ynnys Prydein* 45, Triad 26).

Masefield has Tristan guard the swine while the swineherd Hog goes to warn Isolt not to meet him because of a trap set by Kai. Kai, in turn, wants to punish Hog and Tristan by stealing a pig while the latter is on guard. Arthur, who in this play is a "Captain of the Host" subordinate to Marc, goes along with Kai but is actually sympathetic to Tristan and Isolt. The plot to steal the hog is frustrated by Tristan and Hog, but the comic castigation of Kai and his accomplice Bedwyr cannot prevent the ultimate tragic ending. The comic subplot, in which the transgressions of Kai and Bedwyr are punished, is in fact a way of highlighting the inevitability of the tragic ending, an inevitability suggested at the very beginning of the play by the opening speech of a character called Destiny, who says, "my task is to make / Beginnings prosper to glory and crumble to rotten / By the deeds of women and men and the ways that they take" (1).

But the most interesting twist that Masefield gives to the plot is in the working out of the foreordained tragedy. It is not a vengeful Marc who slays Tristan. Marc is himself killed by "the heathen" at the Battle of Badon Hill (132). During his absence, Tristan, maddened by his separation from Isolt, returns to court seeking her. Since she has come to believe that "This love, that I thought was great, is blindness and greed" (117), she rejects Tristan and has him flogged as a felon (131). Tristan, who has been living "upon leaves and grass"—which is, as Brangwen observes, "No diet to withstand flogging" (133)—dies from the punishment. But Isolt, who is freed from her duty to Marc by news of his death, rushes to Tristan and they have a final moment to express their love before he dies and she stabs herself.

Masefield's main contribution to the legend is to make it truly the tragedy of Isolt. By omitting Isolt of Brittany from his version, he removes any possibility of jealousy or other base motive for her actions. Tristan is unswervingly devoted to her, and it is only her recognition of Marc's basic nobility and of her obligation to him that makes her reject Tristan and order the punishment that causes his death. Thus Masefield's Isolt is a tragic figure who is caught between her love and her sense of duty. This conflict explains why Masefield introduced pre-romantic material from the Welsh *Triads.* It is precisely the blend of this material with the later romantic elements that creates the tragic dilemma for Isolt. The sense of duty she feels and the harsh justice she administers, both consistent with the heroic world of early Celtic literature, are in conflict in her character and in the action of the play with her romantic love for Tristan. By allowing the two worlds to meet, Masefield creates the tragedy of Isolt.

Don Marquis' play *Out of the Sea: A Play in Four Acts* (1927) is also among the best of the dramatic versions of the Tristan story. Marquis avoids some of the pitfalls fallen into by other dramatists by recasting the legend in a modern setting. As a result, the characters, rather than seeming diminished versions of their medieval originals, gain a mythic dimension.

The setting of the play is on the Cornish coast, near where the ancient land of Lyonnesse sank into the sea. Strange sounds echo throughout the play. Characters continually hear the sounds of a ghostly hunt, said to be caused by the spirit of Tristram the hunter who gets restless and rides forth from time to time.

The modern counterpart of Tristram is John Harding, an American poet, who is taken with the romance of Cornwall, where, he says, the ghosts from Lyonnesse speak to him *out of the sea*. The Isolt character is Isobel Tregesal, who was found in an open boat as a child with a very ancient bronze bodkin beside her. Having come out of the sea originally, she comes from it again when her husband Mark Tregesal sails out into a fierce storm and his yawl breaks up.

Mark, who is compared to the ancient giants of Cornwall, is like his original in the Tristan legend in that he is jealous and cruel, crueller "than the old king was to them other lovers," as one of the characters says (62). As Mark begins to suspect that his wife and Harding are lovers, he taunts them, trying to make them wonder about the extent of his real knowledge. His deliberate cruelty to his wife convinces Harding and Isobel that they must run away together, a decision that is supported by her foster-father and by Arthur Logris, the owner of the house in Cornwall where much of the action takes place. Logris, who is on one level a modern King Arthur, is also in love with Isobel, so much so that he puts her chance for happiness with Harding above his own desires.

When Mark discovers Isobel in a cave where the lovers have met before, he knows of their plan and attempts to force her to remain with him. She is defiant, telling him "You have no power over me" (114). But he, like her, is, as Mark himself observes, "elemental" (112). Not only does he try to stop her, but he proclaims his desire for a son and attempts to rape her in the cave. Isobel resists and finally stabs him with the ancient bronze bodkin.

Logris wants to take the blame for the murder so Isobel can live with the man she loves, but she will not allow this. She asks only to see Harding one more time. Confronted with the violent deed, the American poet reveals that he has none of the elemental force of Isobel or Mark or Logris or the Tristram of legend. He says, "I never thought...that it would come...to bloodshed" (130).

When Isobel, now "free even of love" (131), leaps into the sea, Harding says that he should follow her. But Logris, recognizing that Harding lacks the ancient passion that is bred into those who have lived on the coast of Cornwall and in the presence of the legend of Lyonnesse, says "You won't, though. You'll write a poem about it" (133).

Out of the Sea is a fitting rendition of the legend of Tristan and Isolt. Through the setting and atmosphere and through the mythic dimension that he imparts to his characters, Marquis creates a truly tragic play. It is the tragedy not of Mark, who is too cruel to be a tragic hero, or of Harding, who is not noble enough, but of Isobel, whose return to the sea is a tragic victory over both the cruelty of Mark and the pusillanimity of Harding.

Martha Kinross, John Masefield and Don Marquis best achieve the balance between tradition and originality that writers like Antonia Williams and Maurice Baring fail to achieve. Masefield skillfully combines earlier traditions to create a refreshingly new rendition of the ancient story rather than a tired reworking of the old material like Baring's. Marquis demonstrates that one can depart in some radical ways from tradition and still be true to it. Marquis' innovations succeed where Williams' fail because he uses the tragic background of the legend as a way of defining and aggrandizing character rather than denying the tragedy for no better reason than to hammer home a moral. And Martha Kinross shows how a dramatist can be faithful to the tradition and yet give new life to it by seeing a character from an original perspective.

Works Cited

English and American Tristan Plays
Published Between 1900 and 1930

Ankenbrand, Frank. *Tristram and Iseult: A Play in Five Acts.* In *Collected Poems.* London: John Lane, 1911.

Anspacher, Louis K. *Tristan and Isolde: A Tragedy.* New York: Brentano's, 1904.

Austin, Martha. *Tristram and Isoult.* Boston: The Poet Lore Co., 1905.

Baring, Maurice. *Tristram and Iseult: A Play in Five Acts.* In *The Collected Poems of Maurice Baring.* London: John Lane, 1911.

Carr, J. Comyns. *Tristram & Iseult: A Drama in Four Acts.* London: Duckworth and Co., 1906.

Field, Michael (pseudonym of Katherine Harris Bradley and Edith Emma Cooper). *The Tragedy of Pardon.* London: Sidgwick and Jackson, 1911.

Hardy, Thomas. *The Famous Tragedy of the Queen of Cornwall at Tintagel in Lyonnesse: A New Version of an Old Story Arranged as a Play for Mummers in One Act Requiring No Theatre or Scenery.* London: Macmillan, 1923.

Hare, Amory (pseudonym of [Mary] Amory Hare Hutchinson). *Tristram and Iseult.* Gaylordsville, CT: The Slide Mountain P, 1930.

Kinross, Martha. *Tristram & Isoult.* London: Macmillan, 1913.

Lee, Thomas H. *The Marriage of Iseult: A Tragedy in Two Scenes.* In *The Marriage of Iseult and Other Plays.* London: Elkin Mathews, 1909.

Marquis, Don. *Out of the Sea: A Play in Four Acts.* Garden City, NY: Doubleday, Page and Co., 1927.

Masefield, John. *Tristan and Isolt: A Play in Verse.* London: Macmillan, 1927.

Mitchell, D.M. *Sir Tristram: A Tragedy in Four Acts.* London: Fowler and Wright, 1927.

Pilibin, An (pseudonym of John Hackett Pollock). *Tristram & Iseult: A Dramatic Poem.* Dublin: Talbot, 1924.

Symons, Arthur. *Tristan and Iseult: A Play in Four Acts.* London: William Heinemann, 1917.

Todhunter, John. *Isolt of Ireland: A Legend in a Prologue and Three Acts.* In *Isolt of Ireland: A Legend in a Prologue and Three Acts and The Poison Flower.* London: J.M. Dent, 1927.

Williams, Antonia R. *Isolt: A New Telling.* London: Published by the Author, [1900].

Additional Works Cited

Gottfried von Strassburg. *Tristan.* Trans., A.T. Hatto. Baltimore: Penguin Books, 1960.

Starr, Nathan Comfort. *King Arthur Today.* Gainesville: U of Florida P, 1954.

Trioedd Ynnys Prydein: The Welsh Triads, 2nd ed. Ed. and trans. Rachel Bromwich. Cardiff: U of Wales P, 1978.

The Knight-Poets of Logres:
Narrative Voices in Charles Williams' Arthurian Poems

Charles Franklyn Beach

The Arthurian legend fascinated Charles Williams for most of his life, though he did not publish the first poems in his Arthurian cycle until 1930, fifteen years before his death. However, as early as 1917, in his volume entitled *Poems of Conformity*, Williams uses the city of Sarras as an image of the heavenly City of God. His first published novel, *War in Heaven* (1930), tells of a struggle over the Holy Grail between godly and ungodly forces in 1930s England. But Williams' major work in the Arthurian legend came between 1930 and 1944 when he composed and published forty-five different poems, primarily in the two volumes *Taliessin Through Logres* (1938) and *The Region of the Summer Stars* (1944). Thirteen of the poems, however, were published between 1930 and 1931 in *Heroes & Kings, Three Plays*, and the *New English Poems* anthology.[1] Most critics overlook the early poems because they lack the maturity and depth of his later verse, although Williams himself includes them in his definition of the cycle.[2]

Most criticism of Williams' Arthurian poems has focused on the interplay of the metaphysical images, on the organizational structure of the poetic sequence, and on the significance of the verse within the literary world.[3] Little has been said about Williams' use of narration in the cycle; the only analysis of narrative voices to date comes in the appendix to Charles Moorman's essay, "The Structures of Charles Williams' Arthurian Poetry" (114-16), but Moorman's article emphasizes the unity of the poems as an artistic whole and does not focus on the characterization of the narrators. In the cycle, Williams uses eight different knights as narrative voices—Tristram, Lamoracke, Galahad, Mordred, Palomides, Percivale, Bors and Taliessin—although Taliessin features most prominently as a poet: Williams assigns thirty poems to him, two-thirds of the total.[4] Although the eight knights who narrate individual poems demonstrate varying degrees of artistic ability, only Taliessin has the skills necessary to function effectively as the poet-chronicler in King Arthur's court. At the same time, as members of the Round Table, the knights have certain chivalric commitments, and these duties frequently conflict with their artistic aspirations. Of all eight narrative voices, Taliessin is able to balance most effectively the two roles of knight and poet.

Throughout his writings, Williams frequently describes his characters through their attitudes and actions toward the other members of the human community. This community depends on the free and continuous interaction through love of all its members. King Arthur's court serves as a model of an ideal community that, as a result of man's fallen nature, ultimately fails. The greatest danger to this community is individual selfishness; a member of the community who chooses to set himself or his desires above those of other members no longer loves them through his actions. Thus, a prolonged selfishness will isolate an individual from the community, and ultimately, according to Williams' theology, from God.[5] Because they successfully overcome this inherent human tendency toward selfish actions, three knights—Galahad, Percivale, and Bors—achieve the highest goal of the court community, the Grail quest. In his Arthurian cycle, Williams characterizes the knight-poets through a presentation of their attitudes toward their art, their attitudes toward others in the court, and their ability (or lack of ability) to transcend the limitations of their personal experiences.

First, let us consider the knights who fail to be effective poets: Tristram, Lamoracke, Galahad and Mordred. Each knight has a particular weakness which prevents him from achieving the necessary perspective to qualify as a court poet. The knights either see themselves as superior to their peers, or they lack the perception and skill required to fulfill their poetic aspirations.

Tristram, for all of his merits as a knight, fails as an artist because he overestimates his abilities and he isolates himself from King Arthur's court. Elsewhere, Williams calls Tristram a "superfluous" character in the cycle because of his frequent absences from Camelot (*Image* 183). In "Tristram's Song to Iseult," the knight demonstrates his nature by composing a poetic dissection of the queen's naked body, which is gradually revealed "ceremonially" but also "with an intense unceremonious mirth" during a night of love-making. Tristram attempts to turn his love into high art, and in doing so, takes credit for the beauty thus presented:

> For I am Tristram; I have made this sight
> lovely to us and lovely to the night,
> O song, O my great song, O proud and gay!
> (*Heroes* 126-28)

Proud is Tristram indeed, and this pride blinds him to the flaws of his own artistic construction. He mixes his metaphors, comparing Iseult's breasts one moment to Mount Meru, from which the River Ganges "plunges free" (62), while in the next moment he claims to be painting with a "quick brush" her "columned thighs" (71-72). In a final wave of boasting, Tristram declares that his art is equal to—or greater than—"Taliessin's art" (118). Unfortunately for Tristram, his restless refrain of "The dawn must come and I be ridden away!" undermines the poem, for it reveals his lack of dedication to the artistic task: "the stream" of his love and of his art "is running and too soon must go." Tristram's arrogance and restlessness carry over into his other relationships; thinking himself superior to Taliessin and the other knights, Tristram chooses not to frequent the court in Camelot. And this is a dangerous choice, as Williams elsewhere suggests: Tristram "is an individualist as against the State" (*Image* 176).

Like Tristram, Lamoracke's weakness as an artist is twofold—he has a limited range of poetic images, being a man of war in all aspects of his life, and he fails to understand the weaknesses of his lover. Both of Lamoracke's songs are directed to his mistress, Queen Morgause of Orkney. However, his primary occupation as a warrior dominates the imagery of his verse, particularly when he describes his mistress and their love. He portrays his first meeting with the queen in violent physical images: her "hewn eyelids bruised my bone" and "her hand discharged catastrophe" in the yet unformed child in her womb, Mordred (*Taliessin* 38). He compares Morgause to a cleft in a shoreline cliff, a significant image foreshadowing Mordred's future destructive presence in the court. But all of these harsh pictures involve Lamoracke's passion for the queen, a love that is often overtly physical. In "Lamoracke's Song to Morgause," the knight tells a story in verse to his lover—after he has bound her during their love-making. He considers his binding of the queen a conquest, and he sings "for anguish and pity of love" (*Heroes* 72). But the "anguish" is, for the moment, the queen's: Lamoracke does not free her until after his song is complete.

Lamoracke's failure to understand the Queen's weaknesses also undermines his art. Morgause is, for him,

> fashioned without any flaws,
> fair without and fair within,
> body and soul most wondrous fair....
>
> (*Heroes* 112-14)

Lamoracke forgets for a moment that the queen is the mother of the evil Mordred, and also of Gawain and his brothers, who will eventually kill Lamoracke for his affair with Morgause. This inability to recognize the inherent danger to King Arthur and to himself—Lamoracke only sees a potential future danger to Morgause—weakens his credibility as a court poet.

Galahad's contribution to the cycle presents Williams with a problem: How can a knight acclaimed widely for his virtue and humility objectively narrate events at court without falling into the trap of pride, especially since he features prominently in the most important quest of the knights?

In "The Song of the Riding of Galahad," the virtuous knight attempts to dismiss the "great...fame" (*Heroes* 1) which surrounds him. He asks:

> What bishop or king or might
> hath spoken of me right?
> though I be greatly styled
> the Champion, the merciful Childe,
> the high prince Dom Galahad,
> yet most shall they be glad
> that none have at all forgot
> I am also Lancelot.
>
> (*Heroes* 5-12)

Like his father, Galahad is human, mortal, and unworthy of undue praise. Like his father, Galahad faces temptation, though, unlike Lancelot, Galahad successfully resists it. The first sign of Galahad's importance is the "marvel" of his birth, though his audience knows about the deception "the wise woman Briseis" practiced on Lancelot in order to bring the knight to Lady Helayne. But his birth, Galahad reminds us, is not marvelous because of his nature or his heredity but because of his mission. He may be a great knight like his father Lancelot, but he has been singled out for the Grail quest—a task Lancelot had already forfeited by committing adultery with Guinevere. Thus, since Galahad's existence and his task are both substitutionary, the knight rides forth not in his own name but in Lancelot's.

Galahad's quest removes him from the court almost as soon as he arrives; thus, like Tristram, he is in no position to narrate the activities of the court. Once he heals King Pelleas' wound, Galahad "thereafter shall...but kneel / where in a heavenly tongue / the final Mass is sung..." (*Heroes* 128-30). Galahad's divine mission and devotion to the Grail prevent his fulfillment as an artist.

Unlike the first three knights, Mordred lacks both artistic skill and knightly prowess. While Arthur besieges Lancelot's castle in Gaul, the king's son sits safely in Camelot, resting "on [Arthur's] palace roof" and watching the springtime come as "the elms bud in steel points" of civil strife. During the king's absence, Mordred has allowed the city to "become a forest" of "moral wantons" (*Region* 48). Furthermore, he dismisses the spiritual quest for the Grail as a search for "luck": from this perspective, the young prince declares,

> I can manage without such fairy mechanism.
> If it does prove to be, which is no likely thought,
> I will send my own dozen of knights to pull it in.
> (*Region* 48)

He thinks lightly of a quest that most Round Table knights were unable to achieve, and in pride, Mordred focuses on himself:

> I will have my choice, and be adored for the having;
> when my father King Arthur has fallen in the wood of his elms,
> I will sit here alone in a kingdom of Paradise.
> (*Region* 49)

Unlike the other knights, Mordred cares for nothing besides himself, and thus he becomes an enemy of the court, bringing about final ruin to himself and to the kingdom.

While Tristram, Lamoracke, Galahad, and Mordred fail in their poetic efforts, four of Williams' knight-poets succeed in both roles, though the narrative efforts of Palomides, Percivale, and Bors are not as effective as Taliessin's.

The Saracen knight Palomides recounts his personal experience in Logres in several poems that reveal the knight's progression as an artist. In "The Coming of Palomides," he describes the great distances—both physical and spiritual— he travels to reach the court of King Mark. Once there, Palomides is called upon to sing a song, so he composes a poem on the metaphysical identity of Iseult in her role as queen, based on a study of her bare arm. However, Palomides fails to communicate his feelings for the queen to his audience because he sings in Arabic. When the knight "suddenly" ends his meditation, King Mark, thinking the tale is finished, rewards him. The song ends abruptly, Palomides tells us, because he suddenly discovered the "division [that] stretched between / the queen's identity and the queen" (*Taliessin* 36). The knight, alone of the court, recognizes the failings of the queen—failings that her husband Mark and her lover Tristram cannot or will not acknowledge. Iseult cannot fulfill Palomides' vision of a perfect, faithful queen and lover because she is unfaithful in her vows to her husband and to her lover. Only once outside King Mark's court can the knight-poet communicate the queen's true nature, and he does so through this poem.

Despite his recognition of the queen's weaknesses, Palomides has fallen in love with her. In a futile attempt to gain Iseult's love, Palomides takes on the quest of the Blatant Beast—a quest he finally abandons, according to "Palomides' Song of Iseult," because the queen continues to refuse his love. With his dreams "wounded," the knight suggests that

> from all but making of rhymes
> have I, Palomides, ceased
> in these disastrous times
>
> (*Heroes* 4-6)

and later he adds that even the "rhymes" have "saddened me more, / prolonging disastrous times" (*Heroes* 20-21). He refuses to write further because Iseult won't even remember that once "Palomides...sang that my forehead shone" (*Heroes* 83-84).

This failure of quest and rejection of love reveals to Palomides his inadequacies as a knight and a poet: in an attempt to be restored to both roles, he seeks Christian baptism. The final poem he speaks in the cycle, entitled "The Death of Palomides," repeats the refrain "The Lord created all things by means of his Blessing." By this point in his growth, Palomides' vision has expanded from the narrow, subjective sight of Iseult's arm to a broader view of the kingdom and the world; Palomides now sits "with the old men" and sings praises to God (*Taliessin* 80). He concludes his poem with a benediction that offers his life to Christ even as he had earlier offered himself to Iseult. Palomides' progression from human love to the greater love of Christ parallels his greater understanding of world events. But his personal perspective—at first isolated, though he later joins the Camelot community—remains too narrow and individual a view for Palomides to be an effective court poet.

Percivale, who once describes Taliessin as "his verse brother" (*Taliessin* 53), narrates three poems which stand at significant points in the cycle. First, in "Percivale's Song to Blanchfleur," the knight describes Arthur's court for his sister, listing the knights and ladies in the order that they sit at the Round Table. Percivale here emphasizes the relationship of each knight and each lady to the climactic event of the court's history—the quest of the Holy Grail. Thus, he spends the most lines describing Galahad (*Heroes* 86-87). The poem achieves its structure through Percivale's relation of each part of the catalogue to a part of Blanchfleur's body—a metaphorical pattern that emphasizes the importance of some knights over others. For example, Galahad is the throat and backbone, while several of the lesser knights are listed as fingers or toes.

In "Percivale's Song," the Knight defines the nature of "courtesy"—Williams' term for the brotherly love that unites the members of the human community. This love involves the "giving and taking" of human interaction, in its highest "degree" a natural and habitual way of life. Without courtesy, the relationships within the human community fall apart ("Percivale's Song" 345-46).

Indeed, Percivale is courtesy's chief representative at court, as he demonstrates in his final poem, "Percivale at Carbonek." When the three knights arrive at the city of the Grail, Galahad stands outside the gate as a Christlike figure who speaks words of pardon and absolution to the wolflike Lancelot, who has suddenly come among them. As Percivale observes the incident, he courteously fades into the background, allowing the dialogue between Bors and Galahad to proceed uninterrupted. However, despite his accurate perception of real and ideal relationships within the human community, Percivale, by achieving the Grail quest, removes himself permanently from the court; thus, he is unable to chronicle the final events of court history.

The knight Bors reports official events in two poems addressed to his wife Elayne. In "Bors to Elayne: The Fish of Broceliande," the knight recounts an experience he has while serving as Arthur's "lieutenant on the southern coast...from unpathed Broceliande to the eastern forelands" (*Taliessin* 24). During his tour of duty, Bors obtains an unusual fish which he now presents to his wife. The tone and the language of the poem is personal and intimate; clearly, Bors' primary concern is communicating experiences to his individual audience (Elayne).

He also reports on a council meeting in the poem "Bors to Elayne: On the King's Coins." King Arthur has suggested the minting of coins, a proposition that Sir Kay, "the king's steward, wise in economics" (*Taliessin* 44) approves, stating (along with the Archbishop) that "money is a medium of exchange" (*Taliessin* 45). Bors, however, tells Elayne about the dissension of two knights, Taliessin and himself. The two knights argue that the coins are a "convenient heresy" replacing true forms of spiritual and emotional exchange between members of the community (*Taliessin* 44). In the poem, Bors immediately applies the court debate to his relationship with Elayne: he wonders aloud if she, too, will be distanced by the presence of gold in their lives. He is relieved by her promise of continuing intimacy, but he requests Elayne's prayers for the coins, the city, and the king—that all would be placed in their proper places in the lives of the people. In both poems Bors takes an event within the kingdom and communicates it to his wife in a manner that shows the event's significance to their relationship. Using this approach, Bors succeeds in his limited role as a private poet. However, in his narratives he never addresses the significant Grail quest, although he achieves the sacred chalice and later returns to court.

The final knight-poet of Williams' cycle is the most important—all of the other narrators refer to him as the "king's poet." Taliessin's success as a poet is threefold: he does not rely on personal experiences for his subject matter, he narrates most of his poems from a third-person perspective, and he alone successfully unites the two roles of knight and poet.

Taliessin's poems frequently relate matters of the court, especially those involving King Arthur himself. In two poems, "The Calling of Arthur" and "The Crowning of Arthur," the poet figuratively chronicles the accession of the king; "The Last Voyage" concludes with the moment Lancelot learns of the king's death. However, Taliessin is not limited in his perspective; his is not an ethnocentric perception of Logres' importance. Upon the death of Uther

Pendragon, Arthur's father, Taliessin travels to Byzantium, the center of the Christian empire, and studies the Imperial court as well as the books in the Emperor's library. He describes his experience in the Emperor's city and his discovery of a worldwide perspective in "Taliessin's Song of Byzantion." Later, he shares with King Arthur a dream vision that the poet experienced while in Byzantium and that helped broaden his understanding of the world. In "Taliessin's Return to Logres," the poet's narrative combines personal observations with the hidden metaphysical meanings or implications of each place he visits. However, most of the poet's perceptions of Logres and of the Empire are impersonal and objective, whether he recalls the death of Virgil, his artistic mentor, or presents his schematic "Vision of the Empire."

In the first published poems of the cycle, Taliessin often speaks in first person, but in the final two volumes of verse, the poet is as much a character in his narratives as are the knights and ladies he describes. This distance between the narrator and his own actions enables him to create a sense of objectivity the other narrators cannot achieve, and this objectivity results in a more credible court record. Taliessin's frequent third-person references to himself also allow him to compile the work of the other knight-poets and present it with his own as a "complete" chronicle of King Arthur's court.[6] Thus, Taliessin succeeds in his artistic role because his duties to court and to the members of that court come before his personal statements.

These duties, however, do not merely involve his art. For instance, he helps form a "company" of those who "found themselves in common" (*Region* 36). This informal gathering of men and women sought to practice love toward each other, to live courteously, and to depend on each other in a true "community." Taliessin's involvement with this experiment reinforces his dedication to participate within the human community and record the events and ideas of members of that community.

But Taliessin is not only a master poet and a devoted member of the human community; he is also an accomplished knight,[7] who leads a "few" reinforcements in the battle of "Mount Badon." He tarries on the hill, awaiting the right moment, while some of his men question the delay, thinking that "he dreams or makes verse" (*Taliessin* 17). But Taliessin sees a vision of Virgil writing the *Aeneid*, and as the master poet begins a line, Taliessin

> saw, in the long field,
> the point where the pirate chaos might suddenly yield,
> the place for the law of grace to strike.
> He stood in his stirrups; he stretched his hand;
> he fetched the pen of his spear from its bearer;
> his staff behind signed to their men.
>
> (*Taliessin* 17)

This imagery reveals that, for Taliessin, there is no dichotomy between the two roles of knight and poet. They are, instead, part of his complete duty to his king, a duty that does not end with Arthur's death but continues to "Taliessin's Song of Lancelot's Mass." In that poem he reminds us of his dedication to the ideals of the court when he leaves

one last song ere I go;
that if by Thames and Severn
new cities come to be
they shall hear a far sweet echo
of the great king's chivalry.

(343-44)

Notes

[1]All citations to the poetry will be to page numbers, except for citations in *Heroes & Kings* (an unpaginated volume), which will be to line numbers.

[2]In the preface to his *Three Plays*, Charles Williams indicates that the cycle begins with the Arthurian poems in *Heroes and Kings* (vi). Most critics, however, have followed C.S. Lewis' lead in passing over the poems published prior to *Taliessin Through Logres*. See Lewis' "A Commentary on the Arthurian Poems of Charles Williams" for his chronological listing of the poems he includes in his interpretation of the cycle.

[3]The most thorough critical study of Williams' Arthurian poetry is Roma A. King's recently published *The Pattern in the Web: The Mythical Poetry of Charles Williams*. Other valuable studies include Glen Caraliero's comprehensive examination of Williams' life and writings, *Charles Williams: Poet of Theology*; Anne Ridler's introduction to Williams' *Image of the City and Other Essays*; Charles Moorman's book *Arthurian Triptych: Mythic Elements in Charles Williams, C.S. Lewis, and T.S. Eliot*; and articles by Karl Heinz Göller, Stephen A. Gottlieb, Angelika Schneider, and Richard Woods.

[4]For a list of the poems attributed to each narrator, see Appendix.

[5]For a further discussion of these ideas, see Charles Williams, *He Came Down From Heaven*; "The Redeemed City," *Image*, 102-10; "Antichrist and the City's Laws," *Image*, 117-21. An excellent and thorough discussion of Williams' views on theology and human relationships is Mary McDermott Shideler's *The Theology of Romantic Love*.

[6]Williams uses several levels of narration in the cycle:

Williams —→ Implied Author —→ Taliessin —→ Knight-Poet —→ Narrated Event

[7]Richard Woods suggests that Taliessin is "an important figure in Arthur's court," and though primarily a poet, Taliessin is "only casually a warrior" (15).

Appendix

The following is a list of the knight-poets and the poems which they narrate:

Narrators:	Poems:
Bors	"Bors to Elayne: The Fish of Broceliande" (*Taliessin* 24-26) "Bors to Elayne: On The King's Coins" (*Taliessin* 42-45)
Galahad	"The Song of the Riding of Galahad" (*Heroes*)

Lamoracke	"Lamoracke's Song to Morgause" (*Heroes*)
	"Lamorack and the Queen Morgause of Orkney" (*Taliessin* 38-41)
Mordred	"The Meditation of Mordred" (*Region* 47-49)
Palomides	"Palomides' Song to Iseult" (*Heroes*)
	"A Song of Palomides" (*Heroes*)
	"The Coming of Palomides" (*Taliessin* 33-37)
	"Palomides Before His Christening" (*Taliessin* 64-68)
	"The Death of Palomides" (*Taliessin* 78-80)
Percivale	"Percivale's Song to Blanchfleur" (*Heroes*)
	"Percivale's Song" (*New English Poems* 345-46)
	"Percivale at Carbonek" (*Taliessin* 81-83)
Taliessin	"Taliessin's Song of a Princess of Byzantion" (*Heroes*)
	"Taliessin's Song of Logres (*Three Plays* 1-4)
	"Taliessin's Song of Byzantion (*Three Plays* 65-68)
	"Taliessin's Song of the King's Crowning" (*Three Plays* 135-38)
	"Taliessin's Song of the Setting of Galahad in the King's Bed" (*Three Plays* 193-96)
	"Taliessin's Song of Lancelot's Mass" (*New English Poems* 340-44)
	"Prelude" (*Taliessin* 1-2)
	"Taliessin's Return to Logres" (*Taliessin* 3-5)
	"The Vision of the Empire" (*Taliessin* 6-13)
	"The Calling of Arthur" (*Taliessin* 14-15)
	"Mount Badon" (*Taliessin* 16-18)
	"The Crowning of Arthur" (*Taliessin* 19-21)
	"Taliessin's Song of the Unicorn" (*Taliessin* 23-24)
	"Taliessin in the School of the Poets" (*Taliessin* 27-30)
	"Taliessin on the Death of Virgil" (*Taliessin* 31-32)
	"The Star of Percivale" (*Taliessin* 46-47)
	"The Ascent of the Spear" (*Taliessin* 48-50)
	"The Sister of Percivale" (*Taliessin* 51-53)
	"The Son of Lancelot" (*Taliessin* 54-63)
	"The Coming of Galahad" (*Taliessin* 69-74)
	"The Departure of Merlin" (*Taliessin* 75-77)
	"The Last Voyage" (*Taliessin* 84-88)
	"Taliessin at Lancelot's Mass" (*Taliessin* 89-91)
	"Prelude" (*Region* 1-4)
	"The Calling of Taliessin" (*Region* 5-20)
	"Taliessin in the Rose-Garden" (*Region* 21-28)
	"The Departure of Dindrane" (*Region* 29-35)
	"The Founding of the Company" (*Region* 36-41)
	"The Queen's Servant" (*Region* 42-46)
	"The Prayers of the Pope" (*Region* 50-61)
Tristram	"Tristram's Song to Iseult" (*Heroes*)

Works Cited

Abercrombie, Lascelles, ed. *New English Poems: A Miscellany of Contemporary Verse Never Before Published.* London: Victor Gollancz, 1931.

Cavaliero, Glen. *Charles Williams: Poet of Theology.* Grand Rapids: William B. Eerdmans, 1983.

Göller, Karl Heinz. "From Logres to Carbonek: The Arthuriad of Charles Williams." *Arthurian Literature, Volume I.* Ed. Richard Barber. Totowa, NJ: Rowman & Littlefield, 1981. 121-73.

Gottleib, Stephen A. "A Reading of Williams' Arthurian Cycle." *Mythlore* 4.2 (1976): 3-6.

Lewis, C. S. "A Commentary on the Arthurian Poems of Charles Williams." *Arthurian Torso.* London: Oxford UP, 1948. 93-200.

King, Roma A. *The Pattern in the Web: The Mythical Poetry of Charles Williams.* Kent, OH: Kent State UP, 1990.

Moorman, Charles. *Arthurian Triptych: Mythic Elements in Charles Williams, C. S. Lewis, and T. S. Eliot.* Berkeley: U of California P, 1960.

———. "The Structures of Charles Williams' Arthurian Poetry." *Studies in the Literary Imagination* 14.2 (1981): 95-116.

Ridler, Anne, ed. Introduction. *The Image of the City and Other Essays,* by Charles Williams. London: Oxford UP, 1958.

Schneider, Angelika. "A Mesh of Chords: Language and Style in the Arthurian Poems of Charles Williams." *Arthurian Literature, Volume V.* Ed. Richard Barber. Totowa, NJ: Barnes & Noble, 1985. 92-148.

Shideler, Mary McDermott. *The Theology of Romantic Love: A Study in the Writings of Charles Williams.* Grand Rapids: William B. Eerdmans, 1962.

Williams, Charles. *He Came Down From Heaven.* 1938. Grand Rapids: William B. Eerdmans, 1984.

———. *Heroes & Kings.* London: Sylvan P, 1930.

———. *The Image of the City and Other Essays.* Ed. Anne Ridler. London: Oxford UP, 1958.

———. "Percivale's Song." *New English Poems: A Miscellany of Contemporary Verse Never Before Published.* Ed. Lascelles Abercrombie. London: Victor Gollancz, 1931. 345-46.

———. *The Region of the Summer Stars.* London: Oxford UP, 1944.

———. *Taliessin Through Logres.* London: Oxford UP, 1938.

———. "Taliessin's Song of Lancelot's Mass." *New English Poems: A Miscellany of Contemporary Verse Never Before Published.* Ed. Lascelles Abercrombie. London: Victor Gollancz, 1931. 340-44.

———. *Three Plays.* London: Oxford UP, 1931.

Woods, Richard. "The Figure of Taliesin in Charles Williams' Arthuriad." *Mythlore* 10.1 (1983): 11-16.

Contributors

Richard C. Bartone is Assistant Professor in the Department of Communication at William Paterson College, Wayne, New Jersey, and Associate Editor of the journal *Film & History*. He was a contributing writer for *The Encyclopedia of Film*, Perigee, 1991.

Charles Franklyn Beach is a teaching assistant at Baylor University.

Rebecca S. Beal, an Associate Professor of English at the University of Scranton, is a medievalist interested in Dante, Chaucer and popular Arthuriana. A participant in the National Endowment for the Humanities Institute on Arthur of Avalon, she teaches a two-semester sequence on Arthurian literature from its Celtic origins through C.J. Cherryh.

Robert J. Blanch teaches English at Northern University. He has published on Chaucer, Langland, and the *Pearl*-Poet, and edited essay collections including *Sir Gawain and the Green Knight: A Reference Guide*.

Mildred Leake Day took the Ph.D. at the University of Alabama. She taught English at Southern Benedictine College in Cullman, Alabama. Her publications include edition/translations of *De Ortu Waluuanii/The Rise of Gawain, Nephew of Arthur* and *Historia Meriadoci rex Cambrie/The Story of Meriadoc, King of Cambria*. She is co-editor with Valerie Lagorio of *King Arthur Through The Ages*, a collection of essays. She is presently writing fiction and co-editor of the journal *Quondam et Futurus/A Journal of Arthurian Interpretations*, published at Memphis State University.

Kathyleen Ely has just completed her M.A. in English at the University of Wyoming. Her thesis is a history and analysis of the Church Universal and Triumphant.

Maureen Fries is Distinguished Teaching Professor of English at the State University of New York College at Fredonia. She has authored numerous articles and book reviews on Chaucer and other medieval and modern authors as well as on Arthurian literature. Most recently, she has edited the books *Approaches to Teaching the Arthurian Tradition* (New York: MLA, 1992) and *The Figure of Merlin in the Nineteenth and Twentieth Century* (Niagara Falls: Mellen, 1989).

Tom Hoberg is a Professor of English at Northeastern Illinois University where he teaches a little of everything. His area of putative academic expertise is Nineteenth Century British Literature; his first scholarly love, however, is mythology and folklore. He is currently about to embark on a major study of Arthur and the Victorians.

Donald Hoffman is a Professor of English at Northeastern Illinois University in Chicago. He is a contributor to *The Arthurian Encyclopedia* and his articles on Arthurian topics (particularly the legends of Tristan and Merlin) have appeared in *Arthurian Interpretations, Tristania, Philological Quarterly* and other journals.

Alan Lupack is Curator of the Russell Hope Robbins Library at the University of Rochester. He is editor of *Modern Arthurian Literature, Three Charlemagne Romances* (for TEAMS Middle English texts), *"Arthur, the Greatest King": An Anthology of Modern Arthurian Poetry, Arthurian Drama: An Anthology,* and *The Round Table: A Journal of Poetry and Fiction,* and author of *The Dream of Camelot,* a volume of Arthurian poetry, as well as articles on Arthurian literature in *Arthurian Interpretations, Arthurian Yearbook, Studies in Medievalism, Cinema Arthuriana,* etc. He is currently preparing an edition of *Sir Tristrem* and *Lancelot of the Laik* for TEAMS and is working on a book on the Arthurian legend in America.

Suzanne H. MacRae teaches English and Humanities at the University of Arkansas, Fayetteville. Her special interests are Medieval and Renaissance English literature, Medieval romances, Arthurian literature, literature and eros, and interdisciplinary studies of culture.

Jesse W. Nash teaches Anthropology at Notre Dame Seminary in New Orleans and is the Popular Culture Editor of *The New Orleans Art Review.* He is the author of *Vietnamese Catholicism* and several articles on the anthropological study of popular culture.

L.O. Purdon teaches English at Doane College. He has published on Chaucer, the *Pearl*-Poet, and medieval romance. He is currently working on articles on Chaucer and a book on medieval drama.

Constance C. Relihan is an Assistant Professor of English at Auburn University. In addition to work on Cameron's Shakespearean photographs, she has published essays on Shakespeare's *Coriolanus,* Robert Greene's cony-catching pamphlets, and is currently completing a book-length study on authority within Elizabethan novelistic discourse.

Michael Rewa is an Associate Professor in the English Department at the University of Delaware where he regularly teaches a Matter of Britain course. For the last eight years he has co-hosted a weekly three-hour folk and folk-rock program on the University's radio station, WXDR, with his wife, Christine.

Elizabeth S. Sklar is a faculty member in the English Department at Wayne State University. She specilizes in Old and Middle English language and literature, with an emphasis on Arthurian literature in general and Malory in particular.

Sally K. Slocum is Associate Professor of English at The University of Akron, Akron, Ohio. She began the Arthurian Legends Subject Area for the Popular Culture Association in 1987. She teaches courses in Middle English Literature, Chaucer and Arthurian Legend. She has published articles on fiction, pedagogy, Arthurian comic books and Chaucer.

Charlotte Spivack is a Professor of English at the University of Massachusetts at Amherst. Her most recent book is *Merlin's Daughters: Contemporary Women Fantasy Writers* (1984). Forthcoming soon are two Arthurian studies: *Merlin the Wizard: Medieval and Timeless* and *The Company of Camelot.*